Let yourself *feel*

Let ya

And let yourself believe
God is there to catch
each one and hold it,
and you, close to
His heart. ♥

Rick Lawrence

Jesus-Centered
Daily

see / hear / touch / smell / taste

365 Devotions

JESUS-CENTERED DEVOTIONS J.

Jesus-Centered Daily
See. Hear. Touch. Smell. Taste.
365 Devotions

Copyright © 2020 Group Publishing, Inc.
group.com

Author: Rick Lawrence
Chief Creative Officer: Joani Schultz
Assistant Editor: Lyndsay Gerwing
Art Director: Jeff Storm
Production Manager: Melissa Towers
Marketing Manager: Adam Bohlmeyer
Supply Chain Manager: Peggy Naylor

Real. **Bold.** Love.

Unless otherwise indicated, all Scripture quotations are taken from
the *Holy Bible*, New Living Translation, copyright © 1996, 2004, 2015
by Tyndale House Foundation. Used by permission of Tyndale House
Publishers, a Division of Tyndale House Ministries, Carol Stream, Illinois
60188. All rights reserved.

ISBN 978-1-4707-5960-5
Printed in China
10 9 8 7 6 5 4 3 2 1   25 24 23 22 21 20

Acknowledgments

"Life [is] like a box of chocolates; you never know what you're gonna get." Of course, if we simply turn the box over and read the descriptions, the deep-fried mysticism of Forrest Gump is punctured and deflated. But if we unmask the secret identities of the candy we're picking, where's the fun in that? And, by "fun," I mean uncertainty and risk and adventure…

In my 18-month expedition into writing these devotions, I've had plenty of uncertainty and risk and adventure. The key to every successful expedition is, simply, the people paddling in that dugout canoe with you. And I've had the best companions…

- *Jeff Storm*—My longtime friend and art director who designed the cover and interior of the *Jesus-Centered Daily*. It's his brilliance, his sensibilities, and his own passion for Jesus that subtly impact this reading experience. Thank you for going to the mat for this book, and for me, over and over.

- *Joani Schultz*—As always, her dogged determination to make sure my words and ideas never sacrifice clarity for creativity, and never take the reader down a dead-end ally, has been invaluable. Your deft touch as an editor helped cure a thousand little ills in these devotions.

- *Lyndsay Gerwing*—Your flexibility, attention to detail, and patience and perseverance with me have plugged all the holes in the dam that is this book. This is an idiosyncratic work, and I'm grateful for your convictions and your charity.

- *St. Benedict's Monastery*—For 20 years this impossibly quiet mountain retreat has been the setting for the "principle work" of my books. The grace and raw beauty of my surroundings have infected my soul with wonder and seeped into everything I write.

- *My Friends and Family*—Once again, I'm grateful for my wife, Bev, who was the first to read the finished manuscript, the first to tell me of its impact on her life, and always the first to tell me she believes in me. I'm also indebted to Tom and Scotty and Brad and Lucy and Logan and Emma and Radu and Tracy, who all read the manuscript at various stages of the birthing process. And I'm thankful for the insights and stories and influence of my daughters Lucy and Emma, who let me steal whatever I want from them without permission and love me even though I'm weird.

- *The Pursuing the Heart Group*—Finally, I'm so indebted to the two dozen teenagers in the "home ministry" I lead, who've stunned me over and over with their insights into the heart of Jesus. You have been the most influential theologians in my life, for so long…

Introduction

The great 17th-century philosopher and scientist Blaise Pascal said we are all born with a "God-shaped" hole in our souls. Put another way, we're all born heart-hungry. We wander through our lives famished, scouring the world's food-truck menu for the *one thing* that will finally fill us up. The *one thing* that will satisfy our heart's craving. But we eat and eat and eat, and we're never satisfied… We want more, but when we find what we think is more, it turns out to be less…

It is no coincidence that Jesus reveals the answer to our "one thing craving" after he accepts a *dinner invitation* from Martha and Mary of Bethany. After a tired, hungry, and thirsty Jesus arrives at their home, Martha launches into hospitable hyper-drive. And she is frustrated and bitter that her distracted sister has ceded all the work to her. Mary is "seated at the Lord's feet, listening to what he's teaching." And Martha's anger bubbles over: "Lord, doesn't it seem unfair to you that my sister just sits here while I do all the work? Tell her to come and help me."

Martha's hospitality looks like a gift, but it's really a demand. Mary, in contrast, has chosen a different form of soul food. Jesus points out the difference with a rebuke that is both gentle and invitational: *"My dear Martha, you are worried and upset over all these details! There is only one thing worth being concerned about. Mary has discovered it, and it will not be taken away from her."* (Luke 10:38-42).

The *one thing* Martha is looking for is standing right in front of her. But she has settled for *duty and responsibility* in her relationship with Jesus, which keeps him at a respectable distance. What a relief that Jesus will not settle for a rote relationship defined by service and discipline—he's after our hearts, and he's determined to capture them. Our path forward with him leads us to intimacy. Intimacy is scary; duty is predictable. It's safer to follow orders than follow our hearts. Jesus is the most substantial person in the universe because he's the only one capable of filling the hole in our souls. As you move through these pages, lay down your lesser pursuits—the temporary fixes and food-truck appetizers—and find the rich, satisfying meal you've been looking for…

Immerse yourself in these upending expeditions into the heart of the *real* Jesus.

Experience what it means to follow him, through micro-adventures that engage all five senses.

Pursue the "wonder" of his unmatched character and personality.

And pray in response to his movement in your heart.

Together, let's feast a little on Jesus every day, until our thirst and our hunger are satisfied, and the hole in our souls is filled with joy. "Before you know it, a sense of God's wholeness, everything coming together for good, will come and settle you down. It's wonderful what happens when Christ displaces worry at the center of your life" (Philippians 4:7, *The Message*).

The Jesus Reset

Read Luke 7:36-50

Early in the year we do something counter to our natural inclinations: *We actively pursue change.* Whether it's health and wellness, finances and career, or marriage and family, the calendar gives us the leverage we need to reconfigure the chaos of our reality. We buy a new planner, scribble a new bucket list, and declare new vows that certainly seem certain.

On New Year's Day I see two middle-aged women speed-walking in matching jogging suits. They are not running, but they seem convinced they have the capacity for it, like a memory they're trying to recover. And so they sputter forward into an awkward scuffle that quickly degenerates back into a labored walk after 50 feet. This is what makes us human—our vows are both courageous and ridiculous. And I'm reminded that we're captive to our broken best intentions… Maybe the status quo (our first love) isn't so bad after all.

But those who are transformed by Jesus share a common trait: We have given up our quest to summit, on our own, the Everest of deep change. Instead, we push our way forward to Jesus and pour our precious perfume over his feet, bowing and weeping and worshipping. We shift from self-reliance to Jesus-dependence. "Your faith has saved you," he tells the weeping, kissing, perfuming woman. It's in our surrender, not our resolution, that we finally find the immovable force that changes us.

Wonder	**Jesus**	**Do**
What if you simply asked Jesus for the desire to change?	"You cannot be fruitful unless you remain in me" (John 15:4).	Big changes start tiny. Fold your hands; switch the underneath thumb to the top.

Pray: Jesus, I'm trading self-reliance for self-surrender.

Pearls Before Swine

Read Matthew 7:6-7

What's the most valuable thing you have with you right now? Now pause to think about the "standard" you've just used to determine that thing's relative value—is it universal, or would others value it differently?

Early in his ministry, Jesus attracts a huge crowd, so he climbs the side of a mountain and sits down to teach (Matthew 5–7). Out of his mouth comes "shock and awe"—a blast of what he stands for and what the culture of the kingdom of God is like.

- Anger is pretty much the same as murder.
- Adultery is pretty much the same as lust.
- Divorce is pretty much the same as adultery.
- Don't make vows or promises none.
- Don't take revenge, and give your enemy more than asked for.
- Actually, love your enemies.
- Don't pray or fast or do anything spiritual to be praised.
- Forgive, or you won't be forgiven.
- Don't worry about basic needs.
- And, finally, "Don't throw your pearls to pigs! They will trample the pearls, then turn and attack you."

Here, Jesus is revealing the way he values things. And above all, he values the heart. He's telling us to honor and respect the "treasure" of our vulnerability. We don't show our "treasure" to people who can't understand the value of it. Honor our boundaries. Simple. Clear. And brave.

Wonder
Are you more, or less, vulnerable than you would like to be? Why?

Jesus
"Don't waste what is holy on people who are unholy" (Matthew 7:6).

Do
Give your pet a bit of your favorite snack— your "pearl"—and see what happens.

Pray: Jesus, convict me when I devalue my heart.

Self-Help

Read John 14:1-10

A self-help website recommends following a celebrity's morning routine: _Wake up at 5:45 a.m. Sip lukewarm water with fresh lemon and grated ginger. Then yoga followed by 10 minutes of meditation. Wake up your skin with a fresh spritzer of chilled cucumber and lemon water. Wake up your mind by listening to a podcast. Wake up your mouth by spending one minute brushing each tooth. Wake your children gently, then talk with each one for a few minutes. Make their breakfast and a smoothie. Get them to school and yourself to work..._

It is a happy reality for successful people that work and school don't enter the picture until, well, noon-ish. The promise of self-help is, of course, dependent on self-strength—following the right formulas produces the right results. But this is the very mentality Jesus lambastes in the Pharisees, who "crush people with unbearable religious demands." Ultimately, self-help formulas keep us from depending on Jesus and, therefore, divert us from our true hope.

In _Man's Search for Meaning_, concentration camp survivor Viktor Frankl writes, "When we are no longer able to change a situation, we are challenged to change ourselves." Yes, self-renovation gives us a sense of control over the uncontrollable—we prefer to be the foreman on all our personal construction projects. But Paul reminds his protégé Timothy that desperate dependence is the doorway into real freedom: "A true widow... has placed her hope in God" (1 Timothy 5:5).

Wonder	**Jesus**	**Do**
What is your track record with self-help strategies?	"I am the way, the truth, and the life" (John 14:6).	Taste dependence. With a friend, fold a paper airplane, each using one hand.

Pray: Jesus, give me a profound revulsion for my addiction to control.

Jesus Redefines Love

Read John 6:53-69

Jesus redefines "true love" using two metrics: intensity and capacity. He ratchets the *intensity* of love with "all your heart, all your soul, all your mind, and all your strength" (Mark 12:30). And he expands the *capacity* of love with "Love your enemies! Pray for those who persecute you!" (Matthew 5:43-44). The broader, deeper love he's describing is native to the kingdom of God and invites us to escape the prison of our caution.

At the renowned French Laundry restaurant in Napa Valley, one member of the waitstaff every year earns its highest honor—a T-shirt with the slogan "Be the Pig." It references the difference between pigs and chickens: A chicken offers up an egg for breakfast, but the pig gives its life for it. Likewise, when we give ourselves to Jesus with a trusting abandon we're pigs, not chickens.

After the crowds have abandoned him and Jesus wonders aloud if his closest friends will do the same, Peter answers, "Lord, to whom would we go? [Only] you have the words that give eternal life." This is a "pig" abandoning himself to the heart of Jesus. Caution gives way to unreasonable passion. Leonardo da Vinci painted the face of his enemy as Judas in his masterpiece *The Last Supper.* But he simply couldn't paint the face of Jesus until (under conviction) he repainted Judas, dropping his vendetta. When we hate our enemies, our eyes grow scales. When Jesus is in us, and we are in him, we love like pigs...

Wonder
Jesus says true love is defined by its response to enemies. Why?

Jesus
"Anyone who eats my flesh and drinks my blood has eternal life" (John 6:54).

Do
Drink in your environment like a pig. Close your eyes and identify five sounds.

Pray: Jesus, I need you to love my enemies through me.

Still Angry

Read John 11:1-44

All of history orbits around Jesus' execution. He's born in a Bethlehem stable to die on a Golgotha cross. Death is his mission—he intends to embrace it and then conquer it.

On his way to the tomb of his close friend Lazarus (dead for four days because Jesus, inexplicably, shows up too late to heal him), Jesus is fuming: "When Jesus saw [Mary] weeping and saw the other people wailing with her, a deep anger welled up within him." And later, "Jesus was still angry as he arrived at the tomb."

And why is he still angry? This is mystery stacked on mystery. Sherlock Holmes reminds us, "Once you eliminate the impossible, whatever remains, no matter how improbable, must be the truth." We know Jesus is not angry over the shock of his friend's death, so here's what must be true: *Death is at war with Life itself, and any concession to it stirs his anger.* The death of his friend is a necessary prelude—he must demonstrate to the world that he gives life to everything (John 1:4) and eternal life to those who believe (John 3:15) because he is Life itself (John 14:6). And when we eat the "bread of life" (John 6:35), he promises us a "rich and satisfying life" (John 10:10).

Death and Life are like oil and water—they do not mix. So when an angry sun rises in the morning, the lurking darkness must give way.

Wonder
Jesus is intent on proving his authority over death—but why do it *this way*?

Jesus
"Didn't I tell you that you would see God's glory if you believe?" (John 11:40).

Do
Lick some pepper (death), then lemon juice (life). Life wins, and lingers.

Pray: Jesus, stir my own anger over death in all its forms.

A Deeper Taste

Read 2 Timothy 1:3-12

My daughter, home from college, asked me to wake her at 8:45 for a friend's visit at 9:15. At 9:10 I remembered what I was suppose to do. She had five panicked minutes to get herself together before the doorbell rang. Her eyes spilled disappointment. After a lifetime of faithfulness, can our trust be so fragile that even a small failure can diminish it? A proverb reminds us, *we gain trust in drops, but we lose it in buckets.*

The brutal Roman emperor Nero condemns an aging Paul to be chained like a criminal in a dank, forlorn dungeon. Scores of Paul's friends have already betrayed and deserted him. Loneliness pierces his soul, and he knows "the time of my death is near" (2 Timothy 4:6). Is this how the One who "broke the power of death" rewards his friends? Paul confides in Timothy: "I am not ashamed of [my imprisonment], for I know the one in whom I trust, and I am sure that he is able to guard what I have entrusted to him until the day of his return." And what has Paul entrusted to Jesus? Only his heart—*his everything.*

Yes, someday we'll feel let down and abandoned by Jesus. We, like Paul, will feel lonely and forgotten and forlorn. Our circumstances will obliterate our entitlements, leaving only the depth of our trust. Mere circumstantial trust is too shallow to survive disappointment. And so we "eat his body and drink his blood" (John 6) because that feast will carry us through the wilderness.

Wonder	**Jesus**	**Do**
Which of your five senses do you trust the most, and why?	"Do you finally believe?" (John 16:31).	Make a meal wearing oven mitts. How does diminished touch impact your trust?

Pray: Jesus, I do trust you, but help my lack of trust.

What's Good and What's Not

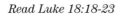

Read Luke 18:18-23

My kryptonite looks suspiciously like a chocolate doughnut. What about you? Candy? Frappuccino? Pie? Pastry? Thin Mint? We all have our own definition of irresistibly *good.* A band you'd kill to see live is the same band you'd have to *pay me* to see. A film you revere is the same I wish I could un-watch. Why do we have so many competing standards for *good*? Well, our definitions of *good* may seem contrary, but in truth they're more like a thousand streams fed by the Amazon river of *Good.*

When a rich religious leader asks Jesus what he must do to "inherit eternal life," he calls him "Good Teacher." Before Jesus answers the man's loaded question, he performs a little surgery on "good" with this: "Only God is truly good." *Yes, yes, yes, Jesus… But what about my question?*

How do we really know what's good and what's not? Well, the preening young man lays his cards on the table: "I've obeyed all [the] commandments since I was young." And Jesus, like a surgeon, decides to cut the cancer of self-sufficient goodness out of his heart: "There is still one thing you haven't done." His *one thing* turns out to be everything: *Sell your possessions, give the money to the poor, and follow me.* When we trade all our sources of "false goodness" for the True Source of goodness, we follow our little stream back to the Amazon.

Wonder
What one word describes your experience of Jesus' goodness?

Jesus
"Apart from me [the Amazon of goodness] you can do nothing" (John 15:5).

Do
Start a "kryptonite" thread on social media: "What's better than [*candy*]?"

Pray: Jesus, remind me of you whenever I use the word *good.*

The Widow's Mite

Read Mark 12:41-44

It's more important to understand and trust the heart of Jesus than it is to apply his "principles." No matter how hard we try to follow his "good person" cookbook, the souffle always collapses when we pull it out of the oven. But the *heart* of Jesus never fails us.

Surrounded by the conspiratorial "teachers of the law" in the Temple, Jesus fights his way through their traps, escaping to a lonely corner near the collection box. There he watches a parade of rich people showboating their large donations. These people bore him. But the poor widow who slides past the box unnoticed, dropping in "two small coins," rivets his attention: "I tell you the truth, this poor widow has given more than all the others… They gave a tiny part of their surplus, but she…has given everything."

The woman offers two *lepta*, which together add up to a *quadrans*, or 1/64 of a day's wage. In today's currency, she's dropping $1.10 into the box, and this is all she has. Jesus trumpets the overlooked courage of those who go all-in because all-in defines his heart and, therefore, defines kingdom-of-God culture. While the rich may obey the biblical principle of tithing, Jesus celebrates the *heart* behind the widow's all-in. She empties herself, the same way he will soon empty himself on the cross. Jesus loves it when we have nearly nothing to contribute but give it all anyway.

Wonder
When you give, do you feel more like a rich donor or the poor widow?

Jesus
"You are not far from the Kingdom of God" (Mark 12:34).

Do
Tape a penny (or a dime) to this page—a symbol of your all-in.

Pray: Jesus, I offer you my *nothing* so that you may make it *something*.

Into the Dark

Read Matthew 23:1-12

In his iconic horror story "A Descent Into the Maelstrom," Edgar Allen Poe narrates the story of three fishermen brothers struggling to survive after their schooner is dragged into the gaping mouth of a massive ocean whirlpool. The older and younger brothers panic and are lost—only the middle brother survives. He notices the casks that slide off the ship's deck into the abyss are dragged down into the chaos but then pop to the surface. So he lashes himself to a cask and throws himself overboard, saving his life.

The middle brother defeats certain death because he's convinced a buoyant cask is capable of delivering him from the darkness of the abyss. He trusts the cask because he has studied what it can do, and so gives himself with abandon to it…

Jesus is not peddling a new set of values; he's offering *himself* as our "buoyant cask." He invites us to give over control of our fate and tie ourselves to him. But we do not easily relinquish control. We must first admit our weakness, our obvious limitations in the face of our challenges, before we gain his strength. "Those who exalt themselves will be humbled, and those who humble themselves will be exalted.." When we lash ourselves to Jesus—binding ourselves to him over and over in ever-growing intimacy—he delivers us from our darkness.

Wonder	**Jesus**	**Do**
What's a "maelstrom" in your life, and what would rescue you from it?	"Practice…whatever [the Pharisees] tell you, but don't follow their example" (Matthew 23:3).	With a black marker, mark a "maelstrom" dot on your palm. Offer it to Jesus.

Pray: Jesus, tie me to you so that we can go overboard together.

The Culture of God's Kingdom

Read Matthew 13:10-17

It's customary to bow instead of shake hands in Asian culture. It's a habit rooted in the past. In India, people once used a jug and their left palm instead of toilet paper. And in Indonesian culture a long fingernail on the left hand served the same purpose. To Western sensibilities, these customs seem disgusting—diverse cultural practices breed comparison and judgment. For example, if you crook your finger to signal "Come here!" in Japan, it's considered obscene. In Serbia, Vietnam, and Malaysia, the same motion is used to call animals—that's why it's insulting.

Jesus understands that the customs of the kingdom of God often seem foreign to us. That makes sense because sin got us kicked out of the Garden, our "home country." So Jesus translates the values and practices of his spiritual home into something we can understand—he tells "cultural translation" stories we call parables.

We learn what's most important to Jesus by paying attention to his parables. After reeling off a string of them (in Matthew 13), he tells his disciples: "Every teacher of religious law who becomes a disciple in the Kingdom of Heaven is like a homeowner who brings from his storeroom new gems of truth as well as old." We won't have treasure to give others unless we embrace the customs and values in Jesus' "treasure house"—the kingdom of God.

Wonder	**Jesus**	**Do**
What's one "foreign" custom in God's kingdom that's hard to follow?	"Blessed are your eyes, because they see; and your ears, because they hear" (Matthew 13:16).	Dab cologne or perfume *here*. Intimacy with Jesus transfers his "smell" to us.

Pray: Jesus, make your "kingdom customs" native to me.

The Jesus Push-Back

Read Matthew 5:21-47

In a culture of competing "truths," how do we discern what's false? For example…

- *Which is more likely to cause hyper behavior—a doughnut or a piece of fruit?* There is no link between sugar and hyperactivity, but there is for pesticide residue.

- *At home, are you more likely to be harmed by a tornado or by a violent assault?* You have the same one in 100,000 chance of experiencing either.

- *Are you more likely to die in an airplane accident or a bathtub?* In an airplane you have a one in two million chance of dying; in a bathtub it's a one in one million.

It's difficult for us to parse fiction and nonfiction in a culture plagued by deception. Jesus lives in this same tension. In his Sermon on the Mount, he repeats the same rhythmic challenge over and over: *"You have heard it said… But I say…"* Here he's debunking conventional wisdom and inviting us to live as "strangers in a foreign land." We are a people longing for home while we sojourn in a broken world. And so we cling to truth by abiding in Truth itself, practicing the "Jesus Push-Back" in our everyday lives. Whenever we hear a "given" in the culture ("You have heard it said…"), we wonder how Jesus would counter it ("But I say…"). Then we commit ourselves to live in the Kingdom we can't see, not the kingdom we can.

Wonder
Jesus' "But I say…" statements seem impossible. Why set the bar so high?

Jesus
"You are to be perfect, even as your Father…is perfect" (Matthew 5:48).

Do
Notice the "cultural givens" in newstand magazines. Ask Jesus for "push-backs."

Pray: Jesus, teach me to push back against the "givens" in my culture.

Being With

Read John 21:1-17

Jesus offers us a blunt invitation into paradise: "Remain in me, and I will remain in you"(John 15:4). Here, everything depends on "remain," but what does that really mean?

In the strange days after the resurrection of Jesus, his disciples are scared and uncertain about what to do. And so Peter decides to go back to the thing he knows best—commercial fishing. He invites his friends to join him, and they spend all night on the Sea of Galilee, catching nothing. At dawn they see the figure of a man on the beach, beckoning them: "Throw out your net on the right-hand side of the boat, and you'll get some!" When they do, they catch so many fish that they can't haul in their net. This bizarre and playful miracle reminds John of another just like it, three years before. "It's the Lord!" he cries.

Peter quickly ties his tunic around his naked body, jumps into the water, and thrashes his way to shore, where he sees Jesus already cooking breakfast. "Bring some of the fish you've just caught," Jesus says. And he serves them bread and fish, inhabiting his friends' fears with his presence. His invitation is as simple as a child's: *Will you be with me?* And when we are *with him,* our confusion and fear and worry slide into the background.

Wonder
Peter betrays Jesus before the cross. Why does he rush to be with him?

Jesus
"Do you love me?... Then feed my sheep" (John 21:17).

Do
Slowly savor a salty chip. Like salt, a little bit of Jesus changes everything.

Pray: Jesus, will you be *with* me?

Jesus On the Job

Read Luke 4

The first few days at a new job can be…hairy. Unspoken expectations, unfamiliar faces, and a fresh herd of sacred cows. But it'd be hard to beat Jesus' first few weeks as the Messiah…

His "pre-employment training" is a solo 40-day fast in the desert, where he's repeatedly tempted by the father of holocausts, Lucifer. Fresh out of desert boot camp, his first business trip is to his hometown, Nazareth, where he promptly infuriates everyone by announcing that God's love extends to all people, not just the Jews. And then his neighbors—the people he grew up with—try to push him off a cliff. Soon after, he's confronted by a man possessed by a demon and scores of people desperate for healing.

All of this before he invites the first disciple to join him.

Jesus' "workday" reflects the brutal reality of a Navy SEAL job description: I have come to set captives free (Luke 4:18). In "You Will Go Free," singer/songwriter Tonio K channels the passion of Jesus' mission in our lives:

You've been a prisoner, been a prisoner all your life. Held captive in an alien world Where they hold your need for love to your throat like a knife… Well, I don't know when, and I don't know how. I don't know how long it's gonna take. I don't know how hard it will be. But I know you will go free.

Wonder	**Jesus**	**Do**
No job is more stressful than the one Jesus has. How does he cope?	"The time of the Lord's favor has come" (Luke 4:19).	Roll this page into the binding and close the book. Feel the impact of stress.

Pray: Jesus, give me the training I need to join you on your mission.

Beautiful Things

Read John 17

Gil Zamora is a forensic artist who worked for a West Coast police department for 20 years, re-creating the facial features of criminals based on victim descriptions of their perpetrators. In a widely viewed advertising campaign for the beauty brand Dove, Zamora tells a succession of women he's going to draw their faces based only on their own descriptions. He remains hidden from them as he asks questions about their hair, chin, jaw, and "most prominent feature." As they talk, he draws. Then he asks each woman to describe *another* woman she met in the waiting room. From this, he produces two portraits for each woman— one self-described, the other from the perspective of a stranger.

In the startling "reveal," the women discover that the "me" they've narrated looks significantly worse than the "me" a stranger has described. Some weep when they realize how much they've allowed their interior insinuations to define their beauty. Then Zamora asks, "Do you think you're more beautiful than you say?" We're formed and shaped by the voices we pay attention to. We must decide if we believe in the "me" Jesus is revealing or the "me" our self-narrative insinuates. Our aching hope is captured in the refrain from Michael Gungor's song "Beautiful Things":

> *You make beautiful things,*
> *You make beautiful things out of the dust.*
> *You make beautiful things.*
> *You make beautiful things out of us.*

Wonder
Why is it hard to believe that Jesus "makes beautiful things out of us"?

Jesus
"I have given them the glory you gave me" (John 17:22).

Do
Draw what your face looks like, then ask someone to do the same. Compare.

Pray: Jesus, describe the "me" you see in me.

Jesus Christ Supernatural

Read John 5:1-15

Stand facing a partner (roughly your size) two feet away. Hold your arm straight in front of you, hovering it over your friend's extended arm, then try to push down against your friend's stiff upward resistance as he/she repeats "My name is [his/her name]" over and over. It'll be difficult to push that arm down. But if you try this again, with your partner repeating "My name is Kermit the Frog" instead, you'll discover he/she can't resist your pressure. The effect seems, well, supernatural—but is it? Well, no… Turns out, *we experience a physiological reaction when we lie about who we are.* Our dissonance saps the physical strength we need to resist that downward pressure. So it's science, not supernatural. And that makes sense, we tell ourselves, because we *should* be able to explain everything, even the inexplicable…

Likewise, we know Jesus amazed people with his supernatural abilities, but so did Superman. These stories are entertaining, but we don't treat them as *real.* Writer Annie Dillard observes, "On the whole, I do not find Christians, outside of the catacombs, sufficiently sensible of conditions. Does anyone have the foggiest idea what sort of power we so blithely invoke? Or, as I suspect, does no one believe a word of it?"

We know Superman will never step off the screen into our living room. And we expect the miracle-working Jesus to stay safely confined to the Bible. But an edited Jesus is no Jesus at all.

Wonder	**Jesus**	**Do**
What's a "supernatural" experience you've had? Why think of it that way?	"You will see greater things than this" (John 1:50).	Find a partner and try the "Kermit the Frog" experience.

Pray: Jesus, open my eyes to your supernatural presence in my life.

Forming Forces

Read Philippians 3:2-11

Look around your environment, then ask yourself: *How is this environment impacting me? What words describe how I feel here?* You're likely unaware, until now, of how your surroundings have been influencing you. Marshall McLuhan says, "Environments are not passive wrappings, but are, rather, active processes which are invisible." Our physical, emotional, psychological, and spiritual environments form us, even when we're unconscious of their sculpting influence.

Most church environments are ruled by two forming forces: *"Try harder to get better"* and *"Understand the biblical principle and apply it to your life."* This means that our spiritual-growth ecosystem is polluted by two fallacies: 1) We assume mere understanding leads to growth, and 2) We falsely believe our own strength is the key to transformation. Satan understood biblical truth when he tempted Jesus in the wilderness, but it didn't transform him. And we have a woeful record of "applying" truths to our lives.

The Apostle Paul reminds us that our willful efforts to achieve goodness smell like an outhouse: "Compared to the high privilege of knowing Christ Jesus as my Master, firsthand, everything I once thought I had going for me is insignificant—dog dung. I've dumped it all in the trash so that I could embrace Christ and be embraced by him" *(The Message)*. We need to know Jesus firsthand, not master our ability to "work the system."

Wonder
Why do we generally prefer "try harder to get better" over grace?

Jesus
"You think [the Scriptures] give you eternal life.. But [they] point to me!" (John 5:39).

Do
Smell a mood-lifter—a plant, fragrance, outside air, food, or person.

Pray: Jesus, how has "try harder to get better" poisoned my soul?

Application vs. Attachment

Read Luke 13:1-9

In an episode of the British sitcom *Outnumbered*, a village vicar at a wedding reception is banished to the kids' table. The minions take advantage of the opportunity, assaulting the bewildered man with rapid-fire and unanswerable questions: *King Herod sent his soldiers to kill the baby Jesus, so why didn't baby Jesus just zap him? Why has God only given us 15,000 billion years left to live before the sun dies? When Jesus was a bit older, and was still being searched by the Romans, why couldn't he shape-shift into a Roman, and when all the other Romans were asleep he could go in and kill them?*

The vicar, understandably, soon plots his escape route.

What makes the vicar's job frustrating and impossible? Well, we expect our religious leaders to be answer-people. It's their job to solve our big mystery questions, because "understand and apply" is our standard for faith maturity. But we don't have all the answers, and real transformation is the fruit of a *right orientation* to Jesus, not the *right answers* about him. Like the branch abiding in the Vine, we draw life from our intimate attachment to Jesus. When our standard is application (doing something), not attachment (being something), we're living like the Pharisees.

Get closer to Jesus and we'll find life, and that life will transform us, and our transformation will produce spiritual fruit—the same fruit we're supposed to apply to our lifes.

Wonder	**Jesus**	**Do**
Why doesn't Jesus simply answer all our questions?	"Why can't you decide for yourselves what is right?" (Luke 12:57).	Pluck a leaf to use as a bookmark—an "attachment" reminder.

Pray: Jesus, bring more fruit in my life, not more answers.

Taking Refuge

Read Luke 7:36-50

We're caught in a social-media hurricane that tears at our souls. Three-quarters of young adults say they experience harassment on the internet. So, to cope, many college students gravitate to "Campus Safe Spaces" created for "civil discourse." But these campus bunker-zones have quickly morphed into walled fortresses built to repel diversity and disagreement. Like many other social cures, the treatment can be worse than the disease.

Jesus calls us *out of, not into,* protective bubbles and hater-free bunkers. To follow him we must exit our safe spaces and enter the fray—*he* will be our battlefield bomb shelter. We know the first part of Psalm 34:8—"Taste and see that the Lord is good"—but rarely focus on the second part—"Oh, the joys of those who take refuge in him!"

Jesus wants to transform us from the inside out, so he will burst all our bubbles. His interactions prove it—from the woman who anoints his feet with perfume and the Pharisees who protest it (Luke 7) to the woman caught in adultery and the haters who want her killed (John 8) to the notorious tax collector Zacchaeus who welcomes Jesus into his home. Jesus, as C.S. Lewis describes him in *The Chronicles of Narnia,* is "good, but not safe."

Wonder	**Jesus**	**Do**
What are the downsides of social media? How do you neuter them?	"I have told you these things so that you won't abandon your faith" (John 16:1).	Fast from social media for one day. Note the impact on your soul.

Pray: Jesus, I want to enter into your refuge today; show me the way.

What to Do With Our Burdens

Read John 15:18-26

In the Western world we believe happiness is tied to our good circumstances. That's a diabolical lie, because circumstantial happiness is like a smoke ring—it dissipates into the atmosphere. We live in the most affluent society in world history, yet we're facing a crisis of depression and anxiety. Our standard of living is higher than ever, but our satisfaction is lower than ever. We don't know what to do with our burdens, because our money (or good circumstances) was supposed to take care of them.

Oswald Chambers upends with this: "Many servants set out to serve God with great courage and with the right motives. But with no intimate fellowship with Jesus Christ, they are soon defeated… Commit to God whatever burden He has placed on you. Don't just cast it aside, but put it over onto Him."

True joy permeates our souls when we pursue two things:

1. Knowing Jesus.

2. Knowing ourselves

We can't relieve the weight of our burdens using our own resources. As we come to know Jesus more intimately, we share everything with him, including what weighs us down. Unburdened, he is kind to reveal what's most true about us. We are what Jesus says we are—members of his royal family, on a mission to set captives free.

Wonder	**Jesus**	**Do**
What's something you've forgotten to give to Jesus today?	"The world would love you as one of its own if you belonged to it" (John 15:19).	Imagine your shoe represents a burden. Take it off and offer it up to Jesus.

Pray: Jesus, I'm asking you to shoulder the weight of my burdens today.

Can You Come Out to Play?

Read Matthew 17:24-27

A pastor observes, "Christian people are a lot more picky and demanding about little details, and whether or not you're 'getting it right.'" We all know this is true. So why do we so often battle a magnetic pull toward criticalness?

We want to get it right, and we really want others to get it right, too.

This is why we don't typically describe our relationship with Jesus as *playful*. And we'd certainly *not* describe Jesus this way. When we read his words, the tone we hear in our heads is serious—grave, even. It's as if his job is to make sure the trains stay on schedule in our lives. But a lot of what Jesus says and does is more playful than we realize. For example, that time he paid his taxes to the IRS agents at his door by asking Peter to go down to the lake, catch a fish, and pull a silver coin from its mouth.

Toward the end of the great theologian Dallas Willard's life, an interviewer asked him to describe Jesus with one word. He chose *relaxed*. When you meet Jesus in the Bible, imagine you're a child who's just arrived at the playground and found your best friend already on the swings.

Wonder	**Jesus**	**Do**
In your life, how are you growing *less* and *more* like a child?	"Anyone who welcomes a little child like this... is welcoming me" (Matthew 18:5).	When you pass by a school or park playground, sit on a swing and pray.

Pray: Jesus, will you teach me to play again?

With All Your Soul

Read Ephesians 3:17-19

What's something besides food, water, and shelter you can't do without? What about music—is it a basic necessity? Jesus invites: *"Love the Lord your God with all your heart, mind, soul, and strength."* We know we're to love Jesus with our belief (heart) and our understanding (mind) and our service (strength). But what about the soul? Music is the language of the soul, because the soul's love-language is beauty.

Paul wants his friends in Ephesus to "know the love of Christ which *surpasses knowledge*, that you may be filled up to all the fullness of God" (Ephesians 3:19, NASB). There is a way to know Jesus that *fills us* more than knowing him with our heads. This is why the Bible includes the Psalms, a lyric collection from the greatest songwriters in history.

As I write, I'm listening to Andrew Osenga's "White Dove," a beautiful meditation on longing that invites my soul to yearn: "Never pin your hopes to the ground, when they're meant for the sky… Though it feels a dam is breaking, like a second coming of the flood. With the promise of not only justice, but mercy and love… And I'm a waiting, waiting for a white dove… Every sad thing will become untrue. Every sad thing will become untrue…" And I raise my hands to worship as the tears roll down my cheeks. And I'm *knowing* Jesus in a way that surpasses knowledge.

Wonder
If music is unnecessary for survival, why do we crave it?

Jesus
"Blessed are your eyes, because they see; and your ears, because they hear" (Matthew 13:16).

Do
Listen to a favorite song with your eyes closed. Invite Jesus to speak through it.

Pray: Jesus, plant your song in my soul.

The Memes of Jesus

Read John 9:1-11

Memes use photos as visual prompts, then turn those visuals on their head with a witty *bon mont*. On the off chance you've never seen one, here's a popular example…

Sometimes our memes are profound, but mostly they're silly or witty or creepy, or some combination of all that. They work because they strip a thought down to its naked impact. Likewise, if we condensed the stories of Jesus into memes, we might discover the naked impact at the core of every encounter. Just picture the face of Jesus, or the one he encounters, in these Jesus-memes…

- John 9:1-11: I might be blind…but that's spit-mud you just smeared on me, right?

- John 3:1-21: Before there is John 3:16…there's the Holy Spirit giving birth.

- Luke 8:16-18: If that lamp is hidden under your bed…you're not paying attention.

- Mark 2:13-17: Do you have a bad reputation? Come on in!

To encounter Jesus using a meme-filter, ask two questions:
1) What truths is Jesus trying to teach through his words/actions?
2) What do I know about the heart of Jesus from this passage?

Wonder
If you created a meme using your face, what would you say to Jesus?

Jesus
"Healthy people don't need a doctor—sick people do" (Mark 2:17).

Do
Search online for "Goofy Jesus Photos"; create your own meme using one.

Pray: Jesus, what meme-message do you have for me?

Proposition vs. Person

Read John 6:52-69

We know a lot about the "whats" of Jesus' mission on earth—we've had *whats* blasted at us through the church firehose for a long time. But the deeper mystery to be explored is hidden in the land of "whys"…

Author Donald Miller writes, "Because we live in a constant sales environment where we are told a certain car will make us sexy…we assume the gospel of Jesus works the same way, that is, if we invest something, we get something more back. But this is not the case… When we let go of the idea of Jesus as a product and embrace him as a being, our path to spiritual maturity begins."

Truth is a *person*, not a *proposition*. That's why we're most drawn to stories in film, songs, and books that intertwine darkness and light. The darkness makes us long for the light, and sin makes us long for redemption. Jesus has somehow planted his rescue message in every great story, because great stories are about people, not propositions.

When we default to reducing the story of Jesus to mere propositional truths (*"All have sinned and fallen short of the glory of God"*), we don't get at the heart of the gospel. Because, at the heart of the gospel is a person, not a proposition.

Wonder
Is your commitment to Jesus more *"If I give, you give"* or *"You are all I want"*?

Jesus
"You are seeing things merely from a human point of view, not from God's" (Mark 8:33).

Do
Read the "stories" of Facebook friends; ask, *"Jesus, show me your heart."*

Pray: Jesus, show me your heart in every great story.

Sheep in Green Pastures

Read John 10:1-16

Ever been challenged to name the zoo animal you're most like? It's a nearly universal embarrassment. Still, it's not crazy to compare ourselves to an animal that captures our essence, because Jesus did that. To him, we are most like…sheep! And he compares himself to a shepherd—a "good shepherd."

When Jesus chooses a metaphor, it's a perfect metaphor, because he is perfect. So the deeper we dig, the more we discover the true meaning of his metaphors. In the iconic beginning of Psalm 2 (NASB), David (a former shepherd) writes:

> *The Lord is my shepherd,*
> *I shall not want.*
> *He makes me lie down in green pastures…*

So how does a shepherd "make" his sheep lie down in a green pasture? Professional sheepherders know: 1) You can *force* the sheep to lie down by holding their legs, pulling them backward, or 2) You can *relax them* into lying down by feeding them, chasing away predators, and leading them to soft grass. Assume the "forced" method doesn't describe the heart of Jesus. Instead, *Jesus wants to feed us into contentment, fight off our threats, and invite us to rest in his presence.*

Wonder
Sheep are the neediest farm animals. How are you a needy sheep today?

Jesus
"[His sheep] follow him because they know his voice" (John 10:4).

Do
Lie down in some grass and stare at the sky for 60 seconds. Exhale tension.

Pray: Jesus, my good shepherd, make me lie down…

The Storyteller

Read Romans 1:19-23

In Eugene Peterson's paraphrase of Romans 1, Paul proclaims, "The basic reality of God is plain enough. Open your eyes and there it is! By taking a long and thoughtful look at what God has created, people have always been able to see what their eyes as such can't see: eternal power, for instance, and the mystery of his divine being."

God has planted his story, like Easter eggs hidden in our living room, all over his creation. It's a story about his attributes, his power, and his divine nature. People often say they feel closer to God when they're immersed in nature. They're not merely describing the beauty around them—all created things are living metaphors that describe the *soul* of Jesus. But we'll miss this if we're not paying attention…

When Adam and Eve betray God in the Garden, the intimate communication they've enjoyed is shattered. Ever since, we've been communication-challenged. But in his humility, Jesus embeds his heart all over our environment. When he enters Jerusalem and the people praise him for his glory, the Pharisees demand that Jesus rebuke them, but he says, "If they kept quiet, the stones along the road would burst into cheers!" These same stones are still proclaiming his glory.

Wonder
When people say they feel "closer to God" in nature, what do they mean?

Jesus
"Notice the fig tree, or any other tree" (Luke 21:29).

Do
Stare at a rock or twig or leaf. Smell it. Touch it. How does it reflect Jesus' heart?

Pray: Jesus, open my blind eyes to your heart, hiding in plain sight.

Hashtag Jesus

Read Matthew 8:5-13

The purpose of satire is to skewer misconceptions. And our misconceptions about Jesus are most often because we're not paying close attention to him. Maybe we make Jesus squirm when we describe him to others.

One Christmas my daughter Emma gave her older sister Lucy a card covered in hashtags that described her heart (a hashtag is a shorthand way of describing the essence of something, like #addictedtoStarbucks). This card is one of Lucy's favorite keepsakes because it uncovers her personality in a witty, insightful way.

If we hashtagged Jesus' encounters with others, we might expose the "chewy center" of his heart. For example, the hashtags about Jesus in Matthew 8:5-13 could be #beliefoverstatus or #paganschmagen or #madeworthy. Jesus longs for a true-you, true-me relationship—where we are mutually, authentically seen. Or playfully hashtagged…

#TrueJesus

Wonder
What's something you believed about Jesus as a child but don't now?

Jesus
"If you only knew…you would ask me, and I would give you living water" (John 4:10).

Do
Pick one of Jesus' random encounters and create your own hashtag.

Pray: Jesus, expose and free me from my misconceptions about you.

No Mistakes in Jazz

Read John 5:1-15

Jazz musicians describe the interplay among players as "sacred," because improvisation requires trust and risk and intimacy. Likewise, "sacred intimacy" is the fruit of a less structured, more relaxed relationship with Jesus. In a TED Talk titled "There Are No Mistakes in Jazz," Stefon Harris, one of the world's most respected jazz masters, exposes a roomful of business leaders to the beauty of improvisation and how it transforms relationships.

After Harris and his band demonstrate the focused, risk-taking, relaxed way improvisational musicians relate to each other, he says, "The bandstand is really a sacred space, because you have no opportunity to think about the future or the past—you're really alive in the moment. Everyone is listening [to each other], we're responding. So, the idea of a mistake, from the perspective of a jazz musician, is [strange]. Every mistake is an opportunity in jazz. Real mistakes happen only when we don't react—when we miss the opportunity to discover where the mistake could lead us."

We recoil from mistakes because we've falsely believed Jesus is judging us for how many "wrong notes" we play. But Jesus wants relationship, and like a jazz quartet, he craves "sacred space" with us—when we are "alive in the moment" because we are taking risks with him.

Wonder	**Jesus**	**Do**
What's a "mistake" in your life that you've never released to Jesus?	"Would you like to get well?" (John 5:6).	Create a short, improvised rhythm with your fingers—an act of playful worship.

Pray: Jesus, I offer my mistakes to you. Please improvise them into beauty.

Inexplicable Belief

Read Matthew 15:21-28

When someone we trust expresses "inexplicable belief" in who we are, it shoots to our core. By *inexplicable*, I don't mean confusing—I mean a kind of deep belief that is both *observant* and passionately *for* us.

Love Does author Bob Goff shares how the gift of inexplicable belief helps set others free from their captivity to destructive self-narratives: "What if, when people meet us, they feel like they have just met heaven? I mean, we tell people who they are turning into. We see people as who they can be. We recognize that they don't want to be told what they want—instead, we tell them who they are…and who they are turning into."

When a pagan woman from Tyre begs Jesus to cast a demon out of her daughter, he first treats her with the sort of dismissive attitude Gentile women are used to getting from Jewish religious leaders: "It isn't right to take food from the children and throw it to the dogs." But when she replies, "Even dogs are allowed to eat the scraps that fall beneath their masters' table," Jesus offers her inexplicable belief: "Dear woman, your faith is great. Your request is granted."

Jesus rescues and redeems our created beauty by paying attention, then appreciating, then surfacing, then celebrating what is "fearfully and wonderfully made" in us.

Wonder	**Jesus**	**Do**
What's something harsh you've believed about yourself, and why?	"I have told you these things so that you will be filled with my joy" (John 15:11).	Pull a weed. As you do, ask Jesus to pull the "weed" you've believed.

Pray: Jesus, what word describes your "inexplicable belief" in me?

Transcending Fear

Read Luke 8:23-25

The most common warning in Scripture is "Fear not!" Fear has poisoned our emotional bloodstream ever since Adam and Eve invited "the knowledge of good and evil" into our DNA. *The Culture of Fear* author Barry Glassner says, "[We] live in what is arguably the safest time and place in human history, and yet fear levels are high." Because fear paralyzes, and is immersive, Jesus is always targeting his disciples' anxieties:

- "Don't be afraid of those who want to kill your body; they cannot touch your soul. Fear only God, who can destroy both soul and body in hell" (Matthew 10:28).

- When they see him walk on water toward their boat, in the deep of the night, across a stormy sea, he calls out, "Don't be afraid. Take courage. I am here!" (Matthew 14:25-27).

- "And the very hairs on your head are all numbered. So don't be afraid; you are more valuable to God than a whole flock of sparrows" (Matthew 10:30-31).

Because fear can hijack our hearts, life is centrally about confronting and overcoming it. And the help Jesus offers us is not the help we typically want—he does not always drive the ogres from under the bridge. Instead, he walks with us into darkness, his arm around our shoulders and a smile on his face. He gives us what author and therapist Edwin Friedman calls his "non-anxious presence"—a *peace* that defuses our fear.

Wonder	**Jesus**	**Do**
Consider one of your hidden fears. What's fueling it?	"Peace be with you" (John 20:26).	Try to crush an empty water bottle with, and without, its cap. Jesus is our "cap."

Pray: Jesus, increase your "non-anxious presence" in me.

Light and Doubt

Read John 14:1-14

I warned the young people in my "home church" that if they looked before I gave them permission, they'd get nothing. And then I said, "If I told you I taped a $1 bill under one of your seats, would you believe me?" And then, "What about $100?" And then, "What's the difference between the two possibilities?" And then, "What if I told you I'd taped a $5 bill under your seat, but you had to pay me $1 to look?" And finally, "What factors into your responses to these possibilities?"

And then I revealed the truth: "I didn't tape $1 or $5 or $100 under a seat. Now, how does that impact your trust? You now have my permission to look—will you?" The air in the room reeked of indignation. That's what happens when you bait-and-switch people who trust you. This was an exercise in doubt-surfacing—I wanted them to feel toward me what they sometimes feel toward Jesus. Doubt is often tied to challenging circumstances or others' behavior. But go deeper and we discover doubt is tied to what we believe about the heart.

Jesus wants everything we keep in the dark out in the light, and that includes our doubts. In the dark, doubts grow like mold, but light shrivels them. So we must be fearless about dragging our doubts out of their dark hiding places. Pat answers don't give us peace in the face of our doubts, but the "the light of the world" will.

Wonder	**Jesus**	**Do**
What is your deepest doubt about Jesus?	"Don't let your hearts be troubled. Trust in God, and trust also in me" (John 14:1).	Hold an empty cup on your head and fill it with water. Give Jesus your doubt.

Pray: Jesus, shine your light on my doubts and shrivel them.

The Skeptic's Undoing

Read Matthew 11:2-6

We live straddled between the Kingdom of God and the Kingdom of Culture, one foot planted in the sacred and the other mired in the profane. And so we face challenges that undermine our default beliefs and arguments that counter the truths we hold self-evident. We need Jesus to show us how to "live and breathe and move" in an atmosphere of skepticism.

A pastor once called to protest a spiritual practice I call "Psalm-o-Rama" I'd included in one of my books. Simply, I ask Jesus to give me a number between 1 and 150 and then a second number to go with it. There are 150 Psalms, so the numbers that surface are chapter and verse. Then I blindly go to the reference, read it, and ask Jesus to speak to me through it. It's very often a profound experience, surfacing issues I didn't know needed my attention and encouragement I didn't know I needed. This pastor's skepticism about my "playground habit" with Jesus fueled a furious indignation. Skepticism blinded him to my heart, and to the heart of Jesus.

Likewise, John the Baptist wrestles with skepticism about Jesus as he languishes in prison—doubt is growing like a cancer in his heart. To counter it, Jesus simply describes to John what happens when people meet him: *My heart is the chemotherapy that kills their cancer, just as it will cure yours.*

Wonder
Jesus tells us we'll "do greater things" than him. What does that mean?

Jesus
"Wisdom is shown to be right by its results" (Matthew 11:19).

Do
Play "Psalm-o-Rama"—read the "Psalm number" that pops up; respond to Jesus.

Pray: Jesus, undermine my skepticism by showing me your impact.

Jesus the Other

Read Matthew 17:14-20

In the award-winning film *Arrival*, linguistics professor Louise Banks leads an elite team of scientists working with military leaders to avert disaster after gigantic spaceships touch down around the world. Banks and her allies must race to unlock the aliens' "language" so they can answer the film's central question: *What is your purpose here?* The answer is almost impossible to discern because the aliens are so *other* that communication seems hopeless.

But "What is your purpose here?" is also our most important theological question, relative to Jesus. The corollaries include: *What is the truth about you? What are your intentions toward us? Is your heart good? And how do you define "good"?*

We crave certainty in his answers to these questions. But some things we see Jesus say or do seem contradictory or in conflict with scientific conclusions or undermining our expectations for how he should behave. Jesus, frustrating as he is, always leaves us a gap to jump over—a "faith leap." He's always pleading with people to have more faith and commending those who *do something* in response to the faith they have in him. And we cannot grow in faith without that gap.

Jesus came to "translate" the other-ness of God for us. His behavior, his stories, and his life are our Rosetta Stone for the God we can't see, but believe in anyway.

Wonder
Faith pleases Jesus more than anything else. Why?

Jesus
"You find it so hard to believe all that the prophets wrote" (Luke 24:25).

Do
Listen to a podcast at learnjapanesepod.com for a bit. Now you are the "other."

Pray: Jesus, I want to know your "other-ness" so well that it is no longer "other."

Favorite/Unfavorite

Read Matthew 5:1-20

Brown paper packages tied up with string… Crisp apple strudel and schnitzel with noodles… Snowflakes that stay on my nose and eyelashes… Van Morrison on the Onkyo with a nice cappuccino… Well, not *every* "favorite thing" found its way into *The Sound of Music.*

When we consider "a few of my favorite things," we're opening a portal—a doggie door—into our hearts. Like the magical wardrobe that leads into the snowy forests of Narnia, the things we love the most invite others into the hidden world of our "fearfully and wonderfully made-ness." The same dynamic is true with the things we *don't* love. Our "unfavorite" things.

So when we consider Jesus through the portal of his favorite/unfavorite things, the passions that drive him come into focus. For example, in Matthew 5…

Favorites	Unfavorites
The Poor	The Proud
The Mourners	The Mockers
The Merciful	The Murderous
The Salty	The Bland

To slow down and savor Jesus, we pay special attention to the sound of his music—to the verses he would certainly add to "My Favorite Things."

Wonder
Ask Jesus: What's your favorite thing about me?

Jesus
"You are…like a city on a hilltop that cannot be hidden" (Matthew 5:14).

Do
Plan a "Favorite Things" outing; include your favorites in all five senses.

Pray: Jesus, what is your favorite thing to do with me?

How We Grow

Read Matthew 13:1-9, 18-23

Consider the mysterious circumstances leading to the death of the Fiddle-Leaf Fig Tree, murdered in the prime of its life...

- Transported home from a reputable nursery, told to expect minor leaf-loss...

- Begins dropping leaves at a shocking rate—already outgrowing its pot?

- Replanted in a larger pot; not as large as a *certain someone* advocated...

- Backyard soil added—not potting soil, as a *certain someone* suggested...

- Moved to new location for more light, accelerating the pace of denuding...

- Moved back to old location, under strict moisture-monitoring...

- Moisture monitoring unnecessary; the Fiddle-Leaf Fig Tree is dead.

- The *certain someone* offers a slow headshake.

Botanicals are like babies—they die if they don't get the care they need. In his Parable of the Soils, Jesus highlights three soils that kill plants and one that's like Miracle Gro. <u>Toxic Soil 1:</u> We hear truth, but don't experience it. <u>Toxic Soil 2:</u> We focus on principles of truth, not the *Person of Truth*. <u>Toxic Soil 3:</u> We pursue the "American Dream," not Jesus. <u>Rich Soil:</u> We long to know Jesus' heart, not plead with him to leverage our happiness.

Wonder
When your relationship with Jesus is stagnant, what's the culprit?

Jesus
"Anyone who does the will of my Father... is my [brother/sister/mother]!" (Matthew 12:50).

Do
Dip your finger into a houseplant's pot. What word describes rich soil?

Pray: Jesus, enrich the "soil" in my soul.

It Is Well

Read Romans 5:1-11

We prefer the repeatability of science over the unpredictability of art. But Jesus is an artist—he's writing a story in our lives, not crunching a formula. And we need an artist, not an accountant, to rework our cataclysms into redemptive beauty.

Devastated by the Great Chicago Fire of 1871, Horatio Spafford, a 19th-century lawyer and businessman, planned to set sail to England with his wife, Anna, and four daughters—to reconnect with friends and emotionally recover. When he had to delay his departure, his family went on. Nine days later, Anna sent this heartbreaking telegram: "Saved alone." Their ship had collided with a Scottish clipper and sunk to the bottom of the Atlantic, killing their daughters and hundreds of others. Debris from the wreck floated under Anna's unconscious head, saving her. On the next ship out of New York, hurrying to join his shattered wife, Horatio passed near the spot where his daughters drowned, spurring him to write this now-iconic hymn:

When peace like a river, attendeth my way,
When sorrows like sea billows roll
Whatever my lot, Thou hast taught me to say
It is well, it is well, with my soul.

We proclaim "It is well with my soul" in the middle of our heartbreak only when we've been driven into desperate dependence on Jesus. There we find a goodness that encloses our sorrow—so real that it is like debris under our heads.

Wonder	**Jesus**	**Do**
More physicists follow Jesus than in the other sciences. Why?	"I wish today that you… would understand the way to peace" (Luke 19:42).	Find the lyrics to "It Is Well With My Soul" online and sing all the stanzas.

Pray: Jesus, make it well with my soul.

Jesus' Intellectual Immune System

Read Matthew 4:1-11

Do you get sick more or less often than others? Getting sick, and getting better, is all about our immune system—the sophisticated network of cells, tissues, and organs that works like our body's Special Forces to repel infectious invaders.

When our immune system is compromised, it has rippling consequences. The same is true for our "other" immune system, the one that "guards our hearts and minds" (Philippians 4:7). The soul's immune system identifies attackers—intellectual viruses or antigens—and targets them. And once these attackers are subdued, our spiritual Special Forces takes a memory picture so it can recognize and defeat them in the future. And then it eats them. The first example we have of Jesus' intellectual immune system (IIS) at work is during his encounter with Lucifer in the desert.

Virus 1—Use your own strength to feed your cravings. _Jesus: Nope, I follow my Father's direction, not my own appetite._

Virus 2—Test God to see if he loves you. _Jesus: Nope, I already know his heart._

Virus 3—You can have it all, if you will worship ambition and beauty. _Jesus: Nope, I don't worship beauty; I worship the Source of it. Now leave!_

Wonder	**Jesus**	**Do**
What habits strengthen or weaken your soul's immune system?	"Worship the Lord your God and serve only him" (Matthew 4:10).	Do standing push-ups against a wall—it's a metaphor for the _feel_ of your IIS.

Pray: Jesus, where has my intellectual immune system been compromised?

The Purpose of Parables

Read Matthew 20:1-16

Parables reveal the heart of Jesus and the truths that define the culture of the kingdom of God. In Romans 1 Paul tells us that everything in the created world has a parable hiding in it, because a Storyteller created all of it. That means we—the "crown" of his creation—are hard-wired storytellers. Even those who resist or decline to acknowledge that God has created them in his image are nevertheless created in his image. It's a truth that does not depend upon our acknowledgment. So, no matter who's doing the creating, we're telling parables—even when we're oblivious to it…

Think of one of your favorite films. Now think of a scene from that film that really impacts you. Now ask yourself, *Why does that scene impact me so much?* Likely, your answer describes a truth about the kingdom of God, or the heart of Jesus, that he's already unveiled in Scripture. Is it the Parable of the Vineyard Workers in Matthew 20? *Grace is not fair—radical generosity will upend you.* Or the Parable of the Wise and Foolish Builders in Matthew 7? *If you want to stand as life's challenges wash over you, your actions need to speak louder than your words.*

Parables reveal the heart of Jesus and the motivation behind his values. And we're swimming in parables—they're all around us, and everywhere in us.

Wonder
What is the parable truth in that scene from your favorite film?

Jesus
"[If you follow] my teaching [you're] like a person who builds a house on solid rock" (Matthew 7:24).

Do
Find "parable truths" in the next episode of your favorite TV show.

Pray: Jesus, wake me up to the parable truths in the stories I love.

The Treasure in the Field

Read Matthew 13:44-46

I heard a pastor say something I often hear in church: *Why don't we celebrate spiritual things—like someone committing to follow Jesus or a prayer answered—the same way we celebrate a touchdown in a football game?* He's implying that we just need to get our priorities straight and celebrate what we *should* celebrate. Like the scoreboard command "Make some noise!" we need prodding to celebrate the "right" things.

I walked in from work one day, and my daughter burst out that she'd won a full-ride college scholarship. I screamed, ripped off the nametag lanyard I wear at work and shot it across the room, then ran into our living room and buried myself in our couch where I ugly-cried for several minutes. I was overcome by the grace of God—and no one had to instruct me on the proper way to celebrate.

When we experience a great joy, we don't need prodding or should-ing to celebrate. And when we encounter great beauty, we can't contain our response. Jesus has an answer for the pastor's question embedded in the Parables of the Hidden Treasure and the Pearl. *When you encounter a treasure so rich that it staggers the imagination, and you recognize what you're seeing, you'll naturally pay what it takes to get it—by the way, my heart is a staggering treasure.*

Wonder
In the last week, what's something you celebrated, and why?

Jesus
"Blessed are the eyes that see what you have seen" (Luke 10:23).

Do
Fold back this page's bottom corner; draw a diamond on the facing side.

Pray: Jesus, open my eyes to your treasure.

A Question of Flaws

Read 2 Corinthians 11:21-29 and 12:1-10

In every mystery story, we miss subtle clues to the criminal's guilt. That's ironic because most of us are *incredibly good* at targeting flaws—in ourselves and in others. But our flaw-radar blinds us to the beauty buried in others and keeps us from embracing the beauty Jesus sees when he looks at us.

Jesus has an intense encounter with Paul about flaws. In the apostle's defense against "false teachers" who are luring his friends in Corinth away from the truth about Jesus, Paul tells them his "thorn" story. It's a fantastical vision, so crazy he's unsure if it actually happened, where he's "caught up to paradise" and overhears inexpressible words.

Paul has been invited into the counsel of the Holy; he has tasted such great truths that the revelation nearly overwhelms him. Now, mesmerized by this beauty, he mistakenly assumes this glory has *transferred* to him. And then Jesus jams a thorn in his side—Paul calls it "a messenger from Satan." But the thorn's purpose, and the purpose of all our flaws, is redemptive, not punitive. The thorn releases Paul's true strength, which is his dependence on the strength of Jesus. The strength we need is the strength Jesus has; it's from him and in him, and we won't drink from his Well unless we know our own well is dry. The thorn in our side pierces our well, draining it. As we acknowledge our emptiness, he fills us.

Wonder
How have your flaws created opportunities for strength to grow?

Jesus
"My grace is all you need. My power works best in weakness" (2 Corinthians 12:9).

Do
Paper-clip this page; let it represent your "thorn." Ask Jesus to fill you.

Pray: Jesus, I acknowledge my thorns and I beg for your strength.

The Talmid's Immersion

Read Matthew 10:1-42

Remember that *one* teacher who really made a difference in your life? How did that teacher's values and habits and beliefs "infect" you? What good things surfaced in you whenever you were around him or her?

In the time of Jesus, the teacher/pupil relationship required "mutual immersion." A young student's goal was to convince a rabbi to extend a life-changing invitation to him—to "take his yoke upon him." If the student (the "talmid") was chosen by a rabbi, he was required to leave his family, synagogue, and community and move into his mentor's home. Here, the talmid learned as much from his rabbi's *essence* as from his teaching. He soaked in every detail of the rabbi's personality—the way he walked and talked and thought. Well-taught meant well-modeled.

When Jesus sends off his disciples in pairs, for the first time without him, he gives them a daunting assignment: to heal the sick, cast out demons, and preach the gospel. As they plunge into this adventure, their immersive experience of Jesus' essence will guide them through their impossible challenges. They will need "the smell of him" permeating their souls as they go out.

We're all talmids who've been chosen by the Great Rabbi—to live with him, learn from him, and become just like him. This is our *good news*.

Wonder
A yoke harnesses the oxen's strength. How are you "yoked" to Jesus?

Jesus
"If I don't [go away], the Advocate won't come" (John 16:7).

Do
Use a loved-one's shampoo. Let the smell remind you of your love.

Pray: Jesus, I want to be "yoked" to you, my Rabbi.

Solving Mysteries

Read Mark 11:12-25

When I was growing up, mystery stories were my favorite. I still have a complete set of (now antique) hardback Hardy Boys books in a bookcase near our front door, greeting friends when they enter our home. At some level, we all have a taste for mystery...

One day I walked outside to grab our newspaper off the driveway and saw a decorative balloon caught in a bush. I plucked it and brought it inside. Only then did I remember it was my birthday. The balloon said "Congratulations!"—somehow, some way, that balloon escaped a graduation party, then descended from the sky and snagged itself in my front yard on the morning of my birthday, as if God himself had delivered it.

Jesus enjoys plunging his friends into mystery. He is purposefully cryptic in his behavior and his teaching because he knows mystery attracts us. For example, one of the great unsolved mysteries related to Jesus is why he decided to curse the "disobedient" fig tree, a truly strange story recorded in Mark 11:12-25. Could it be *"In the presence of LIFE, all of creation MUST bear fruit!"*?

Jesus invites us into his deeper places by scattering mysteries in our path. He's not pointing to solutions; he *is* the solution.

Wonder	**Jesus**	**Do**
What's one of the great mysteries of your life?	"Pray...and if you believe that you've received it, it will be yours" (Mark 11:24).	Be the source of a friend's mystery. Tie a celebratory balloon to their door.

Pray: Jesus, bring a little more mystery into my life.

What Is Truth?

Read John 18:28–19:16

Play "Two Truths and a Lie." In the space below, quickly write two truths about your life and one equally believable lie. Now, whatever you did to make your lie *appear truthful* points to our wider difficulty in discerning truth from deception in life.

A fish in a pond might encounter a bare hook (an outright lie), a baited hook (a lie that looks like the truth), and…real food (the truth). Bare lies can still entice a fish, if the water is murky enough. Baited lies are hard to resist, unless you take a closer look. And though we all need real food to survive, past experience makes us cautious consumers.

When Jesus is standing before Pilate with his life on the line, he tells the Roman ruler that he's a King from another kingdom, and that he's come to "testify to the truth." And Pilate, cynical and frustrated that he has been forced to render judgment on an innocent man, responds with "What is truth?" Jesus leaves that question hanging in the air. *Truth is not something you say; it's something you are.* And Truth is standing in front of Pilate—"the way, the truth, and the life." Like hungry fish, the only way to know Jesus is "real food" is to risk "eating and drinking" him.

Wonder
In a culture of competing truths, how do you decide what's false?

Jesus
"All who love the truth recognize that what I say is true" (John 18:37).

Do
Study tabloid headlines. Pick out the bare hooks, baited hooks, and pure food.

Pray: Jesus, my source of Truth, please strengthen my discernment.

Jesus and His BFF's

Read John 15:13-15

Friends are like oxygen—we can't survive without them. But how do friends become friends, and what makes a friendship "work"? Friend-making is about pursuing what is magnetic about each other. Do they "get" me, and do I "get" them? It's a mutual expedition into the soul—uncovering how the other thinks and feels and believes, then discovering what we enjoy.

Jesus followed his own discovery process as he sought and developed close friendships. Pay attention to why Jesus gravitated to his best friends and we learn what is "mutually enjoyable" to him and what is a magnet for his heart…

• **Mary and Martha and Lazarus**—Outside of his disciples, these are his closest friends. Jesus loves how passionate, headstrong, and blunt Mary is. And he loves how her sister is level-headed, hardworking, and humble. After their brother Lazarus dies of an illness, Jesus (finally) arrives and feels *agapan* for his friend—the Greek word translated "cherish." He loves Lazarus' courage, grace, and humility.

• **Simon Peter**—Like Mary, Peter is passionate and impetuous. He's a risk-taker—a take-charge guy. He is also rough and brave and unsophisticated, the tough and driven owner of a successful family business, a rare accomplishment at a time most people toil without hope as slaves. Jesus loves how he is street-smart, not book-smart—a man to contend with.

Wonder	**Jesus**	**Do**
Jesus didn't easily trust "because he knew all about people." What does this mean?	"There is no greater love than to lay down one's life for one's friends" (John 15:13).	Surprise your BFF with a favorite snack or drink or guilty pleasure.

Pray: Jesus, I want to be one of your BFF's.

What Jesus Wants

Read John 17:20-26

We're captured and consumed by love. Our singers pine for it. Our poets bleed for it. And our filmmakers nearly worship it. So when we sing "Jesus loves me, this I know…" what *species* of love are we describing?

I hear Ed Sheeran declare, *"When my hair's all but gone and my memory fades, and the crowds don't remember my name…I know you will still love me the same."*

Our love songs promise the intimacy we crave will last forever. And yet, we know, the certainty of love very often outlasts the reality of it. My wife and I scrambled through the debris of two broken engagements to reach the summit of our wedding day. Friends showed up half-expecting Act Three—a throw-down-your-flowers, escape-out-the-back-door scene. And this was a reasonable anxiety. Or, for some, a perverse form of entertainment.

How can something that promises permanence feel so fragile?

Love's bait-and-switch creeps like a shadow over *Jesus loves me, this I know…* And this is why he's determined to define what he is after. The love he craves is the same a bride and bridegroom have on their wedding night, the same the grafted branch has with the vine, and the same the vulnerable sheep have with their defender shepherd. "I in you and you in me" is his invitation. He wants it all—he wants… Us. All.

Wonder
Labels list primary ingredients first. What's love's "primary ingredient"?

Jesus
"Father, I want these whom you have given me to be with me where I am" (John 17:24).

Do
Pick your beloved's shirt/top from the laundry; inhale his/her "essence."

Pray: Jesus, I love you, this you know…

The Red Sea

Read 1 Corinthians 2:1-5

The parting of the Red Sea happens every year around Valentine's Day, when card-shoppers wade through a red ocean of glitter-hearts at the grocery store. It's the *Amazing Race*, with a heart-bath at the finish line. I lead a home fellowship that follows this guiding motto: *"Pursuing the heart of Jesus, not his recipes."* It means, simply, that we're more interested in understanding and embracing Jesus' heart than turning his teachings into "recipes for better living." It's the heart of Jesus that transforms us, not the formulas we extract from the things he said and did.

But the "pursuit of the heart" is an adventure fraught with peril. In my favorite novel, Jane Austen's *Pride & Prejudice*, the complicated protagonist Darcy is a wealthy, upper-class gentleman who falls for "middle class" Lizzie, even though it's cultural suicide to marry beneath his class. She despises him, because he seems so haughty. And he's continually frustrated by her willingness to believe the worst about him. Can these two warring hearts ever lay down their emotional WMD's long enough to find love? I'm sure you can guess the answer... Blaise Pascal observes, "The heart has its reasons which reason knows not."

When Paul proclaims, "I determined to know nothing among you except Jesus Christ" (NASB), it's a passion worthy of Valentine's Day.

Wonder	**Jesus**	**Do**
What exactly does it mean to love Jesus with "all our heart"?	"If you love Me, you will keep My commandments" (John 14:15, NASB).	Write a love note to Jesus in a Valentine's Day card. Use it as a bookmark.

Pray: Jesus, I'm determined to know nothing but your heart.

The Deathly Hallows

Read Romans 1:19-20

As people fashioned in God's image, all our *own* creations have embedded in them the "DNA" of God's heart. That means Jesus invades all our created things through a secret trap door, planting parables and metaphors that point to the kingdom of God. Even the Harry Potter stories, the most popular in history, can help us comprehend and embrace the mysteries and motivations of Jesus' heart…

In Potter lore, a good world is invaded by the murderous betrayer Voldemort, who recruits an army of evil wraiths to help him seize power. Most believe this "evil one" was defeated long ago—only a small band of unlikely heroes recognizes Voldemort's activity and is determined to stop him. The plan requires Harry Potter, a boy the enemy tried to kill but couldn't, to offer himself as a willing sacrifice. Secretly, the forces of good know that Harry's "death" will lead to his "resurrection" and the ultimate defeat of their foe.

In Paul's recap of our salvation narrative, the common threads are obvious: "So just as sin ruled over all people and brought them to death, now God's wonderful grace rules instead, giving us right standing with God and resulting in eternal life through Jesus Christ our Lord" (Romans 5:21). The story of God's love wheedles, inexorably, into *all* our stories.

Wonder
What's your favorite death-to-life story, outside of the Bible?

Jesus
"Was it not necessary for the Christ to suffer… and to enter into His glory?" (Luke 24:26, NASB).

Do
Smell frozen food; microwave and smell it again—the smell of "death" and "life."

Pray: Jesus, help me see your death-to-life narrative all around me.

The Blind Will See

Read Luke 4:14-30

Jesus has just spent 40 days in the wilderness alone, fasting and locked in a wrestling match with Satan. He emerges "full of the Spirit." When he returns, he teaches everywhere and is "praised by everyone." And then he travels to Nazareth, his boyhood home. In the synagogue on the Sabbath he stands up to read a prophecy about the Messiah from the scroll of Isaiah. The reading includes a promise that the "anointed one" will help the blind to see again.

When Jesus rolls up the scroll, he's effectively announcing this will be his first day on the job. And his job description has one very specific promise of healing—"the blind will see." Jesus later has six healing encounters with blind people, and John records in great detail an epic story about a man blind from birth whose life is upended by the spit-mud of Jesus (John 9 and 10).

It's clear that Jesus is intent on restoring our sight, both physically and spiritually. We are all blind, but some of us are twice-blind: "Your eye is like a lamp that provides light for your body. When your eye is healthy, your whole body is filled with light" (Matthew 6:22). For the twice-blind he first opens their eyes to the sun, then to the Son. We all need our blindness healed, so we can see the Light of the World.

Wonder
What's a blindness in your life that Jesus has set you free from?

Jesus
"When your eye is unhealthy, your whole body is filled with darkness" (Matthew 6:23).

Do
Close your eyes and walk a bit. What words describe that experience?

Pray: Jesus, open my eyes to you.

Growing Down, Not Up

Read Matthew 18:1-5

Remember what your very first week in school was like? It's easy for me—I wet my pants because the teacher ignored the raised hand of my desperation. That day, I fell off the side of Mount Trauma. It's easy to forget what we were *really* like as children— the pain we endured and the hopes we held. We are born, and then a rushing current hurtles us into the whitewater narrows of "growing up." And that makes sense; everything in the created world is growing, if it's alive.

But Jesus puts an unusual spin on growth. He's more concerned about us "growing down" than growing up. And he repeatedly lifts up children as an example to emulate, advocating a kind of "reverse conversion." We're trying to *grow up* out of childhood, but he's asking us to *grow down* into childhood: "Unless you are converted and become like children, you will not enter the Kingdom of Heaven" (NASB).

Children at the time of Jesus were considered "beneath the dignity of reason"—they were seen as "fearful, weak, helpless, fragile, dependent, defenseless, and vulnerable." But Jesus destroys this conventional wisdom by elevating their trusting, joyous, playful, authentic, and all-in nature. To grow down, we must shed the cynicism and distrust we've accumulated as we've grown into adulthood and open our arms to Jesus, who's waiting for us on the playground.

Wonder	**Jesus**	**Do**
What's one childlike quality you're right now "growing down" into?	"Beware that you don't look down on any of these little ones" (Matthew 18:10).	Sit cross-legged, close your eyes, and listen to a story from lightupyourbrain.com.

Pray: Jesus, free me from the tyranny of growing up.

Three Perfect Days With Jesus

Read Matthew 7

United's in-flight magazine *Hemispheres* spotlights fascinating travel destinations in an award-winning feature called "Three Perfect Days In..." Readers get a savvy three-day timeline for eating, drinking, and experiencing the chosen city—the sophisticated "essentials" for enjoying a new place. It's a strategy that transfers to our relationship with Jesus.

When researchers asked church leaders to pick one "essential" for people who want to "know Jesus [and] be more like him," their top answer was "Time with God." Well, time alone isn't the point—we can sit next to the same person on the subway every day but not know that person's heart. *It's what we do in our time with God that really matters.* To get close to Jesus, we slow down and pay attention to his essentials. So what essentials might be listed on Jesus' own "Three Perfect Days" list? If our "destination" is Matthew 7, we discover...

- Curious persistence—*Jesus loves the heart of an adventurer.*
- Paying attention to what others really need—*Jesus loves giving good gifts.*
- Doing is way more valuable than proclaiming—*Jesus loves it when we live it.*

Wonder
If you planned your own "three perfect days," what's one thing you'd do?

Jesus
"I have told you that I am going to prepare a place for you..." (John 14:2).

Do
Put together a "three perfect days" playlist on your phone or computer.

Pray: Jesus, what would you want to do in "three perfect days" with me?

The Three Bricklayers

Read Matthew 10:16-20

In Edmund Berkeley's classic parable, a traveler meets three bricklayers working on a scaffold. He asks the first, "What are you doing?" and the man answers, without glancing up from his work, "I am earning a wage." To the second bricklayer, the man repeats his question—he turns and answers, "I am building a wall." Then the traveler asks the third bricklayer, "And what are you doing?" He stops what he's doing, faces the traveler, and responds, "I am building a cathedral."

Our words matter… They reveal *what* we believe, *how* we believe, and *why* we believe. The Gospel of John begins "The Word gave life to everything that was created, and his life brought light to everyone." God spoke creation into being through his Word, a reference to Jesus. When God speaks, what comes out of his mouth is Jesus.

And because we are created in his image, our words also have creative power. And so, as Jesus is sending out his disciples on a daunting mission, he warns them that they're about to be persecuted and offers this crucial piece of advice: "Don't worry about how to respond or what to say." He wants them to depend on the Spirit to give them the right words. He promises the Spirit will "speak through us"—and that will require more dependence on Jesus and less dependence on our own ability to navigate our circumstances.

Wonder
How would you describe your work in "third bricklayer" terms?

Jesus
"It will be the Spirit of your Father speaking through you" (Matthew 10:20).

Do
Pray for a friend, first asking Jesus specifically *how to pray.*

Pray: Jesus, show me what to say and how to say it today.

The Heart Before the Head

Read John 17

Jesus' "end game" is always one-ness—he wants a connection with us that mirrors the intimacy he has with his Father: "As you are in me, Father, and I am in you" (John 17:21). We've often translated Jesus' call to discipleship into "learning more"—it's all about the head. But Jesus is after relational immersion, not a spot on our debate team. The heart trumps the head.

How do we experience relational immersion when we can't really see or touch or audibly hear Jesus? James, the brother of Jesus, gives us our best advice: "Come close to God, and God will come close to you" (James 4:8). We "come close" to Jesus when we pay better attention to him... Think of it this way: You meet new friends, and they invite you to their home for the first time. You spend five minutes wandering, stopping to notice their books and photos and artwork and lighting and general décor. You're getting a window into what matters most to them. This is called "noticing what you notice." And our onramp into relational immersion with Jesus is to notice what we notice about him.

When we do that in John 17, we experience the "missional décor" of his heart—wants to fiercely protect us, unite us, fill us with joy, give us courage, and make us holy.

Worship is noticing what we notice about Jesus' heart, not parsing his syntax.

Wonder	**Jesus**	**Do**
What do you "notice what you notice" in John 17, and why?	"I want these whom you have given me to be with me where I am" (John 17:24).	Notice what you notice in your home. What matters most to your family?

Pray: Jesus, when you "notice what you notice" in my heart, what do you see?

The King's Kingdom

Read Matthew 13:31-35, 44-46

Jesus can't stop talking about "the Kingdom of God." He references it 37 times in the gospel of Matthew alone. His mission is to reveal and embody the kingdom, the royal culture of his "home country." To understand the Bible's "meta-narrative," it helps to see the New Testament as an account of what life looks like in the present kingdom of God, and the Old Testament as an account of the coming kingdom of God.

But since most of us don't live in a kingdom, and never will, how do we know what life in one is really like? There are obvious differences between a democracy and living under the rule of a king, and less-obvious differences... In three of his many "kingdom of God" parables, Jesus highlights these important "cultural values": 1) Tiny things planted in the right soil become huge things, big enough to offer sanctuary for others; and 2) If you understand the real value of something, you'll give up everything to get it. These dynamics describe how things work inside the "royal family."

Jesus is inviting us to live in his kingdom, but he knows we're like exchange students plunked down in a foreign culture. So, as a gracious host, he translates for us: "I am the way, the truth, and the life" (John 14:6). Jesus is our translation, because he is formed by the values and priorities of his true home.

Wonder
How is authority in a kingdom different from authority in a democracy?

Jesus
"Seek the Kingdom of God above all else" (Matthew 6:33).

Do
Kneel to pray as an outward way to honor the King of God's kingdom.

Pray: Jesus, show me how to live in your kingdom as a "native."

Persuasion

Read Mark 2:1-5

Christian people are called "the faithful" in the news media—it's a vaguely "holier than thou" label. What's more, *faithful* is open to wide interpretation. The tagline for O Magazine's regular column "You Gotta Have Faith" is *"It doesn't have to be a God thing. You don't have to be religious. But when you're all alone in troubled waters, you need something to hold on to."* Is this what faith is—grabbing anything we can when we're drowning?

The Greek word *Pistos* is translated "faith" in the New Testament. Its core meaning is "trust, confidence, assurance, and belief…in God or Christ." The root of the word is "persuasion." So we are literally *persuaded* into faith. But what are we persuaded by?

Every now and then Jesus is amazed by a person's "great faith." For example, the group of "faithful" friends who dig a hole in the roof of the crowded house where Jesus is staying and, *while he's teaching*, lower their paralyzed buddy down on a mat. What *persuades* them to carry out this crazy plan? Well, Jesus has returned to his hometown after healing scores of people in villages throughout Galilee. The determined friends are persuaded by his obvious power and authority. They are not *grasping at* anything they can get their hands on—they are confident in the *person* inside that house.

Wonder	**Jesus**	**Do**
If a child asked you to describe what faith is, what would you say?	"Jesus said to the paralyzed man, 'My child, your sins are forgiven'" (Mark 2:5).	Close your eyes before you sit in a chair—faith requires a dose of blindness.

Pray: Jesus, I am persuaded by your heart toward me.

Your Special Place

Read John 14:1-11

It is not Jesus' "job" to love us—we are not a "supposed to." When we cherish others, we lay down our lives for them, but not because it's our *responsibility*. Jesus has a real affection for you, down to the hairs on your head. He enjoys your quirky nuances and delights in the small things that make up the big thing that is you. You're not just another bleating sheep-face in the homogenous sheep-herd to him.

On the show *Extreme Makeover: Home Edition*, the construction team kicks off every home rebuild by getting to know the family, scrounging for details about their passions so they can include surprises in the renovation. Hobbies, histories, and hankerings—they all find their way into the "home reveal" at the end of the show. Like Jesus, the designers want to reflect back to the homeowners their quirky (and beloved) nuances.

Jesus offers his disciples a promise you'd give a small child before something hard happens: *I'm leaving to go prepare a special place in my Father's house for you, and "when everything is ready, I will come and get you, so that you will always be with me where I am."* Like a child, Thomas tells Jesus he has no idea where he's going or how to get there. Jesus tells him there is no *way*, there is only the *Way*.

And I can't wait to see your face when you join me at the "reveal."

Wonder	**Jesus**	**Do**
Jesus is preparing a "room" for you. What do you hope to find?	"Have I been with you all this time...yet you still don't know who I am?" (John 14:9).	Send a photo of this page to someone, with: "My special place will include you."

Pray: Jesus, what's something you're preparing for me in my "special place"?

Dangerous Love

Read Luke 11:37–12:3

The great Victorian author and apologist G.K. Chesterton said, *"If you meet the Jesus of the Gospels, you must redefine what love is, or you won't be able to stand him."* This Jesus practices "dangerous love"—the kind of love that wields a surgeon's knife. In the gospel of Matthew alone, he has 18 brutal encounters with religious leaders and scribes. And yet Jesus is never *not* loving the person in front of him. There is no "off" switch for his grace. But real love has deeper intentions than mere comfort, and is after something greater than our circumstantial happiness.

In a hard-to-watch episode of *BBC Earth*, naturalist David Attenborough narrates the gripping story of a family of barnacle geese trying to survive on the cliffs of eastern Greenland. To avoid predators, the geese build their nests 400 feet above their chicks' source of food—the grassy plains below. Once the goslings are big enough, the mother goose flies from the nest to the ground and calls for them to jump. And, one by one, they do. It's a miracle any of them survive the excruciating tumble, as they bounce off the side of the cliff and land in a heap at the bottom. But half of the goslings *do* survive, when all would've been lost otherwise. It's a love story about barnacle geese that endure crushing grief to rescue their kids. It's love redefined…

Wonder
How has Jesus practiced "dangerous love" in your life?

Jesus
"You…tithe even the tiniest income from your herb gardens, but you ignore justice" (Luke 11:42).

Do
Cut off a tiny lock of hair and tape it to this page—a reminder that "love cuts."

Pray: Jesus, your dangerous love scares me; help me open my arms.

Scandalously Nice

Read Mark 14:1-9

Jesus has a scandalous reputation among the religious power-brokers, but they are more upset by the kindness he gives the "wrong" people than by his angry confrontations. He's shockingly tender to the sorts of people they habitually judge and unconscionably kind to the outcasts and lowlifes who pollute their "decent" society.

Jesus is always kind but only sporadically nice. But when he is nice, he is scandalously nice…

Jesus is in Bethany at the home of Simon, a man afflicted with incurable leprosy and ostracized from civil society until Jesus heals him. Simon is throwing a dinner party, something that would've been impossible before Jesus changed his life. A woman, unnamed, walks in while Jesus is eating. She's carrying a jar of perfume made from the essence of nard, an essential oil derived from a flowering plant that grows only in the Himalayas, so rare that it's worth a year's salary. The woman likely imported the oil from Egypt, saving it for a special occasion—the seal is unbroken. She anoints Jesus' head, and the fake do-gooders around the table are outraged: "It could have been sold…and the money given to the poor!"

And then Jesus counters their outrage with his own, because this woman's act is scandalously nice, and that means she's speaking his love language. The expense of her gift reveals the passion of it, and he will make sure she's remembered forever. We are fulfilling that promise right now.

Wonder	**Jesus**	**Do**
Who has offered you "scandalous" kindness in your life?	"You will not always have me" (Mark 14:7).	Put a drop of olive oil on your finger and mark this page with it.

Pray: Jesus, remind me of the ways you have been scandalously kind to me.

The Cycle of Life

Read Mark 4:26-29

Beginning with Ash Wednesday, the Cycle of Life marks a season of the soul when we celebrate the death and resurrection of Jesus. The central revelation of this cycle is abundant, overflowing, eternal life—a tsunami wave of life washing over us, revealing a new creation. The Cycle begins with Lent, then moves through Easter and into Pentecost—from expectation to fulfillment to proclamation.

- In Lent we journey with Jesus toward the cross, learning again to die to the sin that still poisons our lives, discovering how to sustain ourselves by the grace of God instead of our own self-sufficiency.

- On Easter Sunday we summit the mount of celebration, when the barren tomb delivers on all God's promises. Jesus descends and ascends from the dead, and a new age dawns.

- On Pentecost we remember that the mission of God does not end with Jesus' resurrection. When he ascends to the right hand of the Father, he baptizes his followers by immersing them in the deep waters of the Holy Spirit. Finally, he's restored a path to intimacy that was lost so long ago in the Garden of Eden, empowering us to go forth into the world as his body.

Wonder
What's something dead in your life that is now resurrecting?

Jesus
"First the blade, then the head, then the mature grain in the head" (Mark 4:28, NASB).

Do
Tie a string on your finger as a reminder of the death-to-life cycle.

Pray: Jesus, bring life to every incursion of death in my life.

Why Before What

Read John 13:1-17

You could ask friends *what* their favorite film/vacation spot/
restaurant is, but you'd be asking the wrong question. Buried
gold requires a deeper dig into the *why* beyond our *what's*…

- According to a Harris Interactive poll, the favorite film of
  Americans is *Gone With the Wind*. Why? Guardian film
  reviewer Molly Haskell writes, "[People] saw it as their own
  story of survival"—an epic tale of personal and communal
  redemption. It's a story about us that's not about us.

- In an online poll of travel writers, the Daintree Rainforest
  in Australia was voted the top international destination for
  families. Why? The park's attractions draw families closer—
  "It's a relaxed and beautiful tropical destination with plenty
  for all members of the family to love" (YTravelBlog.com).

- The surprising pick for "best family restaurant" by the
  editors of *Parents* magazine? Legal Sea Foods. Why? It's
  a healthy, creative, and fun approach to foods that kids
  typically hate—a family *experience*, not just a family meal.

We don't poke through to the heart of things by asking *what*
questions—*why* targets our deeper catalysts. Put this to the test.
Slowly read the story of Jesus washing his disciples' feet in John
13. Stop often to ask, "Why did Jesus say or do that?" Then finish
this sentence: "The heart of Jesus is _____."

Wonder
What's your favorite
vacation spot ever, and
why?

Jesus:
"Unless I wash you, you
won't belong to me"
(John 13:8).

Do
Ask a friend "what"
questions, then "why"
questions. Observe the
difference.

Pray: Jesus, show me the why's behind all your what's.

Compared to What?

Read Ephesians 1:11-12, The Message

Everyone compares, even though we know we're not supposed
to. Social media demands our highlights, not our lowlights—but
we still compare our "ordinary time" to others' "extraordinary
time." In this mythical promised land, everyone is happy,
interesting, popular, posed, and adventurous. Likewise, celebrity
culture is our aspirational norm, even though it is curated by
personal trainers/chefs/assistants.

Comparison is our soul's aphrodisiac—we can't seem to resist
it. But it's not a sign of weakness; *it's a sign of wiring.* We are
created by God to discover the truth about ourselves by looking
out, not in. Our friends, enemies, family, media, co-workers,
spouse, siblings, and children all contribute to our "identity
formation." But Jesus wants to shift the bounce-back signals we
trust to find ourselves and refocus our identity thirst on him. He
wants to be our only comparable.

One day in the shower, I was churning over a hurtful thing a
close friend said to me. I asked Jesus to enter into my churn,
and his response was simple and piercing: *When will you
leave behind all your other lovers?* He was inviting me to find
myself *not* in the false assessments of others but in the *singular
reflection* of his love for me. We look outside ourselves for our
identity, but find the truth only when Jesus answers our deepest
question: "Who do you say that I am?"

Wonder	**Jesus**	**Do**
What nickname were you given as a child, and why?	"Your Father knows exactly what you need even before you ask him" (Matthew 6:8).	On the corner below, list one way you've compared yourself. Fold the page over it.

Pray: Jesus, who do you say that I am?

The Cat Who Was Nothing

Read John 15:9-11

In *Nothing*, author Mick Inkpen tells the story of a raggedy stuffed cat that's been abandoned and then forgotten under a pile of boxes in a family's attic. On the day the family moves, he's discovered but left behind by a "Voice" that explains, simply, "Oh, it's nothing." And so "Nothing" escapes from the attic to the streets below with the help of a mouse. There he encounters a fox and a frog and, finally, a *real* tabby cat named Toby. Nothing collapses into sobs: "I don't know who I am!" And Toby licks him full in the face, then offers to take him to a new home around the corner.

With Nothing hanging from his mouth, Toby leaps over walls and into trees and on top of roofs until he slips through a back door and delivers Nothing to the lap of an elderly man. He's the grandfather of the family that has just moved in, and he sees something in the wrecked face of Nothing that reminds him of the stuffed cat he loved as a boy—"Little Toby." No longer Nothing, Little Toby is washed and repaired and nestled into the crib of a new baby.

On this day that is a *Nothing* most years, it's good to be reminded that the mission of Jesus is to name us and reclaim us. To love us out of *nothing* and into the truth of our being.

Wonder	**Jesus**	**Do**
Why do so many struggle with this lie: "I am not enough"?	"I am the door; if anyone enters through me, he will be saved" (John 10:9, NASB).	Wash dishes by hand and worship Jesus for "cleaning" and restoring you.

Pray: Jesus, what is the name you like to call me?

The Problem-Solver

Read Mark 5:1-18

Prayer is the great "supposed to" of the Christian life. We know we're *supposed to* close our eyes and use a different tone of voice when we pray—maybe even "preach" a little. We worry about "saying it the right way." And researchers have discovered what we already know from experience: We primarily pray about our problems. Challenges facing "family or friends" (82%) and "my own problems and difficulties" (74%) dominate our prayers.

But is Jesus willing to settle for a problem-solving relationship, where our primary focus is getting the "prayer recipe" right? No. The people in the Gerasene region, on the shores of the Sea of Galilee, are terrorized by a violent demon-possessed man. Jesus confronts the man, ordering the "legion" of demons to leave him and enter a herd of 2,000 pigs, who promptly drown themselves in the lake. The people have a problem, Jesus solves it for them, *and then they ask him to go away and not come back.* Why?

Well, their focus is on their problem, not on Jesus' invitation into relationship. Problem solved, Jesus begone. But what if, instead, we treated prayer more like "pillow talk"—relaxed and intimate conversation—and less like a Christian-y incantation? We might still have our problem, but we'd certainly have Jesus.

Wonder
Pray about the first thing that comes to mind. What's the "category"?

Jesus
"Tell them everything the Lord has done for you" (Mark 5:19).

Do
The first flower you see today, stop and drink in the smell. Exhale your problem.

Pray: Jesus, what's on your heart today?

The Magic Jesus Experience

Read Mark 6:36-56

Who performs the first "magic trick" in human history? Imagine the moment Adam and Eve swallow their very first bite of food. Something solid that exists outside their body suddenly disappears inside their body. Magic…

Of course, the promise of "magic" is what drew colossal crowds to Jesus early in his ministry. When you cast out demons or heal paralyzed people or (!) raise them from the dead, you're (metaphorically) likely to get your own show in Vegas. But Jesus wasn't your typical "magic man"—sometimes he did supernatural things, and sometimes he didn't. Why? If you had supernatural ability, wouldn't you use it all the time?

In the last half of Mark 6, we see Jesus acting supernaturally in two radically different ways. First, he fills the tummies of 5,000 men (and their families) with snack food, then he walks on water in the middle of the night on a choppy sea. Why? In both situations, it's clear that *compassion* is driving him. The people are hungry; they've skipped meals to hear what he has to say, so Jesus opens a fast-food joint on a barren hillside. And his disciples are frightened, their boat about to be swamped by waves, so Jesus decides walking to them would be faster than rowing. Compassion for those he loves makes him blind to the boundaries of the conventional world. It's the size of his love, not the skill of his magic, that matters.

Wonder
Why might Jesus *refrain* from doing supernatural things all the time?

Jesus
"Take courage! I am here!" (Mark 6:50).

Do
Tell a child you can make a piece of fruit disappear—then eat it.

Pray: Jesus, I need your supernatural intervention in my life.

The Name Above All Names

Read Matthew 12:18-21

When we're choosing a name for a baby, parenting experts tell us to consider how our choice *sounds*. Also, avoid trendy names (unique, but not too unique), make it gender-specific, and mull the impact of nicknames and initials. Well, in Jesus' time, parents broke every one of these rules. The ancient Jews named their babies by projecting a prophetic identity. Your name represented your future purpose in the world. "Amos" meant "carry the load," and he went on to protest the vast disparities between the rich and poor. "Dan" meant "he judges," and as the founder of one of the 12 tribes of Israel, he did. And "Yeshua" meant "God is salvation," and Jesus left a red sea of redemption in his wake. A good name was preloaded with meaning and purpose...

- "And she will have a son, and you are to name him Jesus, for he will save his people from their sins." *(An angel, in Matthew 1:21)*

- "And his name will be the hope of all the world." *(Isaiah's prophecy, in Matthew 12:21)*

- "Holy Father, you have given me your name; now protect them by the power of your name." *(Jesus, in John 17:11)*

- "You can ask for anything in my name, and I will do it." *(Jesus, in John 14:13)*

- "At the name of Jesus every knee should bow." *(Paul, in Philippians 2:10)*

Wonder	**Jesus**	**Do**
What name would project the purpose of your life, and why?	"Our Father in heaven, may your name be kept holy" (Matthew 6:9).	Write a new nickname for Jesus in the margin, one not found in the Bible.

Pray: Jesus, like Simon, I'd love to know your "true name" for me.

The Name He's Named You

Read Matthew 16:13-19

After Peter declares that Jesus is the Messiah, the "Lion of the Tribe of Judah" returns the favor: "I say to you that you are Peter…and upon this rock I will build my church." Here, Jesus is answering two big questions for Peter: *"Who am I?"* and *"What am I doing here?"* And, of course, these are also our "two big questions" in life.

Jesus begins his ministry by announcing, "I have come to set captives free." And our great captivity is our imprisoned soul. Jesus intends to set us free from self-recrimination, to release us into our "true name" just as he did when he morphed Simon into Peter. First, Jesus sees and invites him (Matthew 4:18-20). Then he trusts him with responsibility and authority (16:16-19). Then he exposes what needs to be exposed and removes what doesn't belong (16:21-24). Then he takes Peter "backstage" (17:1-9). Then he exposes his false strength as weakness (26:31-35). And finally, Jesus affirms his affection and importance to him (John 21:15-17).

Peter's progression is also ours. Jesus wants to name us for who we really are and launch us into what we were made to do.

Wonder
Peter quickly left behind the business he built to follow Jesus. Why?

Jesus
"You didn't choose me. I chose you" (John 15:16).

Do
Explore your name's meaning on behindthename.com.

Pray: Jesus, please expose my false strengths, and *reveal* me.

Interpreting the Signs

Read Luke 12:54-59

Jesus is full of apparent contradictions—sometimes he's hard and sometimes soft. Happy and angry. Clear and fuzzy. For example, in Luke 12, after the Pharisees are openly hostile to Jesus, the crowds press in. In the chaos, he fires a warning shot aimed at the influence of the hypocritical Pharisees. "Don't be impressed," Jesus urges, "by what the Pharisees will do to you if you disobey them; be more concerned about what God will do if you ignore him." A hard thing, followed by this soft thing: "Five sparrows cost just two copper coins, but God cherishes them. How much more does he cherish you?"

Jesus is challenging the crowds to be more discerning—to contrast what their religious leaders are telling them with the truths about the kingdom of God he's revealing. To decide what is right, based on what they've closely observed. He offers four "teachings" as an exercise in paying better attention to the "signs" of what's really true:

1. On greed: "Life is not measured by how much you own" (v. 13-21).

2. On possessions: "Seek the kingdom of God above all else, and he will give you everything you need" (v. 22-34).

3. On being prepared: "You must be ready all the time" (v. 35-48).

4. On his purpose: "I [will] set the world on fire" (v. 49-53).

Wonder
What is the relationship between "respect" and "cherish"?

Jesus
"Why can't you decide for yourselves what is right?" (Luke 12:57).

Do
Go barefoot sometime today. Consider how hard and soft complement.

Pray: Jesus, what "signs" of right and wrong do I need to focus on?

Conventional Wisdom

Read Matthew 5:21-48

Which of these conventional wisdoms are true?

1. If you swallow poison, induce vomiting right away.

2. Too much salt in your diet is worse than too little.

3. Southerners in the U.S. are more likely to own a gun than people who don't live in the South.

4. It really is darkest right before dawn.

The tally: 1—False *(drink milk or charcoal)*; 2—False *(too little salt is more dangerous)*; 3—True *(42% versus 30% of non-Southerners)*; and 4—False *(it's darkest at midnight)*. Conventional wisdoms feed on assumptions. And Jesus loves to puncture them. Early on he attracts huge crowds, healing "every kind of disease and illness." So time to pop a few CW balloons...

- *Murder is worse than anger.* Jesus: When you call someone an idiot, you're obliterating their sense of self.

- *Committing a sin is worse than contemplating one.* Jesus: You've already done it "in your heart."

- *Adultery is much worse than divorce.* Jesus: Breaking a marriage commitment ignores God's role in the relationship.

- *The punishment must match the crime.* Jesus: Act like your Father, who offers grace to both the guilty and the innocent.

Our CW's, like all other gods, must bow the knee to Jesus.

Wonder
Conventional wisdom says Jesus is "nice." What's a better word?

Jesus
"You are to be perfect, even as your Father...is perfect" (Matthew 5:48).

Do
Your TV remote, not your toilet, harbors the most germs. Clean it today.

Pray: Jesus, expose conventional wisdoms I've held on to about you.

Sheep Revisited

Read John 10:1-16

Jesus calls us "sheep." In the animal kingdom, only "naked mole rat" is a worse comparison. For starters, sheep are timid, easily frightened, and incapable of fighting off any predator. So when Jesus uses sheep as a metaphor to describe us, we have to pry a little deeper to understand the upside of what he's trying to communicate. And the key that unlocks that door is "I am the good shepherd"—it's the relationship between sheep and shepherd that he's trying to highlight.

The shepherd/sheep relationship doesn't immediately resonate because we don't understand the connection the way ancient Middle Easterners did…

Yes, sheep are not the sharpest crayons in the Crayola 64-pack—but they do have a dogged affection for, and obedience to, the voice of their shepherd. They will do anything their master tells them to do because they trust him. And a "good shepherd" is fully invested in his sheep because his heart has been captured by them. He's not in it for a paycheck. In fact, in the face of a threat, he will die defending them. His mission is to invite them into a "rich and satisfying life."

Jesus declares, "I know my sheep, and they know me"—with the same level of intimacy he already enjoys with his Father.

Wonder
Plug "personality of sheep" into a search engine. What's like/unlike you?

Jesus
"I sacrifice my life for the sheep" (John 10:15).

Do
Watch "Do sheep only obey their master's voice?" on youtube.com.

Pray: Jesus, I want to know your voice so well that a whisper is enough.

Little Into Big

Read Luke 7:36-50

In the opening scene of *The Way, Way Back*, an awkward teenager named Duncan is reluctantly traveling with his single mom to her boyfriend Trent's ocean beach house, where they'll spend most of the summer. Duncan's parents have recently divorced, and he doesn't know Trent well. His mom is asleep in the station wagon, and Trent is driving. Duncan is sitting in "the way, way back." From the front, Trent asks, "Duncan, on a scale of 1 to 10, what do you think you are?" Duncan wrestles over the question, not wanting to answer. But Trent pressures him until he mumbles "a six." And Trent responds, "I think you're a three."

That interchange haunts Duncan the rest of the film. All of us have an "interior narrative"—the hidden way we describe ourselves that keeps us in a vice-grip of shame. When we're pegged as a "three," it's hard to dislodge that lie. Maybe that's why the disciples struggled to understand Jesus' teaching about sheep. It's hard to admit how much we're like them... But Jesus takes tiny things and makes them big things. He takes ugly things and makes them into beautiful things. And he takes timid, dependent, helpless, gullible, and stubborn sheep like us and invites us to carry out his mission in the world. We are his allies, his beloved, his most intimate and trusted friends... When we embrace our smallness, we enter into his bigness.

Wonder	**Jesus**	**Do**
In what ways do you feel small, and how has Jesus made you big?	"No one can snatch [my sheep] away from me" (John 10:28).	Sip a glass of water, then drop in an ice cube and sip again. Little changes big.

Pray: Jesus, sometimes I feel so little. I need your bigness in me.

Excuses, Excuses, Excuses

Read Luke 14:16-24

I have a breakfast meeting every Thursday. To get there on time, I have to leave by 6:15. But that almost never happens. Sometimes I wake up too late, or there's a traffic accident or a bad slow-down. Sometimes I forget I have to get gas. The meeting's leaders have heard all my excuses; I'm too embarrassed to open my mouth now. I just sit down and act like everything's fine… They all know that if the meeting's purpose was to claim my lottery winnings, I'd be there on time.

Jesus is invited for a Sabbath-day meal at a Pharisee's home—a great honor. Everyone is watching him closely to see how he'll carry himself, like a rock star invited to meet the Pope. Jesus observes everyone jockeying for the best seats at the table. So he tells them to beware of chasing honor and to invite the poor and needy to their banquets instead of the rich and powerful. And then he tells them a story about a man who prepares a great feast and invites all the "in crowd" to it, but they all have excuses. So the man instructs his servants to scour the streets and alleys of the town and "invite the poor, the crippled, the blind, and the lame."

Jesus is inviting us to a banquet. Whatever excuses we've used in the past don't matter right now. Claim your place at the table.

Wonder	**Jesus**	**Do**
Why do we gravitate to excuses rather than embracing the truth?	"None…I first invited will get even the smallest taste of my banquet" (Luke 14:24).	Slay an excuse today—show up on time, try that food, write that note.

Pray: Jesus, I'm tired of managing my excuses; please give me a redo.

Hard Is Good

Read John 9:1-34

What's the hardest academic course you've ever taken? Mine was a Public-Affairs Reporting class in college—the journalism school's upper-level head-buster. The professor required us to find a publisher for all our assignments, and I had a leg up because I was an editor for the university newspaper. The journalism department chair read one of the lengthy investigative pieces I'd produced for the class and told me he wanted to enter it in a national student journalism competition. On the same day I learned that my piece won *third place* among all college journalists, my PA Reporting professor handed back our graded articles. I got a C-minus on that award-winner...

Now that's setting the bar high.

We have a love/hate relationship with hardship. We want things to be easier than they are, but we also know that we grow the most under the duress of great challenges. In the church we've embraced a "truthy" myth misappropriated from something Paul wrote in 1 Corinthians 10:12-13—we say "Jesus will never give us more than we can handle." But Paul was actually writing about temptation, not hardship. Not only does Jesus embrace the "good" in hard, but he arranges it. In every encounter he injects a little hardship into the person's life, even when he's also extracting it. Jesus believes in healthy hardship because he practices what we preach—that our challenges in life prepare us to persevere as light in the darkness.

Wonder
What's a hardship that Jesus has turned into a blessing?

Jesus
"While I am here in the world, I am the light of the world" (John 9:5).

Do
Serve someone by secretly completing a chore that's not your responsibility.

Pray: Jesus, I know I complain a lot about hardship—I'm sorry.

Jesus Sommeliers

Read John 3:1-21

Over the last half century, fewer than 300 people in the world have earned certification as a master sommelier—a "wine steward" with sophisticated expertise in wine selection and service. In a career that commands average salaries north of $150,000, why so few? Well, only five percent of candidates can pass the grueling three-part exam because, simply, *it seems impossible*. The first stage targets theory; the second requires the candidate to serve a table of demanding master sommeliers. And in the third stage candidates must blind taste-test six glasses of wine. In a 25-minute window, they're required to accurately determine the grape varieties, country of origin, district of origin, and vintage year.

For the trickle of candidates who succeed, the process develops an extraordinary attention to detail. They learn to detect nuanced influences in a wine, training their palate to appreciate a wine's essence. Their secret?

- Slow down to savor.

- Grow acutely aware of nuances.

- Pay much better attention to the wine's essence.

- Taste often and widely.

Likewise, when we savor every "taste" in Jesus, we discover the height and breadth and depth of his beauty, expanding the palate of our worship.

Wonder	**Jesus**	**Do**
If we wanted to "taste (Jesus) often and widely" what would we do?	"You can hear the wind but can't tell where it comes from or where it is going" (John 3:8).	Choose the shirt/top you'd like to wear today. Find it using only touch.

Pray: Jesus, show me the nuances that make up your essence.

The Leverage of the Heart

Read John 14:25-30

We tacitly expect Jesus to honor a basic negotiation: *If I give my faith and allegiance to you, then I expect a happy, fulfilling life.* But he wants nothing to do with our quid pro quo's. He's intent on a transformational relationship, offering his heart, not a prize from his cosmic vending machine. When we become captured and captivated by his beauty, not his functionality, we enter into the "abundant life."

In a story told by Saint Teresa of Avila, the 16th-century Spanish mystic, she "sees" an angel rushing toward her carrying a torch and a bucket of water. "Where are you going with that torch and bucket?" she asks. "What will you do with them?" And the angel answers, "With the water I will put out the fires of hell, and with the fire I will burn down the mansions of heaven; then we will see who really loves God."

When we pursue a relationship with Jesus because he is true and good, not because he will give us what we want, we give the enemy of God no foothold in our lives. If we care less about the transaction than his presence, then it's hard to be tempted into resentment. And if intimacy with Jesus is worth more to us than what we "deserve," we soon become dangerous-for-good.

Wonder	**Jesus**	**Do**
Everyone wants to be happy, but what transcends happiness?	"The ruler of this world approaches. He has no power over me" (John 14:30).	Pay with cash and get your change, then give it to the cashier as a gift.

Pray: Jesus, when I am disappointed in you, please show me your heart.

Look at the Birds...

Read Matthew 6:25-30

Look at the birds...

Look at the lilies of the field...

Look, look, look...

When Jesus invites us to "look," he's pointing at the world's original "art installation"—the created world. We see birds unworried about their bellies and flowers unworried about their wardrobe. Birds and flowers accept their provision as a given, but we toil under the "curse" of Adam and Eve: "The ground is cursed because of you. All your life you will struggle to scratch a living from it" (Genesis 3:17). This curse has us in the vice-grip of anxiety, so Jesus offers an escape route called *parable*...

When his disciples ask Jesus why he so often buries his teaching in botany or zoology or folklore, he quotes Psalm 78, written by the Old Testament prophet Asaph: "Open your ears to what I am saying, for I will speak to you in a parable. I will teach you hidden lessons from our past—stories we have heard and known, stories our ancestors handed down to us. We will not hide these truths from our children; we will tell the next generation about the glorious deeds of the Lord, about his power and his mighty wonders."

When we look, look, look for parables hiding in plain sight, we discover "hidden lessons" about the glory of God. They are hidden only because Jesus wants us to pursue and dig and discover, because that's how we find buried treasure.

Wonder	**Jesus**	**Do**
What's one thing in your life that always triggers anxiety?	"If God cares...for wildflowers...he will certainly care for you" (Matthew 6:30).	Close your eyes and listen for birds. Feel your anxiety lift.

Pray: Jesus, unburden me from worry.

What Jesus Stands For

Read John 4

Many years ago my wife and I were close friends with a couple we met in a birthing class. For years we heard stories about Cathy's globe-trotting, swashbuckling, rags-to-riches-to-rags-to-riches-again father, Leo. He owned and piloted his own Cessna, and one night while he was attempting to re-certify his instrument rating, he slammed his airplane into the side of a mountain.

The next day, Cathy called to tell us the horrific news. A few days later, she called again to invite us to an informal ceremony to honor Leo's life. His family and friends offered speeches, stories, and poems. The last person to speak was a nervous young man who said, "I met Leo when I was 18. A few minutes after I was first introduced to him, he looked me square in the eye and asked, 'What do you stand for?' I didn't even know I was supposed to be thinking of questions like that. But his question has dominated my life."

On our way home, my wife asked, "Well, Rick, what do you stand for?" And I answered, maybe too quickly, "I stand for the glory and honor of Jesus Christ." To stand for his glory, we must know *what he stands for*. If we're going to grow in our relationship with him and trust his heart more deeply, we'll need to understand better what he believes. Kick-start this journey by reading all of John 4, stopping every time you discover something Jesus believes.

Wonder
What's something you "stand for" that others might not know?

Jesus
"I have a kind of food you know nothing about" (John 4:32).

Do
Put this book down and (lightly) stand on this page with your shoe—leave a footprint.

Pray: Jesus, give me something to stand for in my life.

A Drumline Relationship: Part 1

Read Luke 18:18-30

If you've ever tried to play a musical instrument, you know at first the sheet music seems like it's written in Swahili. The "Rich Young Ruler" in Luke 18 finds himself in a similar predicament—he has tried hard to follow all the rules and play the "sheet music" of the law, and yet Jesus doesn't hear *music* coming out of him. He warns his disciples, "It is easier for a camel to go through the eye of a needle than for a rich person to enter the Kingdom of God!" Jesus wants more than a sheet-music relationship...

In his letter to the Roman believers, the Apostle Paul declares that it's impossible to play all the notes, all the right way, all the time. His solution is both simple and euphoric: *"Who will free me from this life that is dominated by sin and death? Thank God! The answer is in Jesus Christ our Lord"* (Romans 7:24-25).

What if the music Jesus is longing to hear is more like the kind a drumline produces—improvised percussion performed by musicians who listen intently to each other, take playful risks, and invite "unscripted" contributions? In a drumline, players treat music-making like a spirited conversation. This is why Jesus invites the Rich Young Ruler to sell everything and "come, follow me." He wants a back-and-forth relationship, not a labored clarinet solo.

Wonder
Watch "Napkin Powder Puff 2015" on youtube.com. What do you notice about the interplay?

Jesus
"Why do you call me good?...Only God is truly good" (Luke 18:19).

Do
Use pens as drumsticks and objects as drums—create your own rhythm.

Pray: Jesus, free me to play the notes, not grind through them.

A Drumline Relationship: Part 2

Read Luke 24:13-32

If Jesus is *not* calling us to discipline ourselves so we can play all the right notes, all the time, then what does he want? Well, even though he often seems to relish making his intentions obscure, he doesn't do that when it comes to the kind of relationship he's longing for. He tells his friends, "I no longer call you slaves, because a master doesn't confide in his slaves. Now you are my friends, since I have told you everything the Father told me. You didn't choose me. I chose you" (John 15:15-16). Jesus is plain here—he wants a…

- "confiding" relationship, where we both share our authentic interior life;

- "sharing" relationship, where we freely give and receive everything we have; and

- "chosen" relationship, where we mutually pursue the other.

This is a relational gumbo called "intimate allies." It's why the improvisation that characterizes a drumline group is such a spot-on metaphor for the life Jesus wants to share with us. He wants an epic shift in the way we relate to him, and it will require us to relax a little, lay down our rutted patterns and rote religious habits, and *play*. We move from a relationship characterized by stiff, fearful obedience to one characterized by joyous and exhilarating improvisation. From a dirge to a jig. From a march to a jitterbug…

Wonder
To "improv" in your relationship with Jesus, what must you stop doing?

Jesus
"You find it so hard to believe all that the prophets wrote in the Scriptures" (Luke 24:25).

Do
Hum a familiar worship song, then improvise your own melody.

Pray: Jesus, thank you for choosing me.

A Drumline Relationship: Part 3

Read Luke 9:28-36

Learning to relate to Jesus in a "drumline" way requires that we understand his character, personality, and value system better than we do now. We find the freedom to play music in our relationship with him by learning his "chord progressions"—what he thinks is important, true, and good. When we understand more intimately what motivates him, we can relax and enter into our relationship with him in a more adventurous way.

First, we play by instinct—we "feel it." We give ourselves permission to *not know* in advance exactly what notes we'll play as we seek his guidance. We learn to trust the *feel* of his influence in our lives rather than demand clarity.

Second, we "play off" Jesus, our Drumline Captain. Every drumline needs a flexible (not bossy) captain as the hub that connects everyone—the one everyone looks to as they improvise. So we never take our eyes off Jesus.

Third, we release the pressure to "be good." It's all about experimenting together. When we face into our insecurities to risk in our relationship with Jesus, we adopt a relaxed, fun, curious, adventurous, humble, and vulnerable attitude.

Fourth, we learn to "speak the language" of music. We understand the "words" before we tell the story. This means exploring and understanding the foundations of truth revealed by Jesus in Scripture.

Wonder	Jesus	Do
Does Jesus seem more "flexible" or "bossy" to you?	"Listen to me and remember what I say" (Luke 9:44).	Trust the *feel* of the breeze on your face. Turn in the direction it is blowing from.

Pray: Jesus, who would you like me to pray for, and for what?

A Drumline Relationship: Part 4

Read John 15:7-8

Remember, Jesus upended forever the way we approach God: "I no longer call you slaves, because a master doesn't confide in his slaves." That means we enter his heart through the door of friendship. We move *from* one kind of relationship *to* a completely new kind of relationship…

From	To	From	To
Have to…	Want to…	Torment…	Compassion…
Cold dedication…	Knowing trust…	Handshake…	Hug…
Slavish obedience…	Collaborating…	Striving…	Abiding…
One…	Two…	Fear…	Trust…
Listening…	Understanding…	Comfort zone…	No limits…
Performance…	Authenticity…	Wanting…	Giving…
Ambiguity…	Clarity…	Bonds…	Bond…
Insecurity…	Freedom…	Salvation by good works…	Good works because of salvation…

This from/to rhythm in our soon feels more like music than discipline. Pastor and author Tom Melton says, "We don't really believe Jesus is beautiful; otherwise, we wouldn't describe our relationship with him as work." We follow Jesus the way we follow the smell of fresh apple pie—beauty entices us forward.

Wonder
Pick the from/to progression above that captures you. Why does it?

Jesus
"If you remain in me…you may ask for anything you want" (John 15:7).

Do
Before others arrive home, bake or cook something that smells enticing.

Pray: Jesus, move me from _____ to _____.

The Possible Impossible

Read Luke 17:5-6

In *Mary Poppins* the title character tosses a one-liner that smacks of Jesus: "Everything is possible. Even the impossible." When the disciples ask Jesus how to increase their faith, he tells them they're working too hard—a tiny micron of belief can move a mulberry bush (or a mountain). That's helpful if the location of your mulberry bush has really been eating at you. But maybe mountain-moving isn't really as rare as we think it is…

I met Tamrat Layne at a small gathering of people invited to hear Dallas Willard speak. He's a tall, soft-spoken man with a thick African accent. We talked a bit about our mutual respect for Willard. Afterward, my friends excitedly asked, "Don't you know—that's Tamrat Layne, the former prime minister of Ethiopia?!"

So I returned to Tamrat and asked if I could buy him coffee and hear his story. He'd led a communist insurgency that ousted Ethiopia's leader. Soon after, a close ally betrayed him, sending him to prison for life. Years later, Tamrat was wrestling with rage and hopelessness when a "shape of light" appeared in his cell. A voice that "came from all directions" said, *"I am Jesus—believe in me and follow me. I am the only one who can give you the life you are looking for."* The visitor returned, repeating the promise, and Tamrat soon risked his micron of faith. His betrayer, inexplicably, then decided to set him free. He now travels the world helping others re-locate their mulberry bushes.

Wonder	**Jesus**	**Do**
What's something you've seen that was impossible but possible?	"Don't be afraid…Take courage. I am here!" (Matthew 14:27).	Use a Q-Tip and lemon juice to write your "impossible dream" in the margin.

Pray: Jesus, I have a mulberry bush that needs relocating: _____.

The Land-Shark at Your Door

Read 1 Corinthians 2:1-5

The first season of *Saturday Night Live* spoofed *Jaws* with a skit called "The Land Shark"—a guy in a shark costume knocked on doors, pretending to be a repairman or a door-to-door salesman.

Woman: *(A knock on the door)* Yes?

Voice: *(Mumbling)* Mrs. Arlsburgerhhh?

Woman: Who?

Voice: *(Mumbling)* Mrs. Johannesburrrr?

Woman: Who is it?

Voice: *(Pause)* Flowers.

Woman: Flowers for whom?

Voice: *(Long pause)* Plumber, ma'am.

Woman: I don't need a plumber. You're that clever shark, aren't you?

Voice: *(Pause)* Candygram.

Woman: Candygram, my foot. You get out of here before I call the police. You're the shark, and you know it.

Voice: Wait. I-I'm only a dolphin, ma'am.

Woman: A dolphin? Well...okay. *(Opens door, foam-rubber shark head chomps down on woman's head)*

The Land Shark is a perfect parable for why so many of us keep Jesus at a safe distance. We may open our door to a dolphin—the Jesus who's a lamb-carrying pacifist—but not the shark the Gospels clearly describe. Just poke your finger anywhere in the Gospels and he'll bite it off...

Wonder
In John 15, Jesus says he lives in us, then asks, "Do you live in me?"

Jesus
"Don't imagine that I came to bring peace to the earth!" (Matthew 10:34).

Do
Tear off a corner of this page as a reminder of Jesus' "bite."

Pray: Jesus, I open my door to you, knowing you're not a dolphin.

Validation

Read Luke 7:36-50

In the short film *Validation*, a man at a kiosk validates
motorists' parking slips. One day he decides to take seriously the
"validation" he's offering; he studies each vacant-eyed person
in line and highlights something wonderful about them. They
arrive like deflated balloons and leave with hope leaking from
their eyes. Word spreads and there's soon a crowd queuing up
for their "validation." But there is one person, a stern and sad girl
who snaps license photos at the DMV, who snubs his attempts to
validate her beauty. He finally gives up, broken by her rejection.
Now when people arrive at his kiosk expecting hope, he confirms
their drudgery instead.

One day tourists on the street ask the man to take their photo.
As he does, he describes what he enjoys about them. Their hope
bubbles over, and he returns to patching holes in strangers' souls.
Later, by chance, he sees the sad girl who broke his heart—she's
now taking passport photos, smiling and validating each person
in line. He is dumbfounded. She lights up when she sees him,
offering him a photo of a smiling, disabled elderly woman—it's
the girl's mother, who hadn't smiled in years. But then the mother
met a certain young man on the street who took her picture and
called out her beauty…

Redemption is validation, spreading like an epidemic of hope:
"I came so [you] can have real and eternal life, more and better
life than [you] ever dreamed of" (John 10:10, *The Message*).

Wonder
When have you felt
validated for who you
are, and why?

Jesus
"If you love only those
who love you, what
reward is there for
that?" (Matthew 5:46).

Do
On youtube.com watch
"Validation Film."

Pray: Jesus, I long to find my deepest validation in your love for me.

Going to War

Read John 12:31-32

A buzzing crowd has gathered in Jerusalem just after Jesus' "triumphal" entry, but he quickly shifts their focus to the earthquake that's about to shake eternity: "The time for judging this world has come, when Satan, the ruler of this world, will be cast out." Here, "cast out" is a legal term that means "the removal of a convicted and condemned prisoner from court so that he may receive his appointed punishment." That punishment is the stripping of the spiritual authority Lucifer once claimed, but *not* his banishment from earth.

Paul later urges us to remain awake to the present "schemes" of this defeated enemy, who now wages guerilla warfare against the children of God: "We are not fighting against flesh-and-blood enemies, but against evil rulers and authorities of the unseen world" (Ephesians 6:12).

When my daughter Lucy was away serving at a demanding summer camp for kids and adults with special needs, she confided that she felt "under attack." So I wrote her this note: *You're a force for the kingdom of God. And that means you're also in the thick of battle with the kingdom of darkness. Stand your ground, assert the authority Jesus won for you, and tell Satan (and his lies) to go back to hell...When you have authority, you're not worried. It's like spraying bug repellant at a mosquito—that pest is going to die...*

Wonder
What's the difference between a spiritual battle and bad luck?

Jesus
"Walk in the light... so the darkness will not overtake you" (John 12:35).

Do
Rub houseplant dirt on this page—a reminder that Satan remains on earth.

Pray: Jesus, be my refuge and strength in the chaos of war.

Treasured Imbalances

Read Luke 12:35-48

Personality tests force us to think about who we are, to wrestle with the mechanics of our identities. The problem: They're a two-dimensional tool for a three-dimensional truth. A number or string of letters represents you, but it isn't *you*. Are our identities chiseled or formed, and why do they seem so fragile? And what does it mean to "find our identities in Jesus"? Well, Jesus revealed Peter's true nature, so let's use his story as a template...

- Luke 5:1-11—Jesus intrudes into his life, exposing the deceptive beliefs he already has about himself.

- Luke 9:1-6, 18-20, 28-36—Jesus gives him more than he can handle, then invites him to embrace his power.

- Luke 12:35-48— Jesus trusts him to give what he has to give, insisting that he live out who he is.

- Luke 22:31-34, 54-61—Jesus allows troubles into his life to expose his false self and invite dependency.

- John 21:1-19—Jesus surfaces his doubts about his identity, then confirms his true nature by giving him a purpose.

What if the weaknesses Jesus exposes in Peter, like ours, are imbalances he "repurposes" to strengthen others? What if real balance happens only when we're connected to others in community—the "body" of Christ? What if we are whole like him only when we're together, our imbalances balanced?

Wonder
What's a "weakness" in you that others have been strengthened by?

Jesus
"Follow me" (John 21:19).

Do
Turn the shower water full cold, then full hot. Find the beautiful balance.

Pray: Jesus, I'm longing for community where my imbalances find balance.

Enemy Sonar

Read Matthew 4:1-11

We live our lives by sonar. We bounce our "signals" off others, then decode the feedback. It's a hazardous practice…

I've been a writer and speaker for a long time—writing is a "natural" outgrowth of my gifting and personality. But I've had to work hard and learn (the hard way) how to speak to large crowds. Once, early on, an established speaker sat through one of my workshops and advised me to stick to my writing and "leave the speaking to speakers." In the crater left by this emotional IED, my sonar feedback was predictable: *You're not enough, and you'll never be enough.* Of course, both Jesus and his enemy, Satan, are acutely interested in my interior narrative. They both want to answer my deepest question: *What is the truth about me?*

In the desert, Satan tries to use his sonar to corrupt Jesus' identity. His strategy then, and now: **1)** Attack when we're weak. **2)** Question if our God-given identities are really true, and tempt us to simply seize what we want. **3)** Goad us into a place of despair by "testing" God's love for us using circumstantial "proofs." **4)** Dangle what our appetites crave—power and glory and riches—as a reward for selling our souls.

Jesus stays awake and alert to the wicked forces attempting to shape his narrative, and actively resists the "phantom" sonar signals that have destructive intent.

Wonder
What's a word people use to describe you that isn't really true?

Jesus
"Get out of here, Satan" (Matthew 4:10).

Do
Dip your finger in turmeric and smear it here. It's the savory *essence* of you.

Pray: Jesus, what is the truth about me?

True Narratives

Read Luke 15:11-32

The story we're telling ourselves, about ourselves, is the foundation for our lives. When we live inside a true narrative, we find our deeper purpose and invite others into intimacy. When we live inside a false narrative, we miss our true purpose and drag ourselves toward self-destruction. The stakes are high, just as they were for the "prodigal son" returning home after he disgraces his father and wastes his inheritance. Will he embrace the plausible lie about his life—*you're a mistake, and not worthy of love*—or will he embrace the truth—*you're a cherished member of the family, worthy of redemption and celebration*?

The prodigal son has a choice: He can allow "the facts on the ground" to define his interior narrative (*I'm an entitled, ungrateful, morally corrupt person*), or he can find himself in his father's response (*the pain I've caused will not overshadow how much I am loved*). In his parable, Jesus is forcing us to confront our choice…

We are wanted—so much so that the God we can't comprehend made himself comprehensible in the fully God/fully man Jesus, just so we could be with him. Our mission is to communicate this fundamental message: "You are wanted, and you are invited into the family of God."

Wonder
When you say, out loud, "I am wanted," what emotions surface?

Jesus
"Bring the finest robe in the house and put it on him" (Luke 15:22).

Do
Go to photofunia.com and create your own "wanted" poster.

Pray: Jesus, I believe I'm wanted, but help my unbelief.

Expecting More

Read John 4:1-30

In Edwin Friedman's fable "The Bridge," a walking traveler is crossing a high bridge when he encounters a stranger tied to a rope. The man hands one end to the traveler, then leaps over the bridge. The shocked traveler struggles to grip the rope. He urges the stranger to climb up, but he repeatedly refuses: "I am your responsibility," he says. "Well, I did not ask for it," the traveler responds. "If you let go, I am lost," responds the dangling man. The traveler concocts a way to haul the man up, with his help, but he refuses again.

At the end of his strength, the traveler tells the man that he "will not accept the position of choice for your life, only for my own; the position of choice for your own life I hereby give back to you." He gives the man one more chance, then releases the rope.

Jesus' encounter with the oft-divorced Samaritan woman from Sychar embodies the traveler's brave strategy. He does not choose rescue *for* the woman: "If you only knew the gift God has for you and who you are speaking to, you would ask me, and I would give you living water." It's her choice to haul herself up on the "rope" Jesus offers. Unlike the stranger, she does. Leaving her water jar behind, she tells the people of Sychar, "Come and see a man who told me everything I ever did!"

Jesus offers us the dignity of *agency* in our rescue—we are participators, not bystanders.

Wonder	**Jesus**	**Do**
Why do you sometimes "over-function" for those who need help?	"I have a kind of food you know nothing about" (John 4:32).	We rescue to circumvent pain. Grip an ice cube, endure the pain until it melts.

Pray: Jesus, give me the strength to endure others' pain.

What Doesn't Belong?

Read Matthew 5:17-48

1. Which word does not belong? A. Fedora, B. Beret, C. Moccasins, D. Sombrero, E. Wig *(Moccasins is right—it's the only thing on the list you don't put on your head.)*

2. Now, which word is the odd one out? A. Alligator, B. Camera, C. Material, D. Casual, E. Salmon *(Salmon is right—it's the only word on the list that does not have two a's in it.)*

Now that you've had a little practice, let's revisit Matthew 5 and look for the "don't belongs" in Jesus' Sermon on the Mount—common-but-wrong assumptions that have no place in his home, the kingdom of God. He first warns the crowds gathered to hear him teach: "Unless your righteousness is better than the righteousness of the teachers of religious law and the Pharisees, you will never enter the Kingdom of Heaven!" And then he spotlights the wrong-ness in their right-ness...

1. **Anger** (v. 21-26)—Resolve differences; don't exact revenge.
2. **Adultery** (v. 27-30)—Don't entertain temptations; crush the source of them.
3. **Divorce** (v. 31-32)—Intimate relationships are not legal bonds; they're spiritual commitments.
4. **Vows** (v. 33-37)—Vows are silly; just say "yes" or "no."
5. **Revenge** (v. 38-42)—Fairness is not the standard; grace is.
6. **Enemies** (v. 43-48)—There is no reward in loving those who love you; "perfection" is loving your enemies.

Wonder	**Jesus**	**Do**
Why would Jesus *launch* his ministry by pointing out wrong beliefs?	"I came to accomplish [the prophets'] purpose" (Matthew 5:17).	Go to wodb.ca and test your skill at picking out what doesn't belong.

Pray: Jesus, what's something that doesn't belong in my life?

Affectations

Read 1 Corinthians 2:1-5

Close friends know our affectations, the obvious quirks that are not so obvious to us. One day, in an online forum, my friend John posted a sardonic checklist of my eccentricities—the strange catchphrases that I (apparently) repeat all the time. Here's how he channeled my persona: "I like to use the phrase 'liminal space' and hate it when people diminish Jesus by calling him 'nice.' In addition, I promote 'The Lombardi Effect' and reiterate 'The Stockdale Paradox.' And, of course, I'm always warning others about the dangers of 'shoulding.'"

John skewered all my favorite tropes. When friends pay attention to you, they know enough to (lovingly, of course) poke fun at what makes you "special." Likewise, the Apostle Paul points out Jesus' "special-ness." Here's his checklist…

- Jesus is both the source of our peace and the *means* of its delivery (Romans 5:1).

- Jesus is, metaphorically, the glorious surprise waiting for us under the tree (1 Corinthians 2:7-9).

- Jesus is a freedom fighter, intolerant of our captivity (Galatians 5:1).

- Jesus intends to make us just as "peculiar" as he is—a people who stand out like light in the darkness (Titus 2:14).

- Jesus is a romantic—his passion is to make sure we're always with him (Romans 8:35).

Wonder
What's a quirk your friends love to point out about you?

Jesus
"Don't let your hearts be troubled. Trust in God, and trust also in me" (John 14:1).

Do
In a grocery store, buy something that reflects your unique-ness and eat it.

Pray: Jesus, thank you for cherishing my affectations.

Keeping Secrets

Read Matthew 6:1-18

I was planning a surprise party for my wife and had to figure out a plausible excuse to stay home from an important event so I could decorate our home. I needed something that wouldn't raise suspicion. We have two cats, so I scooped their litter into a plastic bag, then poured rubbing alcohol on it to break it down. Then I left the bag sitting in the sun. The goal was to create the mother of all awful smells. Mission accomplished. On the morning of the event, I locked myself in a bathroom with the bag, then waited for the smell to obliterate breathable air. When I emerged I tossed the bag in our outside garbage—then told my family I felt sick. The smell emanating from the bathroom was my trump card. They begged me to stay home… And two hours later my wife got the shock of her life.

What's the biggest secret you've ever kept? Researchers tell us that keeping secrets undermines our ability to live authentically and leads to depression and health concerns. But here's a surprise: Jesus is a *big believer* in keeping secrets, including.

- Keeping our goodness secret (Matthew 6:1-4)
- Keeping our prayers secret (Matthew 6:5-13)
- Keeping our fasting secret (Matthew 6:16-18)

Some secrets are meant to be kept, but Jesus vows he won't keep anything from us: "Now you are my friends, since I have told you everything the Father told me" (John 15:15).

Wonder	**Jesus**	**Do**
What are good reasons for keeping secrets?	"Don't do your good deeds publicly, to be admired by others" (Matthew 6:1).	Put a $5 bill in a plain envelope and leave it in a neighbor's mail box.

Pray: Jesus, let's keep some things just between you and me, including…

Setting Captives Free

Read John 8:1-11

In the Oscar-winning film *Dead Poets Society*, an unconventional new English teacher named John Keating arrives at an all-boys boarding school. Early on, Keating asks his students to compose and recite an original poem. Todd Anderson, a painfully insecure student, confesses he didn't do the assignment—he's petrified by the vulnerability it demands. But Keating insists that Todd come to the front, close his eyes, and create a poem on the spot. He challenges and prods and encourages and, when Todd blurts out a string of words saturated in beauty, reacts with awe.

Keating takes great risks to set Todd free from his debilitating insecurities. Jesus does the same, over and over. A sampler from early in the Gospel of John…

The Person	The Captivity	The Freedom
The Samaritan woman (John 4)	Shame, heartbreak, and social rejection	She's the first evangelist ever.
A lame man stuck by the pool of Bethesda for 38 years (John 5)	An identity that is "cursed" because of a lifelong illness	"He rolled up his sleeping mat and began walking!"
Jewish Temple guards (John 7)	Adherence to stifling tenets of Jewish law	"We have never heard anyone speak like this!"
A woman caught in adultery (John 8)	Public shame and death	Life, and freedom from condemnation

Wonder
What's something Jesus has freed you from?

Jesus
"Where are your accusers?" (John 8:10).

Do
Right where you are, free your feet from your shoes. Thank Jesus for freedom.

Pray: Jesus, show me my captivity, and free me from it.

In Pursuit of Unfairness

Read Matthew 20:1-16

In the middle of an exhausting, expensive, and time-consuming effort to replace and restore our water-damaged wood floors, my cellphone rang. It was the flooring contractor telling me our refrigerator had stopped working and was leaking water onto raw wood—I needed to do something right away. My first thought: *Really, Jesus? Now we have to replace our refrigerator in the middle of all of this?* Sometimes life just doesn't seem fair. But we tell ourselves that others have it much worse, which sounds like it should help but doesn't…

What's our standard for fairness? And how does Jesus' standard compare to ours? He begins his Parable of the Vineyard Workers with "the Kingdom of Heaven is like…" And we discover that, in kingdom culture, fairness has nothing to do with comparison—workers are paid the same no matter what time of day they start. Those who protest this "unfair" arrangement use comparison as their defense. Speaking through the mouth of the "landowner," Jesus skewers that assumption: "Is it against the law for me to do what I want with my money? Should you be jealous because I am kind to others?"

For most of us, comparison dictates what is unfair. But the engine that drives justice in the heart of Jesus is kindness.

Wonder
Why is unfairness such a hard thing to accept?

Jesus
"Those who are last now will be first then" (Matthew 20:16).

Do
Invite the person standing behind you to go ahead of you. Don't explain.

Pray: Jesus, thank you for the "unfairness" of your love for me.

The Post-Testament Life

Read John 15:4-27

I pick a random novel from my library (Leo Tolstoy's *Anna Karenina*), open to a random page (*340*), and point to a random sentence (*"Besides the gift of the necklace he wanted to arrange with her about meeting after the ballet"*). Now, is it possible to know what the story is about? Without greater context, no…

Until 2,000 years ago, the people of God lived in the relational reality of the Old Covenant, their lives governed by a soul-crushing load of religious rules and animal sacrifices. And then, for a short time, they lived in the relational reality of the Messiah—the presence of God incarnate. During this time Jesus repeatedly told his disciples that a new time was coming, when the rules and sacrifices would give way to the Holy Spirit, guiding them from the inside out. We must understand the *context* of what life was like under the Old Covenant to fully appreciate the stark contrasts with our New Covenant life in the Spirit…

- Our focus is remaining, not doing and doing (v. 4-7).

- The fruit in our life is organically produced by our *attachment* to Jesus, not trying harder to get better (v. 8).

- We're no longer slavishly subservient in our relationship with God; instead, we're intimates (v. 13-15).

- We're not lead pursuers in this romance—Jesus is (v. 16).

- The Spirit, not the law, will teach us everything we need to know about Jesus (v. 26).

Wonder
What's an Old Covenant habit you still cling to, and why?

Jesus
"This is my command: Love each other" (John 15:17).

Do
The Messiah opened a portal into the New Covenant. Poke a hole in this page.

Pray: Jesus, help me leave the work of the Old and enter the play of the New.

The Ring

Read Luke 15:1-7

In Southern California with my family, I tried boogie boarding for the first time—riding a wave on top of a short, rectangular piece of hydrodynamic foam. I'd never felt the power of the ocean's undercurrents like that, or the pounding of the surf. After one particularly dismembering experience, I washed up disoriented and gasping for air. I looked down at my left hand and saw that the force of the undercurrent had stripped off my wedding ring.

Grief-stricken, I spent the next hours combing the shore, desperate to find my lost treasure. The next morning I went down to the beach early, at low tide. I saw a man with a metal detector, so I told him my story. His eyes lit up. My loss gave John-the-treasure-hunter a great quest. Since I've returned home, he has updated me every month:

- *"I've been back a few times with no luck. I also notified my metal-detecting friends to keep an eye out for it. We may need to get some big storms to move the sand. Here's to big storms!"*

- *"Still looking—had a great low tide couple weeks back and really hunted hard, but no luck."*

- *"Just letting you know it's probably still out there. Will keep looking when conditions improve."*

I may never get my ring back, but I have John out there on the beach, day after day, reminding me of Jesus...

Wonder
What's something you've lost you'd give anything to get back?

Jesus
"If a man has a hundred sheep and one of them gets lost, what will he do?" (Luke 15:4).

Do
On craigslist.org's "Lost & Found" section, pray for a few "lost" postings.

Pray: Jesus, please find what I've lost.

Fundamental For-ness

Read Matthew 25:36-46

At the beginning and end of Jesus' ministry, the fallen angel Lucifer plays a pivotal role. Easter is not merely the story of our redemption; it's the template for the *one story* that goes deepest in our soul—the triumph of good over evil...

In the beginning, Satan appears in the desert to tempt a weakened Jesus—he will appeal to the same primal lust for power and control that bulldozed Adam and Eve into betrayal (Matthew. 4:1-11). But Jesus won't tolerate that. The enemy is banished from his presence, where he stays until he launches a second assault in a lonely garden called Gethsemane (Matthew 26:36-46). In the film *The Passion of the Christ,* this scene is creatively reimagined: Jesus is suffering the agony of the torture he's about to endure while a snake slithers toward his feet. Just as it appears the snake is about to strike, Jesus stomps on its head in a burst of fury. It's a gripping, unforgettable scene that metaphorically mirrors what happens in reality.

Jesus is fundamentally *for us*—in every moment and every circumstance—no matter how our life experience seems to contradict that premise. His refusal to give in to temptation in the wilderness, and his snake-stomping in Gethsemane, is a poetic Alpha and Omega of ferocious for-ness. He is a prizefighter, and the prize he is after is...you and me.

Wonder
Jesus has proven he is for us; why does it sometimes feel like he isn't?

Jesus
"Am I some dangerous revolutionary?" (Matthew 26:55).

Do
On youtube.com watch "Passion of the Christ Gethsemane."

Pray: Jesus, be my refuge and my snake-stomper.

In the Name of Jesus

Read Philippians 2:9-11

As a senior in high school, I was selected to represent my school at a rival school for one day. I showed up and set to work... *representing*. But I had no idea what I was supposed to do. It's important to decode what it means to represent—the phrase "In the name of Jesus" is all over the New Testament, so representing is important.

In the early days of the church, a group of amateur Jewish exorcists travels from town to town trying to make money by casting out evil spirits. They decide to use the name of Jesus in their repertoire: "I command you in the name of Jesus, whom Paul preaches, to come out!" But the evil spirit is unimpressed: "I know Jesus, and I know Paul, but who are you?" (Acts 19:13-16). And then the possessed man attacks, driving the battered men away. This spectacle freaks a lot of people out. If the name of Jesus is powerful, then why didn't it "work"?

Well, the men *used* his name but didn't *represent* his name.

I have a trove of my daughters' early craft projects on my desk—they are not gallery quality, but that doesn't matter. These distorted lumps of clay represent my daughters' hearts, and it's the heart that matters. When we engage others "in the name of Jesus," it's not "gallery quality" he's looking for—it's whether or not our hearts *represent* his heart...

Wonder
In what ways do you *represent* Jesus to those around you?

Jesus
"Many will come in my name...They will deceive many" (Matthew 24:5).

Do
Whisper a bedtime prayer: "Jesus loves you. He's coming after you. He's relentless!"

Pray: Jesus, I don't want to use you; I want to represent you.

Jesus Sings

Read Psalm 116

It's a subtle but glaring omission in our accounts of Jesus' everyday life—there is little mention of music, one of our basic necessities (we spend 18 hours a week listening to it). We're made in the image of God, so music *must be* as intrinsic to God's nature as it is to ours. Perhaps Jesus' singing voice will be our biggest shock when we see him face to face. Or that his favorite instrument is the electric guitar…

According to both Matthew and Mark, Jesus sang on the first night of Passover, after his "last supper" with his friends: "They sang a hymn and went out to the Mount of Olives" (Matthew 26:30 and Mark 14:26). The after-supper hymn was likely from the Hallel—songs recorded in Psalms 113 through 118. Observant Jews sang these songs during evening prayers on the first night of Passover. Here's a line from one of them:

> *Precious in the sight of the Lord*
> *is the death of his faithful ones.*
> *O Lord, I am your servant;*
> *I am your servant,*
> *the child of your serving girl.*
> (Psalm 116:15-16, NRSV)

There is prophetic irony here—though Jesus has sung this song hundreds of times before, this time he's narrating his own story on the eve of his crucifixion. Music opened a pathway into his great sacrifice and our great redemption.

Wonder	**Jesus**	**Do**
Why isn't music referenced as a significant aspect of Jesus' life?	"[I feast and drink], and you say, 'He's a glutton and a drunkard' " (Matthew 11:19).	Find "instrumental music" online; read aloud a Psalm to it (113 to 118).

Pray: Jesus, I long to hear your voice singing over me.

What Jesus Hates

Read Matthew 23:1-36

We can learn lot about a person's heart if we pay attention to what disgusts them. For example, my friends know I despise "smooth" jazz but cherish the old-school jazz masters (Davis, Coltrane, Desmond, Baker). I can't stand safe and predictable and homogenous, but I love risky and surprising and distinct.

Would your close friends guess it was you if they saw an anonymous list of your three pet peeves? What about Jesus' pet peeves? What can we learn about his heart by paying attention to the things he hates? On the heels of another rough debate with a band of conniving Pharisees, he turns to the crowd and lowers the boom, reeling off a litany of traits he can't stand in people…

- Who say things but don't do things.

- Who expect much of others but never try to help.

- Who crave attention and notoriety.

- Who have no compassion for the poor and elderly.

- Who trumpet their giving but ignore justice and mercy.

And Jesus is just getting started… When we appreciate what really upsets him, we get a portal into what he really loves. And when we savor what he loves, our hearts are infected with the redemptive virus in his heart.

Wonder
What's a pet peeve, and what does it reveal about you?

Jesus
"Inwardly you are full of hypocrisy and lawlessness" (Matthew 23:28, NASB).

Do
Try something you hate—smell a used kitchen cloth, for example.

Pray: Jesus, I want to hate the things you hate.

The Sound of Silence

Read Matthew 14:22-23

God created the world in six "days," then rested on the seventh day—*he got quiet.* Because we are made in the image of Jesus, who often retreated into quiet, our need for quiet is deeply embedded in us. Of course, Jesus is not *always* quiet (there was that one time he got table-flipping noisy in the Temple courtyard), but the rest of us are mostly *never* quiet.

For years I've traveled to a retreat center run by Catholic nuns for a "Day Away With the Lord." If you're an elder or staffer, my church will pay the day-rate for a private room once a month. So a group of us cram into a minivan and head down together. Once there, we split up to our assigned rooms for eight hours of silence. Many have never done this sort of thing before. Once, one of the newbies brought no lunch or books or strategy for the day. He assumed someone at the retreat center had that planned for him, so the thought of spending an entire day in silence, one-on-one with Jesus, seemed both ludicrous and frightening to him.

The purpose of going solo and silent in our lives is intimacy. Our close, abiding relationship with Jesus requires "curated" time with him—focused time, connecting time. This is what he means when he says, "Remain in me, and I will remain in you. For a branch cannot produce fruit if it is severed from the vine, and you cannot be fruitful unless you remain in me" (John 15:4).

Wonder
Do you look forward to silence or dread it, and why?

Jesus
"But Jesus often withdrew to the wilderness for prayer" (Luke 5:16).

Do
Take a "Silent Sabbath" by locking yourself in a bathroom for 10 minutes.

Pray: Jesus, I offer you my silence as a "sacrifice of praise."

Which God Is It?

Read John 14:1-14

Let's expose the "elephant in the foyer" for Christians—how can that angry, vindictive God of the Old Testament be the same sheep-defending Jesus of the New Testament? The two seem mutually exclusive. And though Jesus vows that "anyone who has seen me has seen the Father," the differences seem stark, and we wonder how the gap between the two can be bridged.

In the Old Testament, God calls to Moses from a burning bush that never really burns: "'Do not come any closer,' the Lord warned. 'Take off your sandals, for you are standing on holy ground' " (Exodus 3:5). Is this the same God who Jesus says cherishes "the very hairs on our head"—who vows that we're "more valuable than a whole flock of sparrows" and "loves us dearly" and "gives us the same glory" he gave Jesus?

How can this be?

Writer and mystic Brennan Manning says, "It must be noted that Jesus alone reveals who God is...We cannot deduce anything about Jesus from what we think we know about God; however, we must deduce everything about God from what we know about Jesus." We hear the audible voice of God only twice in the New Testament—both times it's a celebration of the heart of Jesus: "This is my dearly loved Son, who brings me great joy. Listen to him." Jesus is the *living translation* of the God we can't see.

Wonder
We can "see" Jesus, so what *must* be true about the God we can't see?

Jesus
"Have I been with you all this time...yet you still don't know who I am?" (John 14:9).

Do
Find a photo online of someone you listen to on the radio. Is it a surprise?

Pray: Jesus, show me the heart of the God I can't see.

The Tension of Kingdoms

Read Matthew 10:37-39

The title of wartime martyr Dietrich Bonhoeffer's classic book *The Cost of Discipleship* raises two obvious questions: What is "discipleship," and what does it cost? Discipleship focuses our life on a growing intimacy with Jesus, but "cost" introduces an edge. Jesus defines cost differently than we do. He lives in the tension between two competing cultures—the kingdom of God (his "native country") and Broken Humanity. When we follow him, we enter into this tension—where the values/customs/truths of one kingdom are at odds with the values/customs/truths of the other. This tension is the true "cost" of discipleship.

In the Kingdom of Broken Humanity...	In the Kingdom of God...
The rich and powerful have organic privilege.	The poor and marginalized have organic privilege.
Relational commitments are fluid, and hatred is the preferred response to enemies.	Relational commitments are sealed by God—grace is the preferred response to enemies.
"Sinners" are disgusting losers who get no voice in the culture and no place at respectable tables.	"Sinners" are Jesus' preferred crowd for hanging out—they know they need him, and that makes him happy.

Humanity declares, "I'm not getting what I deserve." The kingdom declares, "Is Jesus getting what he deserves?"

Wonder
What's something you own that's worth *way* more than it cost?

Jesus
"If you refuse to take up your cross...you are not worthy of being mine" (Matthew 10:38).

Do
Give a personalized gift—costing you more than money to give.

Pray: Jesus, I want you to have what you deserve—my heart...

The End of Compartments

Read Matthew 23:13-30

We circulate in and out of our work, home, church, and "recreational" compartments. But there is one compartment that extends into all the others; it's the stuff we listen to and watch and click on every day—our "media diet." We typically invite Jesus to influence our lives only in *certain* compartments, and that produces dissonance. We know we're not living congruently, but we'd rather not pursue it in all our compartments…

For a research project, I asked thousands of people to answer "always true, sometimes true, or never true" in response to this statement: *"The stuff I watch—TV, movies, and online—doesn't have an impact on my relationship with Jesus."* Almost everyone (88%) answered "always" or "sometimes" true. Apparently, we believe we can "eat" whatever we want with little consequence.

How does Jesus upend the compartmentalized life? "What sorrow awaits you teachers of religious law and you Pharisees. Hypocrites! For you are so careful to clean the outside of the cup and the dish, but inside you are filthy—full of greed and self-indulgence! You blind Pharisee! First wash the inside of the cup and the dish, and then the outside will become clean, too."

Jesus cares what we put in our bodies, but he also cares what we feed our souls: "Eat my body, drink my blood." It's not about self-denial—it's about self-care. So read the "nutrition labels" on your "media soul food."

Wonder
In what ways do you live a compartmentalized life, and why?

Jesus
"Your hearts are filled with hypocrisy and lawlessness" (Matthew 23:28).

Do
Tap the door frame when you enter a "compartment"—an invitation to Jesus.

Pray: Jesus, fill up all my compartments with your presence.

Random Acts of Beauty

Read Mark 12:41-44

In the middle of a three-day sojourn in the wilderness, I'm traipsing up a snowy-mountain road. In my periphery, I notice something I would've missed had I been driving: first one, then three or four, then dozens of fresh rose petals scattered along the shoulder. For a quarter-mile I'm like Dorothy on the yellow-brick road, following a petal-path that leads Home. This haphazard, wallflower beauty annunciates the glory of God.

When we live our lives determined to slow down and pay attention to beauty, we give our souls the living water they crave. A frenzied pace obliterates the details that perch on our periphery, and beauty is always in the details. Jesus models a drink-deep lifestyle—we see it when he notices…

- The widow who slips past the parade of rich posers to drop two pennies ("everything she has to live on") into the Temple collection.

- The sparrows that seem too many to distinguish but are "numbered" for their distinct beauty (Luke 12:6).

- The lilies of the field, dressed more extravagantly than the famously extravagant King Solomon (Luke 12:27).

- The unselfconscious passion of Zacchaeus, the over-eager town scourge (Luke 19:1-10).

Wonder
What's one "beautiful detail" you notice about a loved one?

Jesus
"Now here is a genuine son of Israel—a man of complete integrity" (John 1:47).

Do
Close your eyes and explore the beauty of your fingers by touch.

Pray: Jesus, I'm slowing down right now to appreciate your details.

The Point of the Bible

Read John 1:1-17

The Bible is history's bestselling book—most everyone has one, even if they've not read it. It's history and poetry and teaching and (sometimes) a "handbook for life." But it is foremost the story of an epic romance between God and his creation. In *Love and War*, authors John and Stasi Eldredge condense the meaning of our lives into one sentence: "[We live] in a love story, set in the midst of war." This romance, the way Jesus describes it, is not as PG-rated as we assume. When Christian songwriter John Mark McMillan wrote "How He Loves," one of the most popular worship songs of all time, he included this eye-opening stanza:

So heaven meets earth like a sloppy wet kiss
And my heart turns violently inside of my chest,
I don't have time to maintain these regrets,
When I think about, the way...
He loves us
Oh! How he loves us...

If you're familiar with this song, that first line may take you aback. It's in McMillan's original but not in the now-popular version. McMillan was pressured by music-industry people to alter "sloppy wet kiss" to "like an unforeseen kiss." The reason, of course, is that the original line seems way too *sexual*. Ironic, because intimacy with God is the central narrative of Scripture and the obvious intent of Jesus' bride-and-bridegroom description of our relationship.

Wonder	**Jesus**	**Do**
What's a word that describes your experience of the Bible?	"My prayer is...for those you have given me, because they belong to you" (John 17:9).	Get your lips wet with coffee or tea; leave your sloppy wet kiss here.

Pray: Jesus, I want "belong to you" to become my identity.

Jesus and Revelation

Read Revelation 2:2–3:21

Apocalyptic predictions! Bizarre visions! Indecipherable prophecies! Exclamation points! The book of Revelation is like a French art-house movie—it's thick with obscure allegory, and few make it through the whole thing. The narrative is "delivered" to John, imprisoned on the island of Patmos, by either an angel or Jesus—we're not exactly sure. John is caught up in worship when he hears a trumpet blast and realizes it's the voice of Jesus, who dictates seven letters to seven churches in the "province of Asia." Each one follows a similar structure: *Here's what I like about you, and here's why I have a bone to pick with you...*

- **To Ephesus:** You work hard and don't tolerate lies, but you don't love me the way you first did.

- **To Smyrna:** I know about your poverty, but you're actually rich. Remain faithful through your suffering.

- **To Pergamum**: Satan is enthroned in your city—though you won't deny me, you tolerate false teaching.

- **To Thyatira:** I know how you persevere in love, faith, and service, but you're allowing a liar to lead people astray.

- **To Sardis:** You act like you're alive, but you're not. Wake up!

- **To Philadelphia**: You're weak, but obeyed me anyway. Yes!

- **To Laodicea:** I wish you were hot or cold—because you're lukewarm, I'll spit you out.

Wonder
Which of these "seven summaries" is most convicting, and why?

Jesus
"I am the Alpha and the Omega—the beginning and the end" (Revelation 1:8).

Do
Find "sound of trumpet blast" online—listen to the "voice of Jesus."

Pray: Jesus, do you have a bone to pick with me?

Hide and Seek

Read Matthew 27:45-54

Trappist monk Thomas Keating's poem "Twilight of the Self" invites us into the bowels of his "dark night of the soul"—the description St. John of the Cross uses to describe a spiritual crisis. Keating writes…

My sole desire is You, *And You are always absent…* *I move around in aimless circles.* *Rituals and sacred symbols,* *Once treasured sources of relating* *to You* *Are meaningless to me now.*	*They communicate nothing of You,* *Who are everything to me,* *But for whom and from whom I feel* *no love,* *Nor hope of fulfillment…* *For the God I thought I knew* *No longer exists.*

Keating captures the common cry of those who've been captured and conquered by the heart of Jesus, yet feel an aching distance from him. It's reminiscent of U2's iconic anthem:

You broke the bonds *and you loosened chains* *carried the cross of my shame,* *of my shame* *You know I believe it*	*But I still haven't found* *What I'm looking for* *But I still haven't found* *What I'm looking for*

Jesus endures his own dark night—on the cross, separated from the presence of his Father for the first time in eternity, he cries out, "My God, my God, why have you abandoned me?" In our dark nights, we cry out in anguish, and then we wait for Jesus to find us…

Wonder
What do people most need when they are caught in a "dark night"?

Jesus
"They will mock him, spit on him, flog him with a whip, and kill him" (Mark 10:34).

Do
Sit in a dark room. If darkness were a taste, what would it be?

Pray: Jesus, be the light in my darkness.

Like Little Children

Read Mark 10:13-16

On the University of Chicago Divinity School's "Baptist Day," students eat a picnic lunch and listen to a "celebrity" lecturer. One year it was Dr. Paul Tillich, the influential German theologian. He spoke for more than two hours, quoting scholars to prove that the resurrection of Jesus must be false. His conclusion: Since the resurrection is a sham, the religious traditions of the church are groundless. Then he invited questions.

No one dared, until an old, black preacher with a head of woolly white hair stood up. "Docta Tillich, I got one question." He reached into his sack lunch, pulled out an apple, and ate. "Docta Tillich," CRUNCH, MUNCH… "my question is simple…" CRUNCH, MUNCH… "Now, I ain't never read them books you read…" CRUNCH, MUNCH… "And I can't recite the Scriptures in the original Greek…" CRUNCH, MUNCH… "I don't know nothin' about Niebuhr and Heidegger…" CRUNCH, MUNCH… He finished the apple. "All I wanna know is: This apple I just ate, was it bitter or sweet?"

Tillich paused, then answered, "I cannot possibly answer that question; I haven't tasted your apple." The preacher dropped the apple core into his paper bag, looked up, and said, "Neither have you tasted my Jesus." The crowd erupted with applause, and Tillich left the stage. King David urges us to "taste and see that the Lord is good"—perhaps only children, and the childlike, respond to that invitation literally…

Wonder

How is your intellect both a help and a hindrance to faith in Jesus?

Jesus

"Anyone who doesn't receive the Kingdom… like a child will never enter it" (Mark 10:15).

Do

Buy a candy bar you've never tried before. Taste and see, is it good?

Pray: Jesus, I want to taste you more than I explain you.

Jesus Is the Kingdom

Read Matthew 5:21-48

The National Geographic documentary *God Grew Tired of Us* tells the half-heartbreaking, half-whimsical story of three "Lost Boys of Sudan" relocated from a crowded African refugee camp to a suburban apartment in Pittsburgh. The boys represent more than 20,000 orphaned or displaced children in a civil war that ravaged two million lives. They've never experienced Western culture. On their flight to America, they wonder where the voice on the intercom is coming from. They eat the butter patties served with their meal and guess that it must be soap. They arrive wide-eyed to their new apartment, where a social worker shows them how to work the lights, explains what a refrigerator does, and warns them not to throw their garbage out the window.

The social worker, an African expatriate, plays a key role in the boys' cultural transition. They need someone who understands both worlds to serve as a bridge. That's true for the Lost Boys struggling to understand Pittsburgh, and it's true for us Lost Sheep struggling to understand the kingdom of God. Jesus is acclimating us to a "country" that's our eternal home. This is why he tells stories that begin "The Kingdom of God is like…" Metaphorically, we don't know how to work the electricity in Jesus' native culture—*and what is that big, cold box for?*

The Incarnation describes the lengths to which our "Social Worker" will go to help us acclimate to a new reality. Jesus doesn't explain the kingdom of God; he *is* the kingdom of God.

Wonder
What's a cultural practice that you just don't "get"?

Jesus
"There is more than enough room in my Father's home" (John 14:2).

Do
Watch a "how-to" youtube.com video in a language you don't know.

Pray: Jesus, I'm a lost traveler in your kingdom—find me.

Nothing Owed

Read Luke 18:24-30

In a consumer society, it's tempting to "market" Jesus to potential "customers." This is why prosperity-preachers dangle so many name-it, claim-it "carrots" in front of us. But what if the only real reward Jesus promises those who follow him is…intimacy. Would that really be enough?

After the "Rich Young Ruler" bitterly declines Jesus' invitation to sell everything and follow him, he adds a disturbing exclamation mark as he watches the man walk away: "How hard it is for the rich to enter the Kingdom of God!" Peter and the other disciples can't get their minds around this—Jesus' conditions for following him seem near-insane. And they are disillusioned, to put it mildly: "Then who in the world can be saved?" Peter, obviously frustrated, adds his own passive-aggressive complaint: "We've left our homes to follow you."

That little jab hangs in the air for a moment…

And then Jesus reveals what they will get in return for their sacrifice: "I assure you that everyone who has given up house or wife or brothers or parents or children, for the sake of the Kingdom of God, will be repaid many times over in this life, and will have eternal life in the world to come." Likely, the disciples are translating what Jesus has said concretely—but Jesus is speaking relationally. "Repaid many times over" is what it feels like to know Jesus, to love Jesus, and to die for Jesus. Because they all did.

Wonder	**Jesus**	**Do**
What's the greatest "reward" you've received from Jesus?	"I assure you, today you will be with me in paradise" (Luke 23:43).	Mess up your hair in front of a mirror, then invite Jesus into your mess.

Pray: Jesus, you don't owe me anything—but I would like your heart.

Effortless Discipline

Read Colossians 2:16-23

In the classic *Celebration of Discipline*, author Richard Foster funnels our spiritual life into Inward Disciplines (meditation, prayer, fasting, study), Outward Disciplines (simplicity, solitude, submission, service), and Corporate Disciplines (confession, worship, guidance, celebration). The appeal of spiritual disciplines is the promise of greater control over our growth, but control is not a lover's language…

A friend once belonged to a men's group organized around a "Discipline Checklist"—every week he checked off "duties" on a standard list of marriage disciplines. Then he'd score himself and submit the results to the group for accountability. The higher the score, the (theoretically) better the husband. But how did his wife feel about him scoring his intimacy with her? My friend grew to hate that "checklist mentality" and left the group.

Intimacy is not defined by checklists and discipline. In his first letter to the Corinthian believers, Paul compares spiritual discipline to athletic discipline: "I run with purpose in every step." But later, in his letter to the Colossians, Paul clarifies what he means, urging his friends to dump their "checklist scorecard." He labels religious disciplines "mere human teachings about things that deteriorate as we use them" and "shadows of the reality yet to come…Christ himself is that reality."

When discipline is our focus, we can subtly substitute a scorecard for passion—and Jesus wants our hearts, not our checklists. When he gets our hearts, discipline is the fruit.

Wonder
When you do something you love, what role does discipline play?

Jesus
"I want you to show mercy, not offer sacrifices" (Matthew 9:13).

Do
Eat something that takes discipline for you. Why does it?

Pray: Jesus, give me the desire for discipline as I draw near to you.

The Cure for Self-Doubt

Read Matthew 17:14-20

Self-doubt, like cancer, kills under cover of darkness. A friend's father died suddenly of a heart attack when he was 10. Of course, he was not prepared for this cataclysm. And so "preparation" became the antidote for self-doubt: *If I can over-prepare for every variable in my life,* he reasoned, *I can keep trauma at bay.* This is why trust and faith and vulnerability require extraordinary courage for my friend—there is no pre-certainty in them.

Dr. Timothy Smith was a pastor with two young sons when his wife died, leaving him heartbroken and paralyzed by self-doubt. That's when he stumbled into this bit of advice from the Scottish mystic George MacDonald: "What God may hereafter require of you, you must not give yourself the least trouble about. Everything He gives you to do, you must do as well as ever you can, and that is the best possible preparation for what He may want you to do next. If people would but do what they have to do, they would always find themselves ready for what came next."

"Do the next thing you know to do" propelled Smith to take his next step—and the next and the next. And my friend who lost his father came to the same conclusion. He's finding his way out of the prison of control, making one tiny, courageous choice to trust after another. Jesus encourages us in the face of our self-doubt by nudging us into the next good thing.

Wonder	**Jesus**	**Do**
What's the most courageous thing you've ever done?	"You're not yet taking *God* seriously" (Matthew 17:20, *The Message*).	Grab a random spice from your pantry and taste it—how are you acting in faith?

Pray: Jesus, show me the "next good thing" to do.

Jesus, Down and Dirty

Read John 3:1-21

Jesus breathes in ugly and breathes out beauty. At the beginning of his ministry, in the hillside poetry-slam called "The Sermon on the Mount," he recalibrates our reality with the rhythm of redemption… The mourning get comfort, the humble inherit the world, the wronged get justice, the persecuted get the kingdom of God, and the mocked and lied-about get a "great reward." *I know how bad things seem*, he is saying, *but your focus is on the brush strokes, and I see the whole canvas.*

Yes, we have the promise of Jesus that he is working redemption, like yeast, into the lump of dough that is our broken life. But it's hard for us to imagine the sight and smell of fresh bread when we open the oven door. We comprehend this kind of beauty only in retrospect, like cresting a hill to look back on the landscape we've left behind.

Of all the epic miracles recorded in the New Testament, the restoration of trust overshadows them all. Children who once trusted as if trust wasn't dangerous are rendered incapable of trust as adults—ashes have clogged our arteries. And so, Jesus tells the curious Pharisee Nicodemus, "You must be born again." When we're born over, we discover we can trust like a child again. And trust, like mountain rain, showers our burn zones and coaxes new growth up through the heart's mantle of ash.

Wonder
What happened in your childhood that's made it harder to trust?

Jesus
"The Holy Spirit gives birth to spiritual life" (John 3:6).

Do
Blow out a lit match, then use it to circle the words "restoration of trust" above.

Pray: Jesus, fertilize my life with the ugly thing that broke me—grow new life.

The Mingled Blood

Read Luke 13:1-3

When we read the Bible like an Instagram account—coagulated truisms—we diminish the weight of its impact. The Bible is more like a narrative hurricane stripping our frail belief systems of their facades…

Jesus hears that the Roman prefect Pontius Pilate has executed innocent Galilean Jews as they're offering atonement sacrifices at the Temple. Historians confirm that Pilate, intent on magnifying the offense, mingles the blood of the executed with the blood of their animal sacrifices. It's a cynical brutality—a mockery of their purity ritual. And Jesus knows what everyone is thinking: "Do you think those Galileans were worse sinners than all the other people from Galilee? Is that why they suffered?"

He is poking at a universal mystery: Why do bad things happen to good people? The Jews think they've already solved this one; they believe in a God who doles out circumstantial punishment to sinners and circumstantial blessing to the righteous. It's a purity proof by the random lottery of tragedy.

But Jesus scatters this house of cards with a thundering rebuke: "Not at all!" *Bad things are not God's bludgeon for guilty sinners. And I will soon prove this truth by submitting myself to scourging, humiliation, and crucifixion. Purity will be co-mingled with the guilt of mankind, bleaching the souls of all who will lower themselves to drink of me.*

Wonder	**Jesus**	**Do**
Why doesn't Jesus protest the brutal rule of the Roman occupiers?	"It is not [God's] will that even one of these little ones should perish" (Matthew 18:14).	"Mingle" cream with coffee or sugar with tea; thank him for his purity.

Pray: Jesus, you are the purity running through my veins.

Governor Jesus

Read Luke 23:1-25

Most of us have no idea what it's really like to live in a kingdom. I saw the changing of the guard in London once. And a long time ago, in a New York City coffeehouse, JFK Jr. stood behind me in line. That's the extent of my experience with royals. Our relative ignorance about kingdom culture matters, because Jesus is always talking about it.

Historian Michael Grant says, "Every thought and saying of Jesus was directed and subordinated to one single thing…the realization of the Kingdom of God upon earth," and "this one phrase [Kingdom of God] sums up his whole ministry and his whole life's work." When Jesus spoke about the kingdom, he described a structured, authority-based governance—that's why both political and religious leaders saw him as a threat and why they hatched a plot to execute him.

Jesus' "kingdom talk" extends the driving theme of the Old Testament. Biblical scholar John Bright says, "Had we to give [the Old Testament] a title, we might with justice call it 'The Book of the Coming Kingdom of God.' That is, indeed, its central theme everywhere. Old Testament and New Testament thus stand together as the two acts of a single drama." And that "single drama" is the conquest of sin by the great champion Jesus, who then ushers in a royal culture that replaces "an eye for an eye" with "love your enemies and pray for those who persecute you."

Wonder
A kingdom is not a democracy. Why is that a good thing?

Jesus
"You would have no power over me… unless it were given to you from above" (John 19:11).

Do
We bow in the presence of royalty. Make bowing habitual when you pray.

Pray: Jesus, plant your kingdom culture in me.

The Beauty of Risk

Read Matthew 14:10-21

In June of 2018, 12 boys from a Thai soccer team and their coach ventured into a complex cave system and got trapped after heavy rains drove them more than a mile deep into the inky dark. A worldwide rescue effort kicked in, and divers discovered the emaciated teenagers 10 days later. The monsoons were filling the cave system like a bathtub, and rescuers faced long odds to get them out in time.

The checklist of potential risks facing the divers was long; one bad guess or poor decision could cost the boys (or them) their lives (one rescuer died when he miscalculated the oxygen level in his tank). Rescues require risk—true, also, in every aspect of our lives with Jesus. We're part of a massive rescue operation, with a Commander who's determined to beat the odds and invite as many as he can out of their dark caves…

To join him, we'll need to recapture our childlike habits, including our openness to risk. Observe kids on a playground for a few minutes and you'll notice that risk fuels their play. The spirit of play—and, therefore, the essence of risk—is what leaks out of us as we get older. We know that childlikeness is the engine that drives the kingdom of God, and risk fuels that engine. So when we risk, we engage our hearts, souls, minds, and strength—the forceful propellant behind transformational love.

Wonder	**Jesus**	**Do**
When and why have you "invited trouble" instead of avoiding it?	"[If you don't] receive the Kingdom…like a child [you] will never enter it" (Mark 10:15).	Ask Jesus who to serve today, and how—then follow through.

Pray: Jesus, move me toward the tipping point of risk in our relationship.

The Poison Pill

Read John 21:20-23

In the cult classic *The Princess Bride*, the farm-boy-turned-pirate-hero Westley rescues the kidnapped princess Buttercup, who has lived in a protective bubble of privilege her whole life—she is safe, but her entitlements have been shattered by trauma and pain. When the princess mourns her lost love, Westley is not impressed. "You mock my pain!" she cries. And Westley retorts, "Life is pain, Highness! Anyone who says otherwise is selling something."

Not your typical inspirational meme, but it's a turning point for Buttercup—the dawning of a love that is rooted in deeper soil. Brutal truth will open her eyes to beauty if she will summon the courage to embrace it. Of course, we want to spit in the eye of pain. But, like Buttercup, we can't help recoiling from it, then digging our hole deeper by bemoaning our troubles in light of others' (supposed) blessings.

After Jesus tells Peter, three times, to "feed my sheep," he gives him ominous news—Peter, like Jesus, will one day be executed on a cross. It's a swallow-hard moment. Peter sees John walking behind them and asks, "What about him, Lord?" And Jesus shoots back, "If I want him to remain alive until I return, what is that to you?" Our pain is not reduced or altered by complaining or comparing our shattered entitlements—the way out of pain is through it, not around it.

Wonder
How effective is comparison in helping you feel better?

Jesus
"Others will...take you where you don't want to go" (John 21:18).

Do
Compare the feeling of sun and shade on your shoulders as you walk.

Pray: Jesus, I give you my shattered entitlements as a worship offering.

The Differentiated Jesus

Read Matthew 15

Poet Ralph Waldo Emerson says, "To be yourself in a world that is constantly trying to make you something else is the greatest accomplishment." Emerson is describing *self-differentiation*—a term first coined by family-systems pioneer Dr. Murray Bowen. It's the ability to "distinguish our experience from the experience of people we are connected to." Self-differentiated people maintain a permanence of self even when they're under duress—when failure or criticism try to hijack what is true about them.

Self-differentiation matters because we live in a "cauldron of critique." In a massive survey of Americans by *Allure* magazine, two-thirds say the first thing they notice about someone is their attractiveness; half say that their appearance either "significantly" or "completely" defines them. With so many victims of shallow critique, it's no wonder 40 million American adults struggle with anxiety. Meanwhile, Jesus is the most self-differentiated person in history. In Matthew 15 alone, he…

- resists the Pharisees' pressure to honor an "old tradition,"

- shunts his disciples' fear that he's offended these leaders,

- ignores cultural and religious restrictions and celebrates the extraordinary faith of a pagan, and

- insists on feeding thousands, though others say it's folly.

Jesus maintains the boundaries of his identity because God is never leveraged by critique.

Wonder
How has Jesus helped you become more differentiated?

Jesus
"They teach man-made ideas as commands from God" (Matthew 15:9).

Do
Use a physical cue—a finger-flick on your palm—to differentiate from stress.

Pray: Jesus, be my boundary between peace and stress.

The Strength to Lament

Read Psalm 3

A close friend is emerging from a long season of lament—in the last two years, she has endured...

- The disintegration of her marriage after she discovered her husband's secret life of drug abuse, sexual affairs, and criminal activity—layered on top of his physical abuse.

- The sight of a moving truck pulling out of her driveway, on its way to a storage facility to offload her life.

- The loss of her job after she fled to another state.

- The loss of her community and her entire support system.

- The loneliness of starting over in a new place, with no financial foundation.

The seasons of the year are a living metaphor for the seasons of our lives. We move through a cycle of death to life. But in the fall and winter of our sorrows, we struggle to cope with the certainty of loss. Lament is our Spring-bridge into Summer-hope. And lament—a vulnerable release of grief—is a major theme in the Psalms, because it was a normal part of life for ancient Jews. Jesus was no stranger to it. In John 16 he tells his disciples that he'll soon be leaving them, and he knows they'll "weep and mourn" over what's about to happen. But their lament will give way to joy, like a mother in labor. Mark the onset of Spring by "going into labor" with your mourning.

Wonder
What's something in your life that you've not yet lamented?

Jesus
"You have sorrow now, but I will see you again; then you will rejoice" (John 16:22).

Do
Choose a "memorial" object to represent your lament; keep it on your desk.

Pray: Jesus, give me the courage to lament.

How, Not What

Read Luke 11:1-4

Jesus wants prayer to be as organic as breathing—instead, it's often rife with misconceptions and assumptions and even manipulation. When we pray, we're conditioned to…

- Use a softer voice and close our eyes.

- Repeat strange vocal patterns (abnormal cadence, or using "just" or "Jesus" or "God" to substitute for "umm").

- Adopt formal body language.

In the conventional approach to prayer, we treat it like a tool to leverage God for what we really want in life. But Jesus models prayer as a way to get what _he_ really wants—a deep, playful, intimate relationship. John the Baptist taught his disciples how to pray, so Jesus' disciples ask for their own tutorial. He responds, "This is how you should pray…" And then he launches into "The Lord's Prayer." Because we're like sheep, we've turned "This is how you should pray…" into "Pray exactly these words because they're magical…" _This is how_ means, simply:

- Talking to God in a relaxed way—as loving, doting children talk to their loving, doting Daddy.

- Pledging our passion to his mission in the world.

- Vulnerably revealing our needs, whatever they are.

- Admitting the harm we cause, and seeking reconciliation.

- Pleading for help in the spiritual war we're fighting.

Wonder
What's the first descriptive word that surfaces for "prayer"?

Jesus
"To everyone who knocks, the door will be opened" (Luke 11:10).

Do
Ask Jesus to prompt prayer for certain homes as you pass by.

Pray: Jesus, teach me how to pray.

The Epidemiology of Unbelief

Read Mark 6:1-6

Eight out of 10 people in the world identify with a religion, and nine out of 10 Americans believe in God. But this is a default definition of belief—like listing "brown eyes" on your driver's license. We get a portal into the mechanics of belief (and unbelief) when we pay attention to what people pray about…

What people typically pray for…	Have you ever prayed for…?
Family or friends (82%)	People who mistreat me (41%)
My problems & difficulties (74%)	My enemies (37%)
Good things to happen (54%)	Winning the lottery (21%)
My sins (42%)	Success with little effort (20%)

Obviously, our emotional and physical challenges drive us to "try out" our belief—just as they did for the crowds who flocked to Jesus whenever he surfaced in public. But when he returns to hometown Nazareth riding a groundswell of popularity, the locals are first impressed by his teaching and then offended by the "uppity" way he performs miracles. "He's just a carpenter" is a snarky version of "Who do you think you are?" Their unbelief, dripping with arrogance, is a fortress that repels the invasion of healing in their town. Pride is a form of blindness, because you can't see the Messiah standing in front of you.

Jesus is looking for believers who have the humility to bow down to drink from him.

Wonder
Who in your life do you wholly believe in, and why?

Jesus
"Go home to your family, and tell them everything the Lord has done" (Mark 5:19).

Do
Write "Believe!" on a dozen sticky notes; stick them to car windshields.

Pray: Jesus, you're way more than a carpenter to me…

Jesus Beyond the Bible

Read Luke 24:13-34

It's a three-hour walk from Jerusalem to the little village of Emmaus. It turns out, that's enough time to get a Master's-level education in biblical studies. We sometimes forget when we're studying Scripture that Jesus pored over these same words. But his relationship to the Bible is radically different from ours. With a roomful of raised-in-the-church people, I point to four corners labeled with these signs: "Instruction Manual," "Reference Book," "Dust-Gatherer," and "God's Love Story." I ask them to move to the corner that represents how they saw the Bible when they were young—the "Love Story" corner is always lonely.

When we make coverage the goal of Bible study, we treat it like CrossFit—we're mainly concerned with "getting our reps in." But when Jesus Incognito joins two friends on their long walk home, his mission is to help them understand the "meta-narrative" of Scripture. They don't yet realize that the Old Testament is the onramp into the climax of an epic love story. On the road to Emmaus, we get Jesus' best Bible-study tips…

- Ask the Spirit to "remind us of everything Jesus has told us."

- Slow down and approach it like a conversation.

- Don't over-read—just as we don't overeat. Eat a healthy meal, but leave room for "snacking" on truths during the day.

- Pay better attention to Jesus—ask "why" he said and did the things he did.

Wonder	**Jesus**	**Do**
In what "Bible Corner" would you stand today?	"The Messiah [had] to suffer all these things before entering his glory" (Luke 24:26)	A car symbolizes independence; every turn of the key, re-commit to dependence.

Pray: Jesus, I want to walk the road to Emmaus with you.

Hugging the Porcupine

Read Mark 7:36-37

Jesus is wholly unreasonable—it's maybe his most distinctive characteristic… We host Friday Film Nights in our home. With 15 or so young people, we "watch a film that's not about Jesus, then talk about Jesus." One night our choice was a superhero blockbuster that left the bitter aftertaste of predictability. But when I asked why the flawed-hero-who-finds-redemption storyline is so common in films, a college student offered this insight: "That thread of redemption is universal in great literature. But even though the Bible is considered a great literary work, what sets it apart from every other great literary work is that no one has ever had a 'character' like Jesus—he breaks every mold and violates every expectation." To love Jesus means to develop a taste for hugging a porcupine.

- He launches his ministry with a shotgun-blast of impossible morality, upending our addiction to self-righteousness.

- He dumps over religious apple carts, celebrating the heart behind our obedience, not the arrogance of self-discipline.

- He intentionally provokes both his enemies and his friends, calling out their stubborn refusal to believe in him.

- He asks for everything—he wants us to hold nothing back because that's the engine of passion.

Jesus can be prickly—when we get close to him, we're likely to get poked and prodded into living unreasonably ourselves.

Wonder
Jesus clearly has an edge. Why is his popular persona so different?

Jesus
" *'Ephphatha,'* which means, 'Be opened!' " (Mark 7:34).

Do
Feel the edge of a sharp knife; consider the ways that edge is a necessity.

Pray: Jesus, poke and prod me into a life of unreasonable passion.

Lord of Right and Wrong

Read Luke 12:54-59

"Why can't you decide for yourselves what is right?" It's not a rebellious, disrespectful teenager asking the question—it's Jesus, and he's not asking it ironically... With the red-faced, rule-keeping Pharisees fuming in front of him, he challenges a crowd of thousands to pay attention to him and choose their own moral path. We're driven by what we believe is right and wrong. But we know we're not supposed to simply decide for ourselves—so why is Jesus promoting such a reckless standard?

He first warns his disciples to beware of the "yeast" of the Pharisees. We know that yeast makes bread dough rise, but how? It's actually a *fungus* that remains dormant until warm water is added, when it reactivates. It then feeds on the sugars found in flour, releasing the carbon dioxide that makes the bread rise. In essence, Jesus is warning his friends that the teachings of their religious leaders are like a dormant fungus that, once activated, radically changes the bread—but not in a good way. So don't tolerate what they're trying to add to the truth. Instead, pay attention to the Source of all truth, then act on what you know to be true—the same way we pay attention to weather patterns.

Jesus wants us to pay attention to the kingdom of God culture he is revealing—to be so transformed by the way he thinks and behaves that outside "control" is unnecessary.

Wonder	**Jesus**	**Do**
What primarily influences your standards of right and wrong?	"I have come to set the world on fire" (Luke 12:49).	A test of open-eyed truth—lay down the book and drop a pen here on "Do," then do it with your eyes closed.

Pray: Jesus, I need your help discerning what is true, and what isn't.

Too-Much-Ness

Read Matthew 26:36-46

Alvin Toffler's 1970 bestseller *Future Shock* popularized the term "information overload," until then a little-known dynamic. Today, for a people awash in a daily information tsunami, "overload" seems quaint. Hunter College professor Bertram Gross says, "Information overload occurs when the amount of input to a system exceeds its processing capacity." That means "too-much-ness" can fry our circuits. We see too much/hear too much/know too much. Do you have visual proof of what your friends ate for dinner last night? If not, you forgot to check social media…

Too-much-ness also extends to our spiritual lives. We're weary of what Paul, in Ephesians, calls the "fiery arrows of the devil." We expect life to be hard but not *too-much* hard. When the unfair hard happens anyway, we wonder why Jesus doesn't do something. Well, he knows how that feels. In the Garden of Gethsemane, with the torture that awaits him looming, Jesus…

- reveals to his best friends the truth about his too-much-ness;

- asks those friends to enter into the darkness with him, to be with him through it;

- gets alone with his Father to ask for relief, and to pledge his love and obedience no matter what; and

- endures the disappointment of his friends' response to his need, then keeps returning to his Father in a spirit of humility, dependence, and deference to his mission.

Wonder
What feels like "too much" in your life right now?

Jesus
"If this cannot pass away unless I drink it, Your will be done" (Matthew 26:42, NASB).

Do
Drink down a whole glass of water. How is that like life right now?

Pray: Jesus, "too much" is too much for me—I give it all to you.

Un-Used

Read John 17:22-26

In the church we promote "common heresies"—they sound true but don't reflect the way Jesus describes our relationship with him. For example, "I just want God to use me…" The verb is the problem here—*use*. We use a tire iron to fix a flat or a password to access our bank account or GPS to find our way home. But Jesus doesn't *use* us—we are God's beloved sons and daughters, and no good Father has a relationship with his children that is user-based. We've extracted this heresy from something Paul writes to Timothy: "If you keep yourself pure, you will be a special utensil for honorable use. Your life will be clean, and you will be ready for the Master to use you for every good work" (2 Timothy 2:21).

Paul uses the "utensil" metaphor to describe the difference between "expensive" and "everyday" kitchen tools. He's urging Timothy to live a "clean" life, free from the leverage of sin. He is not defining our relationship with Jesus as user-based. Jesus emphatically tells us that we're partners, not tools (John 15). So, because our words matter, let's reject this common heresy and replace it with "partner with" or "move through" or "live out" or "give what I have to give." And let's not identify ourselves as "the used"—we are, instead "beloved" and "salt and light and yeast" and "precious" and "forgiven" and "treasures."

Wonder
What words describe your relationship with your best friend?

Jesus
"Father, I desire that they also be with me where I am" (John 17:24).

Do
Tighten screws around your home. Thank Jesus that you're more than a tool to him.

Pray: Jesus, I want to change the way I think and talk, to honor you.

The Benevolent Vending Machine in the Sky

Read Romans 8:26-30

You've probably heard a chopped version of the Apostle Paul's Romans 8 proclamation: "All things work together for good." It's a comforting, magic-spell promise— the kissing cousin of "Trust the universe that everything will work out." And like many of the Bible-ish myths that infect our everyday life, it's not true…

- **Trust exists only inside of a relationship, and it's impossible to have a relationship with "the universe."** We say "trust the universe" because we'd rather hope for a vending machine in the sky than pay the cost of intimacy in a relationship.

- **Paul is exploring how the Spirit of Jesus actually works in our everyday lives.** The Jesus who lives in us—our Rabbi Inside—"helps us in our weakness," shows us how to pray in concert with God's will, and advocates for us. Because Jesus is influencing our lives from the inside out, he "causes" everything in our lives to "work together for good," as long as we commit ourselves to an intimate relationship and are "called according to his purpose for [us]."

Jesus will take the dumpster-dive of our circumstances and re-craft that mess into performance art—but he won't trespass our boundaries to do it. "All things work together for good" is a shiny, happy spin on fatalism, not the symphony of trust the Paul is really describing.

Wonder	**Jesus**	**Do**
How is Jesus "causing everything to work together for good" for you?	"When the Spirit of truth comes, he will guide you into all truth" (John 16:13).	On a rock, write a word representing a mess in your life, then toss it away.

Pray: Jesus, I don't trust the universe; I trust you.

"Disciple" in 15 Words

Read Luke 10:38-42

A friend posted this challenge on Facebook: "Can you define *disciple* in 15 words or less?" Here's a response sampler:

- "Doing the things that you should do, even when you don't want to do them. Just a bunch of do-do."

- "A dedicated student and practitioner."

- "1 John 2:6: 'Those who say they live in God should live their lives as Jesus did.' Repeat encore."

- "One who lives to be more like their master."

- *(Quoting Dallas Willard)* "One who systematically and progressively rearranges one's life to become like Christ."

- "Someone who follows the teachings and rhythms of Jesus."

I chewed on this challenge myself—but couldn't get past Paul's thunderclap: "For I determined to know nothing among you except Jesus Christ, and Him crucified" (1 Corinthians 2:2, NASB). To the "Pharisee of Pharisees"—a brilliant student schooled by Gamaliel—*determined to know nothing except Jesus* is a full-stop in the discipleship debate. "Know nothing" is translated from the Greek "to be conscious of nothing."

When we abide in Jesus, we soon become conscious of nothing other than him. This hyper-attention to the presence of Jesus is what made Mary oblivious to the housekeeping tasks that fell to her sister. Mary's "conscious of nothing" passion is a living definition of *disciple*.

Wonder
What's your 15-words-or-less definition of *disciple*?

Jesus
"There is only one thing worth being concerned about" (Luke 10:42).

Do
Follow (discreetly) a random person. How is it like following Jesus?

Pray: Jesus, I want to know you so well that I'm "conscious of nothing."

Pushing the Envelope

Read Matthew 15:21-28

We have a complicated relationship with risk... Entrepreneurs want to master it, fearful parents want to eradicate it, sports fans want to maximize it, and betrayed lovers want to mourn it. A few years after college, after a breakup with a longtime girlfriend that left me feeling empty, I decided it was time to branch out. I took a girl I barely knew out for dinner and did what I always do—I asked risky questions and pursued her with creative curiosity. Two hours later I could tell we were never going on another date. She looked like she'd been caught in a wind tunnel...

Risk-taking can be overwhelming. At the end of the night, that first-date girl told me, "You're just too much." But Jesus treats risk as the lifeblood of our relationship with him, because real intimacy requires it. To give our hearts, we have to risk our hearts. A sign in a fitness center captures it: "If you're not outside of your comfort zone, then you're not going to change."

The one thing we know for sure about Jesus' encounter with the Canaanite woman in Matthew 15 is that he is bowled over and amazed by her willingness to risk. She shows up where she doesn't belong, asks what she shouldn't ask, invests what she can't afford to lose, gives what she's not supposed to give, and moves toward Jesus when he seems to push her away. In the wind tunnel of her risk, he faces into the hurricane, raises his arms, and exults in it.

Wonder	**Jesus**	**Do**
What's a risk you've taken that no one but you knows about?	"Keep on seeking, and you will find" (Matthew 7:7).	Write "Consider Jesus" on a dollar bill, then spend it.

Pray: Jesus, take me outside my comfort zone with you.

Don't Just Listen

Read John 1:1-5

Words form our reality—we are created in the image of God, and God formed all reality with his words (Genesis 1:1-26). So the way we talk about ourselves, inside, shapes our souls. All outside voices either confirm or challenge the me I've already told myself I am. We solidify that image by acting on it, generating evidence for the case we've made about ourselves. James tells us, "Don't just listen to God's word. You must do what it says. Otherwise, you are only fooling yourselves. For if you listen to the word and don't obey, it is like glancing at your face in a mirror. You see yourself, walk away, and forget what you look like" (James 1:22-24).

We typically translate this advice as *read and obey what the Bible says to do.* But we're missing the elephant in God's living room. John opens his gospel: "In the beginning the Word already existed. The Word was with God, and the Word was God." Jesus is "the Word." Plug that definition into James' mirror-metaphor and we get: *Don't just listen to Jesus, live out what he says about you. Otherwise, you're telling yourself a lie. You'll forget who you really are, quickly, if you acknowledge the "truth about your being" but don't act on it. So give what Jesus says you have to give.*

We make Jesus Lord of our lives when we do more than merely listen to his words...

Wonder
What do you do that blesses others, but they don't know it?

Jesus
"Is it easier to say 'Your sins are forgiven,' or 'Stand up and walk'?" (Matthew 9:5).

Do
Use your phone's "Voice Memo" to record a truth about you. Play it back often.

Pray: Jesus, help me remember what I look like.

Better Than Glory

Read Matthew 20:20-28

A month after I moved into my first post-college apartment, I invited an old friend over and gave him my 15-second "grand tour." *That's my kitchen with no pots and pans, my dining area with no table, my family room with no couch, and my bedroom with the single bed from my parents' house.* Above my bed on both walls I'd mounted my high school and college award certificates. My friend stared at this pathetic spectacle and remarked, "It looks like you lie in bed at night and look up at your walls to remember who you are." His laugh told me he was oblivious to the sting of his observation. After he left, I took down all of those framed "immortality symbols" (props for a false identity)—he'd punched through to the hollow core of my accomplishments.

Our performance can't satisfy our longing for transcendent purpose. Columnist David Brooks says, "I remember a few years ago…I got a call from my editor that my first book had made the *New York Times* bestseller list, and I felt nothing. It was just something happening out there…I would trade that away for one dinner with my wife or one meal with my kids."

It's in our character, formed by Jesus in the crucible of hardship, that we discover our true nature. Our accomplishments are like cotton candy—all sugar, no substance.

Wonder	**Jesus**	**Do**
What's an "immortality symbol" you use to prop up your insecurity?	"Whoever wants to be a leader among you must be your servant" (Matthew 20:26).	Choose one of your immortality symbols and get rid of it.

Pray: Jesus, I want to trade my insecurity for your security.

Necessary Disruptions

Read Matthew 10:5-31

In *The Lion, the Witch and the Wardrobe*, Lucy Pevensie escapes into a dark wardrobe full of musty winter coats—she does not realize she's inches away from a beautiful apocalypse, but she can sense it. If she pushes through the back of that wardrobe, she'll find Narnia, a land ruled by a White Witch and populated by talking animals, fauns, and ogres. So will she leave behind the safety of her predictable life and risk it all on an uncertain adventure? The tipping point will come down to "Why not?"—the nudge we need to step into the unknown. And so she gives up her life to gain her life.

"Why not?" is a way of life. It's diagnostic, because we're forced to consider what's going on inside of us when we freeze in the face of adventure. Our fears bully us into backing out of the wardrobe and closing the door. This is why Jesus did a great deal of his teaching "on the road"—the unpredictability of the road is defined by "Why not?"

Jesus invites us to drink his "living water" and tells us we'll "never be thirsty" if we do. When we live in the momentum of "Why not?"—pushing through the wardrobe coats into the great unknown—we invite disruption and make ourselves perpetually thirsty for him. Answer "Why not?" to the challenges you know are beyond your capabilities, expertise, and courage… You'll find yourself camped out at the well of Jesus.

Wonder
What's the fruit of one "Why not?" in your life?

Jesus
"Don't carry…a change of clothes and sandals or even a walking stick" (Matthew 10:10).

Do
Step into a coat closet; savor the smells and sensations. Consider "Why not?"

Pray: Jesus, help me find the portal into my own Narnia.

Roadside Vistas

Read Romans 8:31-39

We need "rest stops" along our road—to savor how far we've come and relish where we're headed. When we take the offramp out of the fast lane, we notice the ways Jesus has crept into our brokenness. In the quiet of our roadside vistas, we worship. We remember how he has worked beauty into our ugly…

- In the adults who sacrificed their comfort and sanity to nurture our growth when we were young, Jesus was there.

- In those who entered into our our grief with a generosity of spirit after our world crumbled, Jesus was there.

- When a great hardship yielded a painful lesson and left us stronger and wiser, Jesus was there.

- When circumstances crushed our hopes and a new and better hope rose up from the ashes, Jesus was there.

- When danger cornered us, but a miraculous way out opened in front of us, Jesus was there.

- When we left the "path of life" to sample "the path of death," but found a surprising "guide" who led us back through the thicket onto the "narrow way," Jesus was there.

- When we decided we had our fill of eating pig food and dreamed of eating at our Father's table again, and set our face toward home, Jesus was there.

Jesus was there. Jesus is here. Jesus will always be with you…

Wonder	**Jesus**	**Do**
Ask Jesus, "Where are you creeping, unnoticed, into my life?"	"I am the way, the truth, and the life" (John 14:6).	Pull off the road and spend a few minutes drinking in the beauty.

Pray: Jesus, I'm going so fast, so intent on my destination, that I've missed you.

Speaking of Jesus

Read John 10:14-16

Carl Medearis has been a missionary to the Middle East for decades—he reminds me of Indiana Jones, without the fedora and bullwhip. And, also, he looks nothing like Harrison Ford. In the aftermath of the allied invasion of Iraq, he and some friends sneaked into Fallujah and were forced off the road by militants. The armed men commandeered their vehicle and drove them into the desert, intending to execute them. But miraculously, the militants dumped them in the wilderness and left instead. That's the sort oft cliffhanger Carl reels off in casual conversation, so you get the idea…

He's a bold, courageous, determined person. For years he worked to build relationships with Muslims and invite them into the Christian life, but with zero impact. He considered quitting. But then he noticed that Muslims really, really like talking about Jesus. In fact, they love Jesus, even though they don't believe he's God. So Carl spent a whole year focusing his devotional reading on the Gospels alone, just to rivet his attention on Jesus. And then he stopped talking about the Christian life and started talking exclusively about Jesus. And then his ministry began to get traction, then momentum, then explosive impact.

Turns out, the cost of trading the Muslim life for the Christian life is impossibly high, but the cost of laying down your life for Jesus doesn't seem so high when you've fallen in love with him.

Wonder	**Jesus**	**Do**
What does Jesus mean: "I have other sheep… not in this sheepfold"?	"They will listen to my voice, and there will be one flock with one shepherd" (John 10:16).	Risk by adding "Jesus loves you, this I know" to your email "auto signature."

Pray: Jesus, I want my love for you to infiltrate my conversations.

Beyond Category

Read Ephesians 1:11-12

Not long ago a reader posted a review of one of my books: "Worse [sic] book I ever read. The book reads as one run-on sentence from beginning to end. One minute the author portrays Jesus as loving and then as insensitive…" I've been a writer for more than 30 years, so I'm used to criticism. But that phrase, referencing my confusing portrayal of Jesus as both loving and insensitive, really stopped me.

Umm… Sorry, buddy—that really is Jesus.

When we encounter Jesus in the raw, he is both tough and tender. Author and Boston College philosophy professor Peter Kreeft describes Jesus as a "shocking wonder"—he's both shockingly tough and shockingly tender. He offended people not just because of the hard things he said ("You brood of vipers!"), but because he was way more tender than he was supposed to be with people he should've avoided and ignored ("Neither do I [condemn you]").

On a work retreat I completed the Keirsey Temperament Sorter—a personality test. Spoiler alert: I have one. After I got my results, I wondered how Jesus would've "scored." If he is the source of all personality—everything made is mashed together out of him—then he transcends category. And because he's beyond category, he has an unparalleled ability to see, understand, and appreciate our particular brand of personality.

Wonder	**Jesus**	**Do**
How much stock do you place in personality tests, and why?	"Now here is a genuine son of Israel—a man of complete integrity" (John 1:47).	Go to personalityperfect.com and take a free personality test.

Pray: Jesus, show me what is "fearfully and wonderfully made" about me.

Jesus on Hell

Read Matthew 7:13-14

Illusionist Penn Jillette, a self-proclaimed atheist, has a surprising take on hell: "I've always said that I don't respect people who don't proselytize... If you believe that there's a heaven and a hell, and people could be going to hell or not getting eternal life, and you think that it's not really worth telling them this because it would make it socially awkward...How much do you have to hate somebody to believe everlasting life is possible and not tell them that?"

On the other side of the atheist "hell debate," physicist Stephen Hawking once said, "There is no heaven or afterlife for broken down computers. That is a fairy story for people afraid of the dark." For atheists, hell is fair game. Ironic, because we rarely hear it talked about in church. But Jesus talked about hell all the time—nine times in the gospel of Matthew alone. In the Parable of the Rich Man and Lazarus (Luke 16:19-31), he covers the mechanics of hell. We learn...

- No one can cross over from heaven to hell or back.

- Hell is separation from God—something we can choose—and because it's a choice, we're accountable to its consequences.

- Hell must exist, because Jesus has paid the ultimate price to make sure we can choose relationship with him—but it's not a default setting.

Wonder	**Jesus**	**Do**
How does the reality of hell make a difference in your everyday life?	"The prophets have warned them. Your brothers can read what they wrote" (Luke 16:29).	Open a bottle of vinegar and give it a long, deep whiff. If hell were a smell...

Pray: Jesus, I never want to be separated from you.

The Irritability of Jesus

Read Luke 4–7

If we pay better attention to everything Jesus said and did, we discover a man who seems, well, often irritated…

- In Luke 4:4 he's irritated with Satan for pressuring him to turn stones into bread.

- In Luke 4:23-27 he's irritated with the "townies" in Nazareth for doubting that he's the Messiah.

- In Luke 5:22-24 he's irritated with the Pharisees who accuse him of blasphemy after he forgives a man's sins.

- In Luke 6:8-11 he's irritated with the Pharisees again (get used to it) after they complain that he broke the Sabbath by healing a man's deformed hand.

- In Luke 6:32-34 he's irritated with the crowds for "loving only those who love you"—even "sinners" can do that.

- In Luke 7:31-32 he's irritated with "the people of this generation," comparing them to whiny children.

- And in Luke 7:44-46 he's irritated with Simon the Pharisee for neglecting basic hospitality.

Why is Jesus so often irritated? Well, real people get annoyed with each other, and Jesus is a real person. The most enjoyable person in your life likely has a broad emotional bandwidth. We're spending eternity with Jesus; it's good he's not like Siri.

Wonder
If Jesus never sins but is often irritated, is irritation "okay"?

Jesus
"From the time I first came in, she has not stopped kissing my feet" (Luke 7:45).

Do
Rub something rough. What "good purpose" does irritation have?

Pray: Jesus, I'm grateful you can handle the things that irritate me.

Off the Sidelines

Read Matthew 10

It's the quiet crescendo of an epic adventure story—the "coming home" scene at the end of _The Lord of the Rings_ film trilogy. Four friends, mounted on the backs of travel-weary ponies, drag themselves into their village after an epic battle against an overwhelming evil. They leave home as clueless boys, wasting their days pranking each other and drinking beer; they return as warriors seasoned by terror and triumph. Together they order pints at the pub as their old friends, oblivious to their sacrifices, giggle and dance and tell bad jokes. Then the four friends silently raise their mugs to each other and linger, haunted by their memories but grateful they've survived.

The adventure has clearly changed them—there's a gravity to their presence that seems out of place in "normal" life. They've left "childish things" behind on the sidelines.

And when Jesus invites us into his family, our "yes" moves us off the sidelines and into his version of an epic adventure— the advance of the kingdom of God on earth. Jesus wants his disciples to "freely give" to others and to feel utterly dependent on his ability to take care of them. They will be at the mercy of people around them, and they will be betrayed and opposed and misunderstood and even hated. But he reminds them that they are treasured by God no matter how bad their circumstances seem. They (and we) will enter into the unknown as children and return Home as warriors.

Wonder	**Jesus**	**Do**
What is the greatest adventure you've ever been a part of?	"Don't be afraid of those who threaten you" (Matthew 10:26).	At meals, raise a glass or mug to Jesus instead of "saying grace."

Pray: Jesus, what's a "childish thing" you'd like me to leave behind?

The Thief Inside Us

Read Luke 23:39-43

Two thieves and a Savior hang on crosses buried in the blood-soaked dirt of the terrible hill the locals call "the place of the skull." One of them, with nothing left to lose, hurls abuse at Jesus: "Some Messiah you are!" But the other, also with nothing left to lose, rebukes the first man and defends Jesus: "Have you no fear of God? We deserve this, but not him—he did nothing to deserve this." And Jesus, always and eternally aware he has nothing to lose, offers the second thief a "hail Mary" hope: "Today you will join me in paradise."

Tortured and locked in the deepest sorrow anyone has ever experienced, Jesus responds to this petty criminal and part-time terrorist with tender assurance. "Today you will join me in paradise" is a reiteration, because to be with Jesus is to be in paradise. Historians have named this second thief St. Dismas—a man we're certain is right now in heaven, because Jesus said so.

Our great temptation in life, as God's enemy insinuates, is that we can be "little gods." But Dismas is the face of desperate dependence—there is a redemptive invitation in his total loss of control… One thief holds on to this control until the end. The other has the courage to let down his guard, own his need, and turn to Jesus like a child. When we do this, Jesus says we will "find" ourselves in him.

Wonder	**Jesus**	**Do**
How do you explain the vastly different responses of the two thieves?	"For whoever wishes to [control] his life will lose it" (Matthew 16:25, NASB).	Clench your fist hard, then release control and turn your palms up.

Pray: Jesus, I recognize how tightly I hold on to control—please release me.

Doubt, Our Frenemy

Read John 20:24-29

Tick down the list of apostles until you get to "Thomas." What's the first word that pops into your head? *Doubting*, of course… We're shorthand people—we slot things and people in categories. It's lazy, but we do it all the time, even with the apostles. Peter is the loose cannon. John is the favorite. Nathaniel is the smart aleck. Simon is the revolutionary. Judas the betrayer. And Thomas? He's the doubter…

He is defined and reduced by one honest moment in the middle of the chaotic scramble after Jesus' death and resurrection. But he's so much more than that. In John 11, Jesus says he's heading back to Judea because his close friend Lazarus is "sleeping"—the disciples are shocked, because an angry crowd just tried to stone him there. But Thomas leads with his heart: "Let's go, too—and die with Jesus." In John 14, Jesus tells his disciples he's going away to prepare a place for them, and they can follow because they "know the way." Thomas, desperate, asks, "We have no idea where you are going, so how can we know the way?" Jesus responds, "I am the way."

Thomas is later the first missionary to India, where he's martyred after giving his whole heart to Jesus. In a charged Upper Room atmosphere, he just wants evidence that it's really Jesus. He doubts, yes, but everyone is doubting—he's just honest about it. His doubt is a marker for his passion, the very quality Jesus prizes most.

Wonder	**Jesus**	**Do**
What's the difference between "healthy" and "destructive" doubt?	"Put your hand into the wound in my side" (John 20:27).	Give a friend $5—to "pay it forward." What's the basis of your trust?

Pray: Jesus, I have honest doubts about you, including _____.

Water for Insecurity

Read Luke 7:36-50

Ever feel like you'll never belong at the "cool kids" table? My wife and I were cultivating a relationship with a couple we'd always respected. We met for coffee, and they came over for dinner a few times. But something always seemed a little off. Soon our friendship, like a dying campfire, smoldered into ash. They avoid spending time with us, and we don't know why. The burn of insecurity is the universal "tie that binds"—we all know what it's like to feel empty and exposed and unwanted…

Fred Rogers created the groundbreaking PBS show *Mr. Rogers' Neighborhood*. His influence on American culture is enormous. But in a documentary about his life, he reveals the haunting question that stalked his life: "Am I a mistake?" How can someone so successful still be wracked by self-doubt? Well, insecurity is no respecter of success; it's an indiscriminate predator.

Jesus had many encounters with the flawed and the marginalized. A "scandalous" woman crashes a high society party and makes a beeline for the guest of honor, then covers his feet with her sobs, anointing them with perfume. Jesus responds with a tenderness that seems dangerous to his outraged hosts. But he sees in her a child's courageous response to insecurity. What do children do when they're hurt or rejected or ashamed? They do what this woman did. They kiss his feet and cry. Kiss his feet and cry. Kiss his feet and cry…

Wonder	**Jesus**	**Do**
Are you more open or more closed about your insecurities, and why?	"Your faith has saved you; go in peace" (Luke 7:50).	When you apply lip balm, thank Jesus for offering "balm" for your shame.

Pray: Jesus, thank you for inviting me to your "cool kids" table.

Family-Hunger

Read John 17:20-26

The film *Lion* is based on the true story of Saroo, a five-year-old boy from India who is scavenging for freight-train coal with his older brother when he falls asleep at a train station—he awakes to find himself all alone. He boards an empty train looking for his brother but can't escape when the train departs, racing thousands of miles across India. At the end of the line, he has no idea where he is or what has happened to his brother. And he can't explain to others where "home" is. This begins a harrowing quest to reunite with his family. He eventually lands in an orphanage in Calcutta, where an Australian couple adopts him. He leaves the fear and squalor of his shattered life and emerges into the shiny, happy comfort of suburban affluence.

As Saroo grows up, the child of improbable privilege, he remains restless for home. Yes, he's lost and found—but he is not yet restored. Something stirs in his heart, a longing for a deeper *found*. He scours images from Google Earth, looking for his needle in a haystack. Like him, we all hear the siren call of "home." Jesus wants us to find our way Home, against impossible odds, and rejoin our true family. Saroo sacrifices the life he has inherited for a life of fundamental reconnection. And this is what Jesus means when he says, "You must lose your life to find it."

Wonder
What's a longing tied to your family that has never been met?

Jesus
"Father, I want these… you have given me to be with me where I am" (John 17:24).

Do
Paper-clip a photo of your family to this page.

Pray: Jesus, a longing for home stirs in me—lead me back to you.

Art Is Pointless...

Read John 14:11-14

For a design assignment, University of Texas student Jasmine Kay Uy created a double-message poster (a "syncopated poem") she attached to a building's corner walls. On the left side is a sentence-column that makes sense on its own, but has new meaning when combined with sentence-extenders on the right...

Art is pointless	Without passion.
You have to go out	And create art.
Get an actual job	Doing what you love
And make a living	By being yourself
You can't just let	Other people define
The rest of your life	And say you will
Be a joke, a failure.	Follow your heart.
You will end up	Happy and free, not
A starving artist.	Love your art and
Contribute to society	By inspiring people
Instead of wasting time	Letting others tell you
You're worthless.	You can change the world.

Drawn from John 14:12, Jesus' own syncopated poem might read:

Life is pointless	without faith.
If you believe in me	you can change the world.

Wonder
Which is a higher calling—duty or passion?

Jesus
"Believe because of the work you have seen me do" (John 14:11).

Do
Use John 14:11-14 to create your own corner-message battle cry.

Pray: Jesus, your call to "greater works" seems impossible, but I believe.

Purity, Inside Out

Read 1 Corinthians 8

In the era of the Old Testament, the people of God knew their mission was to remain "unstained" by the polluted influences of idol-worship and false gods. Purity was both their practice and their standard. But it was a lifestyle doomed to failure and rife with self-righteous temptations, as Jesus tried to point out to its chief proponents: "What sorrow awaits you teachers of religious law and you Pharisees… For you are so careful to clean the outside of the cup and the dish, but inside you are filthy— full of greed and self-indulgence!… First wash the inside of the cup and the dish, and then the outside will become clean, too" (Matthew 23:25-26).

Jesus promises us an inside-out car wash, but we still prefer our own systems of purity management. *We decide* whether or not something is "unclean." *We choose* the music we listen to, the TV shows we watch, the language we use, the books we read, and the websites we visit using our private sensibilities. But, Paul reminds us, a life of intimacy with Jesus does not include private sensibilities—everything is public, because everything we say and do influences others.

Paul says consumption is like marriage—the two become one. When we are in Jesus, and he is in us, we're always in a dependent posture. He's our personal chef, always guiding what we consume, and what we don't.

Wonder	**Jesus**	**Do**
What's something you're currently consuming that you'd like to give up?	"Do not call something unclean if God has made it clean" (Acts 10:15).	As you wash your hands, invite Jesus to wash you from the inside out.

Pray: Jesus, wash the inside of my cup and make me clean.

Stranger Things

Read Ephesians 6:10-19

Jesus engaged in "spiritual warfare," modeling for us an uncomfortable and inconvenient lifestyle. It's uncomfortable because the "dark" supernatural unnerves us. It's inconvenient because we've mostly ignored the demonic influences Jesus engaged all the time. Yet our lives are about following Jesus, and this is what he did. Jesus had 11 encounters with the demonic in the New Testament, plus many more that are unrecorded. Later, in his letter to the Jesus-followers in Ephesus, Paul writes, "For we are not fighting against flesh-and-blood enemies, but against evil rulers and authorities of the unseen world." So what does this "fight" require of us, and how do we enter in?

In Watchman Nee's classic book on spiritual warfare *Sit, Walk, Stand,* he argues that our "fight" comes from a place of rest, because the battle has already been won. But why must we fight a battle that's over? Jesus gives us a clue: "[The devil] has always hated the truth, because there is no truth in him. When he lies, it is consistent with his character; for he is a liar and the father of lies" (John 8:44). Deception is cotton-candy power—it looks real but is mostly hollow. But it still must be fought. Since Jesus gave us authority over the demonic, our role is to simply exercise it. We stand in the gap, like the wizard Gandalf confronting the demonic in the Mines of Moria, and declare, "You shall not pass!"

Wonder	**Jesus**	**Do**
What is your experience with "spiritual warfare" in your life?	"He was a murderer from the beginning" (John 8:44).	Declare "You shall not pass!" over your home—hang a symbol of faith in your entryway.

Pray: Jesus, I assert the authority you won for me over the evil one.

The Servant Mentality

Read John 15:9-17

Psychologists studied the Torah (first five books of Bible) and discovered the most frequent "relational theme" is "God is helpful." Two less frequent but also repetitive themes are "God controls or hurts." There is obvious tension between these two insights—God is helpful but could hurt you. The implication is that he's the demanding master, and we're the obedient servants. That's why the presence of God in the Old Testament is mitigated by ritual, sacrifice, rote practices, and mediation.

And Jesus upends all of this...

First, early in his ministry, Jesus appears to embrace the Torah's servant/Master relationship: "Anyone who wants to serve me must follow me" (John 12:26). But then comes a tipping point, when Jesus reveals a new way of relating to God: "I have loved you even as the Father has loved me. Remain in my love. When you obey my commandments, you remain in my love, just as I obey my Father's commandments and remain in his love" (John 15:9-10).

Jesus is calling us out of a Master/servant relationship—where our primary focus is obedience and the relationship is functional and hierarchical—and into something much more intimate, immersive, and collaborative. Living obediently is safer than living passionately. But the greater the risk, the greater the potential for intimacy. The point is restoration—restoring, then advancing our relationship beyond the intimacy Adam and Eve experienced in the garden.

Wonder	**Jesus**	**Do**
How do you still live out the "expired" Master/servant relationship?	"Don't begin until you count the cost" (Luke 14:28).	Sing a worship song as you complete a chore—passion over service.

Pray: Jesus, show me how to "remain in your love."

What We Have to Do, But Can't

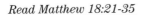

Read Matthew 18:21-35

Let's explore something Jesus said we have to do but knew we couldn't do, and how that impossible standard is at the core of our calling as disciples. For the ancient Jews, the law set a "forgiveness limit" of three pardons for the same offense. So when Peter suggests to Jesus, with some bravado, that he'd be willing to extend that limit to an almost-incomprehensible seven, he's shocked by the response: "No, not seven times, but seventy times seven!"

It's human nature to take up offense, and our cage-match political culture and technologies feed it even more. We're hyper-connected but not typically in grace-filled ways. Because they obliterate face-to-face consequences, our devices make it easy to flambé people. We walk around, and especially drive around, with buffalo chips on our shoulders—fairness is our god. But Jesus tells us our path into discipleship will require us to swallow massive amounts of unfairness. And that means we're competing in a pole-vault event without a pole…

In his Parable of the Unforgiving Debtor, he tells us how to do the impossible—we can give others "forgiveness without borders" because we've been given the same. We are simply passing on what has already been given to us. We are not generating "Amazing Grace"; we're transferring it. To do that, we'll have to get in touch with our "wretch-ness." We don't offer amazing grace unless we already know our profound need of it.

Wonder
Ask Jesus, "Who needs my forgiveness right now?"

Jesus
"That's what my heavenly Father will do to you if you refuse to forgive" (Matthew 18:35).

Do
On youtube.com play "Aretha Franklin Amazing Grace." Close your eyes.

Pray: Jesus, I need you to extend your impossible forgiveness through me.

Infected by Maturity

Read 1 Corinthians 9:19-27

What is the viral path of maturity? I mean, how does it spread from others to us? We can measure how much others know, but it's hard to measure their transforming influence in our lives—we get infected by their maturity.

The first book I ever wrote, more than 20 years ago, was *The Family Friendly Church*—co-authored with Ben Freudenburg. Ben is a pioneering "family ministry" innovator who wanted to write about his approach. But he needed help. I was asked to consider co-writing the book, but I had no interest. And then I had second thoughts. Ben, I knew, was a mature, transformational person. If I agreed to write this book with him, it would give me an excuse to be around him…a lot. And that might change my life. So I agreed, and I was right. Immersing myself in his presence infected me, changing my life forever.

This approach is exactly what Jesus modeled: "Don't let anyone call you 'Rabbi,' for you have only one teacher" (Matthew 23:8). He's referencing the immersive way rabbis infected the growth and maturity of their students. Once "yoked" to a rabbi, the young man would then morph into his shadow. The rabbi became the air he breathed. The goal was to "taste and see" (or "know by experience") the rabbi's heart. Our Rabbi's infectious presence is what changes us, so we invite him into all our compartments.

Wonder	**Jesus**	**Do**
Who has "infected" you with their maturity? What's been the impact?	"Follow me, and I will show you how to fish for people!" (Matthew 4:19).	Wear something that reveals the influence of a loved one.

Pray: Jesus, I want to get your "smell" on me.

Not a Tame Lion

Read Luke 12:49-53

Just after I returned from a 10-day ministry trip to Kenya, where I spent one long day on safari in the Maasai Mara National Reserve, I saw a widely shared social media video of a group of safari tourists "welcoming" a wild lion into their vehicle, stroking him like a housecat. I couldn't believe what I was seeing. I saw plenty of wildlife from the safety of an open-sided Land Rover, including many lions, but the thought of inviting one of them onto my lap never occurred to me…

Lions are not tame. Not something generally known, apparently. Tourists are sometimes surprised to discover this insight the hard way.

"Not a tame lion" is also the profound way author and apologist C.S. Lewis envisions Jesus in his metaphorical fantasy series *The Chronicles of Narnia*. Theologians often point to this 50-year-old set of children's books as their favorite "reference" work, because Lewis uses the fierce lion-character, Aslan, to plumb the depths of Jesus' heart. In the Narnia narratives, he's fearsome and tender, ferocious and restrained, simple and mysterious, kind and demanding, possible and impossible… Jesus through and through.

A housecat does not have the capacity to win our redemption. The weight of it is too heavy for "tame." If the real Jesus climbs into your Land Rover, watch out…

Wonder	**Jesus**	**Do**
When have you experienced Jesus as both tender and fierce in your life?	"I have come to divide people against each other!" (Luke 12:51).	At freesoundeffects .com listen to a cat, then a lion.

Pray: Jesus, I know I've sometimes tried to tame your wildness—forgive me.

Talismans

Read Matthew 20:1-16

The bad things we experience in life often seem indiscriminate—and because unpredictable trauma scares us, we're desperate to snatch back control. We need something that will promise us the life we want as long as we "meet the conditions"—a "talisman" for happiness we call success. So if we "live a good life" and excel in a career, we expect to gain more control over the pain and uncertainty we fear. We just need to…make a little more money or finally find our soulmate or get the promotion we deserve or get that one person in our life to change or earn that diploma or stick to that diet/fitness plan/financial strategy…

If we can just…just about anything.

After a friend discovered his spouse stealing to finance an opioid addiction, he was shattered. In the aftermath, the obvious question so many of his friends asked was "How did you not know this was going on?" At its root this question is a defense of the success talisman—*if you'd been more on top of things as a husband, and paid better attention to your wife, you'd be happy now.*

Jesus told the Parable of the Vineyard Workers because he's intent on destroying our success talismans. We are not owed anything because we've done everything the right way. Grace is the great leveler; control is the great cancer. And the cross is our only true talisman.

Wonder
What has been an "If I can just…" success talisman in your life?

Jesus
"Should you be jealous because I am kind to others?" (Matthew 20:15).

Do
Buy a small cross to keep in your pocket. When you touch it, remember.

Pray: Jesus, I lay all my success talismans at your altar.

Fight Club

Read John 18:1-10

Fight Club is a film about two bored losers who launch a string of underground bare-knuckle "fight clubs" so other bored losers can vent their frustrations and feel alive again. They find meaning and identity in brutality because it feels real. And it's an improbable metaphor for the life Jesus has called us into…

Jesus says, "The thief's purpose is to steal and kill and destroy. My purpose is to give [the true sheep, those who come to Me and enter into life through Me] a rich and satisfying life" (John 10:10). And then "The Son of God came to destroy the works of the devil" (1 John 3:8). When we attach ourselves to Jesus, like a branch in the Vine, we join his "Fight Club." And we find our identity and purpose in the context of his fight.

It's tempting, however, to get drawn into lesser fights and forget who our true enemy is. Political battles, social-justice campaigns, and philanthropic causes are micro-battles worth fighting, but they're not the macro-battle Jesus describes. We have an Enemy who transcends all our lesser enemies. This is why, in the Garden of Gethsemane, Jesus tells Peter to put away his sword. And why, on trial before Pilate, he says, "My Kingdom is not an earthly kingdom. If it were, my followers would fight to keep me from being handed over to the Jewish leaders" (John 18:36). Jesus wants us to fight *his* battles, not *our* battles.

Wonder
What's a "lesser battle" you're fighting?

Jesus
"Shall I not drink from the cup of suffering the Father has given me?" (John 18:11).

Do
Throw a few "air punches." How does that impact your mindset?

Pray: Jesus, I want to fight your battles, and I give you mine to fight.

See It, Say It

Read Luke 7:36-50

It's easy to believe the worst about ourselves. John Williams, one of the great film composers in history (*Star Wars* and *Jurassic Park* and *Schindler's List,* among others), has been nominated for more Academy Awards than any other person not named Walt Disney. With his 90th birthday on the horizon, an interviewer asked if he ever listens to music. "No," he replied. "I'm writing music all the time… And therefore, it's no comfort to listen to it… If I listen to great classical composers, I would only think, 'That's much better than anything I could write.' It isn't comforting."

We may be giants to others, but not to ourselves. This explains Jesus' habitual practice of "speaking truth to power"—in this case, the "power" wielded by our own brutal inner critic…

- Nathanael, a cynic by reputation, is recalibrated by Jesus as "a man of complete integrity."

- The "woman at the well," well-known for her scandalous lifestyle, is "dear woman" to Jesus.

- Simon, the headstrong commercial fisherman who's ashamed of his sin, is renamed by Jesus "Rock."

- The "immoral woman" who anoints his feet with expensive perfume is lauded for her "great love" and remarkable faith.

When Jesus sees beauty in others, he describes it, because words have a forming influence on our soul. When he sees it, he says it.

Wonder
What's something others enjoy about you but you always diminish?

Jesus
"From the time I first came in, she has not stopped kissing my feet" (Luke 7:45).

Do
For one week, speak out the beauty you see in another. Watch what happens.

Pray: Jesus, speak truth to the false power of my inner critic.

The Music of Jesus

Read Romans 9:27-33

Few things have more power to form our worldview than the music we love. In college the music of singer/songwriter Michael Card was fertilizer for my rapidly growing faith. His three-album narrative of the life of Jesus—*Known By the Scars*, *Scandalon*, and *The Final Word*—seeded an insatiable thirst for a Jesus in me. A snippet from Card's masterwork "Scandalon":

> *Along the path of life there lies a stubborn Scandalon*
> *And all who come this way must be offended*
> *To some He is a barrier, To others He's the way*
> *For all should know the scandal of believing*
> *It seems today the Scandalon offends no one at all*
> *The image we present can be stepped over*
> *Could it be that we are like the others long ago*
> *Will we ever learn that all who come must stumble*

The Jesus I "tasted" in Card's lyrics shattered the Jesus I thought I knew. The churchy music I grew up with was pablum compared to "will we ever learn that all who come must stumble." In fact, some music we call "Christian" operates like a Trojan Horse—it looks like a gift from a friend, but it's actually hiding an enemy inside. It gives us a Jesus who sounds biblical but isn't. He's more like a vending machine or a divine butler than a "Scandalon." Faith depends on its focus, and faith in a milquetoast Jesus limits us to a milquetoast relationship. Music matters…

Wonder
What role does music play in your relationship with Jesus?

Jesus
"Families will be split apart, three in favor of me, and two against" (Luke 12:52).

Do
Press your finger into a butter knife's blade—Jesus is more knife than spoon.

Pray: Jesus, you are my Scandalon, not my vending machine.

Reverberations of the Heart

Read Matthew 14:6-23

"Hello darkness, my old friend, I've come to talk with you again"—the iconic opening words to Simon and Garfunkel's classic "The Sound of Silence." It's a lonely homage to the spare beauty of…nothing. The unfilled space that reverberates like our own heartbeat, calming and recentering us. Silence is no luxury; it's a necessity. If we don't have seasons of it in our lives, we live reactively. And what are the signs that we are silence-starved?

- Impatience, restlessness, and anxiety…

- Words that harm…

- Silly thinking…

- Withdrawing into our own small world…

- A "shallowness" of soul…

- Emotional instability…

Silence will cure what ails us. Jesus balances the demands of his life with long stretches of it. After his friend John the Baptist is beheaded by the treachery of Herodias, Jesus slips away in a boat to lament in silence. But the desperate crowds track him down, and he heals the sick late into the day. They are hungry, so he feeds them. And now the silence can wait no longer. He sends his friends away and melts into the stillness of the hills.

We embrace Jesus-silence when we listen before we speak, cut distractions, observe "fallow" time, and eliminate noise.

Wonder	**Jesus**	**Do**
Are you grateful for silence in your life, or do you resist it?	"I have a kind of food you know nothing about" (John 4:32).	Plug your ears for one minute and observe the impact.

Pray: Jesus, I see the impact of noise in my life. Draw me to silence.

At Play With Jesus

Read Matthew 18:1-6

On a war-ravaged street in Syria, children on bikes pick their way through the rubble of their bombed-out homes, unconsciously reminding us that we are hard-wired to play, even in the shadow of trauma. For children, the urge to play is relentless. And this is why Jesus

Source: CFP - Globaltimes.cn

marries childlike habits to kingdom of God culture. A playful spirit makes it possible to maintain close relationship with him.

The words *child* and *children* appear more than 180 times in the New Testament, and Jesus often refers to his closest friends as "little children." In Luke's gospel he prays, "I praise you, Father, Lord of heaven and earth, because you have hidden these things from the wise and learned, and revealed them to little children" (Luke 10:21, NIV).

It makes Jesus happy when we embrace a spirit of play in our relationship with him, because play gives faith its momentum, and it's "impossible to please God" without it. Play means we move through life with a willing belief that Jesus is good and all will be well—we embrace a "preference for joy" over a "preference for worry."

Wonder	**Jesus**	**Do**
What area in your life is overshadowed by anxiety, and why?	"I tell you, I haven't seen faith like this in all Israel!" (Luke 7:9).	Stare at the photo; ask Jesus, "How is this a metaphor for my life?"

Pray: Jesus, recover my ability to play like a child again.

The Laughing Jesus

Read Luke 5:1-11

"What would Jesus do?" Well, "laughs all the time" is probably not on our checklist. If we're created in God's image, and laughter is one of our "basic necessities," it must be true that God laughs often. So why don't we see more obvious examples of laughter in the life of Jesus?

I'm a comic-strip fan—I have a few book-length collections piled on our coffee table where everyone can see them. It's not very "adult," and sometimes I'm a little self-conscious, but humor is one of Jesus' "love languages." A lot of things he said and did reveal an edgy, sardonic sense of humor. Try an experiment—imagine Jesus is smiling or laughing when he says the things below, rather than the holy scowl we usually assume…

- "The servants who are ready and waiting for [the master's] return will be rewarded. I tell you the truth, he himself will seat them, put on an apron, and serve them as they sit and eat!" (Luke 12:37).

- "Put your finger here, and look at my hands. Put your hand into the wound in my side. Don't be faithless any longer. Believe!" (John 20:27).

- "We played wedding songs, and you didn't dance, so we played funeral songs, and you didn't weep" (Luke 7:32).

The Bible gives little context about the tone and tenor of Jesus—we just assume he's grave-serious all the time. But that can't be true…

Wonder
What's the "purpose" of laughter in our lives?

Jesus
"Don't be afraid! From now on you'll be fishing for people!" (Luke 5:10).

Do
Search for "laugh sound effects" online and listen for a minute.

Pray: Jesus, help me "hear" your voice more broadly than I do.

Chewing the Bible

Read Romans 2:17-29

Most Bible-reading plans make quantity, not depth of understanding, the goal. And the church has conditioned us to treat Bible-reading as quasi-academic: *You have to do your homework.*

But if we want a deeper experience of Jesus, our Bible-reading must move from a discipline to a hunger. In college I developed a life-threatening illness—I had to drop out of school to get treatment. When I returned, I felt isolated, stressed, and worn out. Some friends invited me to a church that emphasized "the life of the Spirit." There, I asked the church's leaders to pray that I would have a "deeper in-filling" of the Holy Spirit. The effect was like turning on a light switch in my soul. I had an insatiable desire to read Scripture, with Jesus looking over my shoulder to help me understand everything.

In his letter to the Jewish believers in Rome, Paul exposes their academic approach to Scripture as bankrupt: "You are convinced that you are a guide for the blind and a light for people who are lost in darkness. You think you can instruct the ignorant and teach children the ways of God. For you are certain that God's law gives you complete knowledge and truth. Well then, if you teach others, why don't you teach yourself?" They have comprehended God's truths but haven't yet ingested them. We don't get the "nutritional value" of God's Word until our hunger leads us to eat it, as Jesus invited us to do.

Wonder
When you read the Bible, is it more like work or play?

Jesus
"What are you discussing so intently as you walk along?" (Luke 24:17).

Do
Try reading the Bible conversationally. Pause to ask Jesus questions out loud.

Pray: Jesus, I'm inviting your Spirit to plant a desire for the Bible in me.

Inside Enemies

Read Luke 4:16-20

In his hometown synagogue, Jesus stands to read from "the scroll of Isaiah" on Sabbath day. During the time of the Babylonian exile, handwritten copies of the Torah and the Prophets were systematically destroyed. To preserve them, the scrolls were divided among the families in Nazareth. Isaiah 61 was long ago "entrusted" to Jesus' family—remarkable, because the focal point of this section of Scripture is the mission of the Messiah.

> *"The Spirit of the Lord is upon me,*
> *for he has anointed me to bring Good News to the poor.*
> *He has sent me to proclaim that captives will be released,*
> *that the blind will see,*
> *that the oppressed will be set free,*
> *and that the time of the Lord's favor has come."*

Jesus rolls up the scroll, hands it to the synagogue attendant, and sits (rather melodramatically) in "the seat of Moses." Then he proclaims, "The Scripture you've just heard has been fulfilled this very day!" This is shocking to the Sabbath crowd because no one but the coming Messiah is allowed to sit in the seat of Moses—it has been empty for centuries.

Jesus intends this to be a defining moment, highlighted by what he *doesn't* read in the scroll. He plants a period where Isaiah had a comma, excising this: "…and with it, the day of God's anger against their enemies." Jesus will be targeting "the enemy within us," not the enemy without.

Wonder
In what area of your life are you craving freedom the most?

Jesus
"I tell you the truth, no prophet is accepted in his own hometown" (Luke 4:24).

Do
Shine your phone's flashlight behind the Isaiah 61 quote. Read it slowly.

Pray: Jesus, thank you that I'm no longer an enemy, but a friend.

Fishing All Night...

Read John 21:1-12

In the chaos surrounding the death and resurrection of Jesus, Peter copes with his restless anxiety by returning to what he knows best—fishing. He tells (not invites) his friends that he's heading out on his boat for the night. And they quickly jump on board. Stripped for work, they trawl the shallows until morning and catch nothing. Nothing. Ever feel like you're working as hard as you can but accomplishing nothing?

Jesus intends to send them out into the world to announce the good news of redemption, raining down on a parched people like a thunderstorm, and to "heal the sick, raise the dead, cure those with leprosy, and cast out demons." But they must wait before they go, and it's driving them crazy. So they stop "remaining and abiding" and get busy doing something. Anything. So Jesus meets them in the middle of their nothing and does something sly—just as he did three years before, he tells them where to throw their net. And they catch so many fish that their boat starts to sink.

There, on the shore, waiting for them, is Jesus holding a frying pan… They couldn't wait for him, so now he's waiting for them. And when they get there, he feeds them and sends them. If your life feels like a whole lot of work with nothing to show for it, there's a guy on the beach holding a frying pan who's waiting to fill you and send you.

Wonder	Jesus	Do
What area of your life feels like "fishing all night but catching nothing"?	"Fellows, have you caught any fish?" (John 21:5).	In your grocery store's fresh fish section, smell what Jesus smelled.

Pray: Jesus, I've fished as best I can. Show me where to throw the net.

The Congruent Jesus

Read Matthew 5:1-12

Jesus is the only person in history whose actions were perfectly congruent with his beliefs. Everything he taught, he lived. Everything he lived, he taught. For us, congruence means we embrace what Jesus believes. The late evangelist and activist Tom Skinner, a former street-gang leader, once said, "We're meant to live as models on Earth of what is already happening in heaven." So, a congruence-starter…

What Jesus believes…	How we can believe the same…
Kingdom-of-God love is defined by the way we treat our enemies.	"Love" is not the same as "be nice to"— love means the other's freedom from captivity is paramount.
Marginalized and needy people are insiders, not outsiders.	We make no distinctions about the value of others by race, social status, economic resources, or mental/emotional health.
Hope must be paired with the courage to face brutal reality.	We develop a ferocious determination to embrace reality while trusting Jesus more than we trust ourselves.
The arrogant need to be opposed, and the humble need to be lifted up.	Arrogance is a form of captivity, so we help release people from its prison by knocking the knees out from under it.

We are saboteurs working under the radar with Jesus to confront and destroy systems and patterns of belief that are not in harmony with the love of God.

Wonder
On this list, what's most challenging about what Jesus believes?

Jesus
"What good is salt if it has lost its flavor?" (Matthew 5:13).

Do
Say "musty" aloud while you smell something musty—that's congruence.

Pray: Jesus, I want my walk and talk to match.

Jesus and Trick Questions

Read Luke 20:19-26

If we love as Jesus loves, we'll have to embrace awkward encounters with enemies. My missionary friend Carl Medearis often meets with a leader of the terrorist group Hezbollah in his Beirut home. It's a paramilitary force loyal to Ayatollah Khomeini and trained by Iran's Revolutionary Guard—its mission is to harass Israel and eradicate Western influences from Lebanon. And Carl is determined to reach its leaders with the love of Jesus…

One night, Carl and his friends were about to leave, so they asked if they could lay hands on the Hezbollah leader to pray for him. While their eyes were shut, a camera crew from the Hezbollah TV station entered to record the scene. On a live feed, they asked Carl, "Why do you love the Hezbollah, and why you hate Israel?" With no time to think, he asked Jesus for help— "Jesus does funny things with trick questions," he told me later. Guided by the Spirit, Carl answered, "That reminds me of a story Jesus told—the story of the Good Father, or the Prodigal Son…" And then he told the story. "The Hezbollah camera crew," he said, "was shocked by this story. In that culture, family patriarchs don't run to embrace their reprobate sons. If the father ran, he would do it only to kill his son and restore honor to his disgraced family."

The story upended the camera crew's agenda, planting a redemptive seed in the most unlikely of "soils."

Wonder
Is "shrewdness" a positive or negative thing, and why?

Jesus
"Render to Caesar [what's] Caesar's, and to God [what's] God's" (Luke 20:25, NASB).

Do
Pick an "enemy" from your phone's contacts. Send a short, supportive note.

Pray: Jesus, I trust you, in the moment, to show me how to love my enemies.

The Power of Gratefulness

Read Luke 17:11-19

People who are habitually grateful in life also tend to have greater persistence and courageous resolve—that's one of the surprising insights from new research into the long-term impact of "grit." The finding is so strong that the U.S. military changed its basic training regimen to emphasize gratefulness as a "survival habit" for new recruits.

A grateful posture in life rivets our attention on the random acts of grace that litter our path—it means we take regular inventory of the relationships and advantages we're already enjoying but may have taken for granted. Jesus spotlights the stark contrast between the entitled and the grateful when he heals 10 lepers in the Samarian wilderness. He's on his way to Jerusalem, where he will be celebrated, then arrested, then crucified. The desperate men call out to him from a distance, afraid to get closer because they are pariahs twice—once because of their disease, and then because they are Samaritans.

Ten are healed, but only one returns to prostrate himself before Jesus in thanks. Like us, the nine others are desperate right up until the moment they're not. Once they get what they want, they quickly revert to self-sufficiency. Jesus redefines the grateful leper's passion as "great faith"—why? Because faith is humbly grateful for the beauty and goodness of Jesus, not merely what he can do. This man recognizes Jesus as a wonder, and wonder then fuels his gratefulness.

Wonder
What are you treating as an entitlement instead of a blessing?

Jesus
"Has no one returned to give glory to God except this foreigner?" (Luke 17:18).

Do
Touch something near you. Pause to give thanks for what it represents.

Pray: Jesus, I lie down to rest in the palms of the Giver of all good things.

What God Looks Like

Read John 14:1-10

I once gathered a large collection of unusual "Jesus pictures" I found online, then showed them to a group of people and asked them to mark on a handout whether each image was true or false. They had to make a quick decision. After they'd voted on each picture, I had them explain to a partner why they voted the way they did. Then I asked them, "What did you learn about the way we expect Jesus to look by rating these pictures?" Most of the "false" votes went to the Jesus pictures that were funny or quirky or playful.

Youth With a Mission leader Floyd McClung says, "When she was little and we were living in Amsterdam, my daughter asked me, 'Daddy, what does God look like?' She saw a lot of old men wandering the streets in Amsterdam, so I told her God didn't look like an old grumpy grandfather. God's not like a judge, measuring every wrong thing we do… I told her God looks exactly like Jesus. Jesus took children into his lap and told them stories. Jesus wasn't afraid to be seen with a really bad woman. Jesus went to a wedding feast and saved a family from terrible shame. We have images of God that have been imposed upon us by others. Nobody gets to do that—we need our own experience of Jesus that defines him for us. The most incredible thing in the universe is that God has broken into our world to show us who he is, through his Son, Jesus."

Wonder
What's one thing about Jesus that proves no one could have made him up?

Jesus
"If you had really known me, you would know who my Father is" (John 14:7).

Do
Find a "goofy Jesus" image online. Make it your phone's wallpaper for a day.

Pray: Jesus, here's looking at you, kid…

Don't Say Jesus—Be Jesus

Read Matthew 10:5-10

Jesuit priest Greg Boyle's memoir *Tattoos on the Heart* plumbs the depths of his 30-plus years working with gang members in Los Angeles. He's founder of Homeboy Industries, the world's largest (and most successful) gang intervention and rehabilitation program. At a conference for Jesus-lovers, I heard Father Boyle tell this story…

I was speaking at Gonzaga, my alma mater. I picked two homies who are in rival gangs to go with me—Mario and Bobby. Mario was really terrified to fly; he was hyperventilating before we even got on the plane. The passengers were scared by him, but he's determined to be the kindest person in Homeboy.

Mario and Bobby told their stories, which were full of horror and pain. Afterward, during the Q&A time, a woman asks Mario: "What advice do you give your kids who are about to enter adolescence?" And Mario blurts out, through his tears, "I just don't want my kids to turn out to be like me." And then the woman says, "Why wouldn't you want your kids to turn out like you? I hope your kids turn out to be like you."

Everyone stands to clap; they won't stop. Mario just holds his face in his hands and weeps. These strangers returned him to himself. The kingdom of God is about kinship, no daylight separating us. Jesus says, "That you may be one." We're not invited to say Jesus—we're invited to see Jesus, and invited to be Jesus.

Wonder
When and how has someone "returned you to yourself"?

Jesus
"Anyone who believes in me will do… even greater works" (John 14:12).

Do
Surprise a friend with lunch—a gift "out of nowhere," just as Jesus did.

Pray: Jesus, return me to myself, and help me return others to you.

Fighting Accusation

Read Revelation 12:7-12

Jesus was criticized more often than a baseball umpire…
- "You are a law-breaker" (Matthew 12:1-14).
- "You get your power from Satan" (Matthew 12:22-37).
- "You're useless unless you perform" (Matthew12:38-45).
- "You're a disappointment" (Matthew 16:21-28).
- "Who do you think you are?" (Matthew 21:23-46).

We have an enemy who intends to "kill, steal, and destroy"—death beyond our physical death is this enemy's aim. What he wants to kill in us is the you that makes you, you. He does this, Jesus reminds us, by accusing us…

Let's say your best friend suddenly drops off the radar—your texts and calls and emails don't get a response. It has been two weeks of slow-cooker anxiety. The dissonance creates a gap you're driven to fill, so you generate imagined explanations for this disappearance—some benign ("I'm sure she's just been very busy") and some not ("I must have said or done something wrong"). And now the seeds of accusation take root, your greenhouse of insecurity, accelerating their growth: *"Maybe my friend has finally seen through my facade."*

The gravitational pull of our insecurity drags us down into accusation because we live in a "kingdom" ruled by the Accuser (Luke 4:6). But Jesus tells us worship is our weapon against this onslaught—in his own response to the Accuser, he counters with "You must worship the Lord your God and serve only him" (Luke 4:8).

Wonder
What's the most common accusation you "hear" inside?

Jesus
"When he lies, it is consistent with his character" (John 8:44).

Do
When you feel accused, sing (out loud) "Jesus loves me, this I know…"

Pray: Jesus, you are my refuge—a mighty fortress for my soul.

The Greatest Bad Teacher

Read Luke 10:25-37

At first, an "outcome-based" assessment of Jesus' teaching belies his reputation as the greatest teacher of all time. He didn't seem to convince many, some hated his "lessons," and his illustrations often required explanation. He skirted clear answers and often ducked questions altogether. But when he taught, Jesus planted redemptive time bombs in the hearts of his listeners…

The impetus for one of his best-known teaching stories—the Parable of the Good Samaritan—is a Pharisee's trick question: "What should I do to inherit eternal life?" Jesus asks him to answer instead, and he responds, "Love God, love your neighbors." But then the conniving man wants to know who he's required to love and who he can ignore. So Jesus tells him a story about a man beaten by thieves, lying by the side of the road. The Pharisee knows Jesus is going to insert him as a character in the story—but he's not the first passerby (a Sadducee), not the second passerby (a Levite), and not even the third passerby (a man who doesn't even belong in the story—a Samaritan). London School of Theology professor Conrad Gempf says, "It's like Jesus is telling a story about the Civil War, and a guy in a space suit floats in." Jesus makes the neighbor-loving Samaritan the hero of the story, so the person he helps (the only "unassigned" character) must be…the Pharisee.

Jesus makes transformation, not mere learning, the goal of his teaching.

Wonder
What teacher has impacted your life the most, and why?

Jesus
"Do this and you will live!" (Luke 10:28).

Do
Jesus teaches "time-bomb" lessons in nature. Go outside to listen and learn.

Pray: Jesus, I'm ready to learn, so teach me.

Spider Bites

Read 1 Corinthians 1:18-25

A spider falls into a pond—he's drowning until a boy playing nearby sees him and saves him. The spider responds by biting the boy. Startled, the boy drops the spider back into the water, where it sinks again. Time after time, the boy saves the spider but is bitten in return. Finally, the spider asks, "Why is it that you save me? You know that I am a spider, and biting people is what I do!" And the boy responds, "Well, I am the Son of God, and loving is what I do."

Our one hope in life is that Jesus will never stop rescuing us, even though it's just a matter of time before we bite him again. The cross represents much more than our salvation—it's the great "spider bite" that Jesus endures, only because it's in his nature to love no matter how we respond. Paul tells the Jesus-followers in Corinth, "The message of the cross is foolish to those who are headed for destruction! But we who are being saved know it is the very power of God."

The true "power of God" is his determination to save and save again—until the spider is born over. Jesus has made this his mission. To Nicodemus he says, "I tell you the truth, unless you are born again, you cannot see the Kingdom of God." We desperately need the persistence of a Savior who intends to re-birth our "natural inclinations" so completely that we still look like spiders but don't act like them.

Wonder	**Jesus**	**Do**
How have you "bitten" Jesus this week?	"The Holy Spirit gives birth to spiritual life" (John 3:6).	Pinch between your thumb and forefinger—then thank Jesus for persisting.

Pray: Jesus, thank you for your "seventy times seven" heart.

The Grace Reversal

Read Genesis 50:14-21

CNN interviewed a prominent Christian leader soon after his daughter-in-law was diagnosed with a brain tumor. Seven weeks earlier she'd given birth prematurely via C-section because the baby was breech, with the umbilical cord wrapped around its neck. If she'd given birth on her due date, the contractions would've stressed the undiscovered tumor and likely killed her. "So what we thought was a problem was actually a protection saving her life," observed the pastor.

This story has a happy ending. But Jesus is not "good" only when a hidden catastrophe is avoided—when a hard thing seems "worth it." No, Jesus is good regardless of our outcomes. Sometimes we solve the dissonance of our good-God/bad-experiences conundrum by tacitly framing him as an abuser, as this quote from another well-known church leader implies: "[God has] already counted on the trials to come. They were part of his foreknowledge and his design from the beginning."

Jesus doesn't "design" evil for us. We live in a fallen world, and things are *not* as he designed. It's truer to say that he's an Artist, repurposing what was intended to harm us into a life-giving grace. To cope with a difficult childhood, I often descended to our dark basement to work alone on my hobbies. In that long season of lament, Jesus planted in me a love for the light. That is redemption feeding on catastrophe. Gratefulness *before* our good outcome is a "sacrifice of praise."

Wonder	**Jesus**	**Do**
What's your sacrifice of praise today?	"He gives his sunlight to both the evil and the good" (Matthew 5:45).	Use hand lotion to smooth what is rough; thank Jesus for doing the same.

Pray: Jesus, repurpose my circumstances into good art.

What Jesus Believes

Read John 17

Professor and pastor Bart Tarman, longtime chaplain at Westmont College, says the great theologian Dallas Willard once told him, "You believe in Jesus; it would be so awesome if you believed *like* Jesus." That zinger kick-started an adventure in excavation—Tarman pored over all four gospels, highlighting what Jesus believed. He used three filters to dig: 1) What Jesus said. 2) What Jesus did. 3) What Jesus refused to do.

At the end of his "big dig," Bart had created a list of 57 things Jesus believes. Then he posted those beliefs on one side of a page, listing "what Bart believes" on the other side. "I believed about 24 things on that list of 57," he says, "and I wanted to close the gap. But you can't close the gap if you don't know what he believes."

In the time of Jesus, obedience in a disciple-rabbi relationship was the fruit of close relationship, not an ongoing effort to maintain discipline. Put another way, obedience had more to do with your being than your doing. Willard says, "We come to Jesus to become like Jesus so we can live like Jesus." Living like Jesus will mean we see the world through his eyes and believe the way he believes—and Jesus believes he is secure, provided for, and cherished. Author Brennan Manning describes it best: "I have been seized by the power of a great affection."

Wonder
Does Jesus believe "God helps those who help themselves"?

Jesus
"I have revealed you to the ones you gave me from this world" (John 17:6).

Do
Try Bart Tarman's idea using John 17. Read aloud beliefs you don't yet embrace.

Pray: Jesus, I want to believe what you believe; help my unbelief.

Jesus Is Both/And

Read Matthew 5:17-48

In Western culture we've embraced the Enlightenment, a worldview inspired by the ancient Greeks that elevates reason, individualism, and skepticism. Under its influence, we've reduced music, a fluid and "soul-ish" art form, into a digitized progression of numbers. That's in contrast with the Hebrew culture of Jesus, which promoted a both/and mindset. That means, to Jesus and his disciples, the pursuit of truth was not a linear progression toward a "solution"; it was more like dancing the tango. The waltz is a linear form of dance, with prescribed and repeated steps. But the tango is "free-form"—partners follow nuances, responding to slight changes in leverage and hand pressure. Dancing the tango requires a focused, dependent, trusting attention on the other—it's an intimate art form.

Oxford economics professor John Kay says, "The process in which well-defined and prioritized objectives are broken down into specific states and actions whose progress can be monitored and measured is not the reality of how people find fulfillment in their lives, create great art, establish great societies or build good businesses." Rather than reducing Scripture to a list of principles to follow, Peter Kreeft compares reading the Bible to standing under "a big sprig of [God's] mistletoe."

The both/and of the tango fits Jesus well; he is fully human and fully divine. And he's inviting us to read the Bible as a lover's invitation, not a mechanic's checklist.

Wonder	**Jesus**	**Do**
Jesus came to "fulfill the law," not abolish it. What does that mean?	"You think [Scriptures] give you eternal life. But the Scriptures point to me!" (John 5:39).	Search for "Basic steps of the tango" on youtube.com—watch, then try it.

Pray: Jesus, I want to feel the slight pressure of your guiding hand.

Three Loaves of Bread

Read Luke 11:1-10

Jesus is finishing a conversation with his Father when his disciples ask if he'd teach them to pray. So he models for them *how* to pray, not necessarily *what* to pray ("This is how you should pray…"). Nevertheless, we've turned his *how* into a what-formula we call The Lord's Prayer—"Father, hallowed be your name. Your kingdom come…" It's important to recognize that Jesus' lesson on how to pray leads directly into a story I've nicknamed "The Parable of the Pushy Friend"—an extended teaching on how to relate to God.

In the story, a desperate man knocks on the door of his friend at an ungodly hour, asking to borrow three loaves of bread to feed unexpected guests. At first the friend, irritated, refuses to get out of bed. Finally, he grumpily opens the door and gives his friend what he's asking for. Metaphorically, God is the "master of the house" who refuses to help his friend (and metaphorically, that's all of us). Jesus tells the story to encourage us to develop the kind of relationship with him that is trusting enough to accommodate our persistent, inconvenient requests.

He wants us to relate to him as we would to our closest friends, trusting his generosity and love for us more than our circumstances say is appropriate. He wants us to knock and knock and knock on his door because we know his heart well enough to "shamelessly persist."

Wonder	**Jesus**	**Do**
Do you know Jesus well enough to "shamelessly" inconvenience him?	"Suppose you went to a friend's house at midnight…" (Luke 11:5).	Give a solid surface near you a few knocks—hear the sound of persistence.

Pray: Jesus, I'm knock, knock, knocking on your door because…

The Giver

Read Matthew 6:22-23

After a brutal stretch of disappointments, I couldn't dig my way out of sadness. Ashamed and arrogant, I hid the truth. And then, one day, I found a plain white box in our mailbox, labeled with my typed name on it. Inside was a figurine from the cartoon show *Phineas and Ferb* and a laminated Scripture passage.

Clearly, someone was working hard to encourage me and knew that I loved watching *Phineas and Ferb* with my third-grade daughter. My family was delighted by the mystery, brainstorming possible "culprits." The following week (and for the next seven weeks), it happened again and again. Another box, another figurine, another laminated Scripture. But the eighth week I got a typed ultimatum—I had 24 hours to guess the "bandit's" identity or it would stay a secret.

But I had a secret of my own: This massive effort had not moved the needle in my soul. The darkness inside was even deeper. *Sometimes encouraging messages aren't enough.* But that afternoon, as a joke, I asked my daughter Emma if she was the culprit. She paused a micro-moment, hiding a tiny upturn in her lips. And then reality washed over me—my two young daughters had planned and pulled off this epic subterfuge. The dam holding back my tears burst, and I cried into the night.

Good news often isn't enough—*what matters is the Giver.* Jesus proclaims, "I am the way, the truth, and the life." It's the heart of the Giver that ultimately breaks through our defenses.

Wonder
Why are others' attempts to encourage us sometimes not enough?

Jesus
"If the light you think you have is...darkness, how deep that darkness is!" (Matthew 6:23).

Do
Breathe deeply from a flower's aroma; worship the "Giver's" beauty.

Pray: Jesus, I need you, the Giver, even more than I need your message.

The Scandal of Childlikeness

Read Matthew 18:1-4

In the middle of a sermon, I asked if any children would volunteer to perform a cartwheel in the aisle—five or six did. Then I asked for adults to do the same, and I got…crickets. Cartwheels in church are not on the approved list of adult behaviors. Adults, unlike children, are shaped by responsibility and imprisoned by self-consciousness.

For example, when my daughters want to go to the pool, I tell them I have deadlines to meet. When they're on a break from school they can sleep in, but I get up at 5:30 to stay on top of my responsibilities. They get to enjoy summer Drama Camp, but for most adults, the workplace is our permanent "drama camp." Adulthood means we've left childhood (and often childlikeness) behind. That's a problem, because Jesus said, "I tell you the truth, unless you [change] and become like little children, you will never get into the kingdom of heaven." Not entering the kingdom of heaven means, essentially, we're not living the way Jesus lives.

George MacDonald writes, "There is a childhood into which we have to grow, just as there is a childhood which we must leave behind…" This is why Jesus invites Nicodemus, a Pharisee imprisoned by adult-ness, to descend into childhood again. In the kingdom of God, we honor responsibility but live in the spirit of deep delight.

Wonder
Today, if you knew failure didn't matter, what would you try?

Jesus
"[Those who are like] this little child [are] the greatest in the Kingdom" (Matthew 18:4).

Do
Practice childlikeness—use a curly straw to drink, or wear funky socks.

Pray: Jesus, transcend my adult mentality with a child's freedom.

The Red Thread

Read Isaiah 53

Jesus is the focal point for *all* Scripture—he's the "red thread" running through God's story, from Genesis to Revelation. If we dip a toe into the Old Testament's flowing stream, we discover…

In Genesis, he is the promised seed of the woman.

In Exodus, he is the Passover Lamb.

In Leviticus, he is the high priest.

In Deuteronomy, he is two laws—love God/love your neighbor.

In Joshua, he is the captain of the lord of hosts.

In Ruth, he is the kinsman redeemer.

In Samuel, he is the root and offspring of David.

In Kings, he is greater than the Temple.

In Esther, he is the savior of God's people.

In Psalms, he is the song.

In Proverbs, he is the wisdom of God.

In Song of Solomon, he is the bridegroom of the bride.

In Jeremiah, he is our righteousness.

In Ezekiel, he is the true shepherd.

In Daniel, he is a rejected stone that became the cornerstone.

In Jonah, he is our salvation.

In Nahum, he is the stronghold in the time of trouble.

In Habakkuk, he is our joy and confidence.

In Zephaniah, he is our mighty lord.

In Haggai, he is the desire of the nations.

In Malachi, he is the Son of righteousness.

Wonder	**Jesus**	**Do**
Of these descriptions of Jesus, which is most meaningful?	"Destroy this temple, and in three days I will raise it up" (John 2:19).	Across the page-tops of your closed Bible, side-to-side, use a red marker to draw a line,.

Pray: Jesus, you are my beginning and my end.

The Scary Path

Read Luke 9:1-6

Jody, a middle-aged woman on the eve of her first cross-cultural mission trip to Nicaragua, pinpoints the question that will later define her experience: *"Jesus, what is my role in this adventure?"* Jody's question is also the central question of our lives—interchangeable with "What is the meaning of life?"

Most of us have held on to the wrong definition of *adventure* since childhood. We have a giddy interpretation of it—a Disneyland dream. But real adventures feel dangerous when we're inside them. The difference between a tropical storm and a hurricane is wind speed, and the difference between everyday life and an adventure is danger.

So when we decide to follow Jesus, we enter into danger, because he is at home in the hurricane. To live out his mission in our lives, we will risk our vulnerability and our status and our safety and our complacence and our inadequacies. We will speak when others are silent, run toward when others run away, and open ourselves when others close down. Fear will tell us we are likely to be misunderstood and opposed and maybe even betrayed. But in the eye of the hurricane, we discover the calm of his great affection for us. So we live and breathe and move inside that eye, like Tabernacle tents moving through the wilderness. With Jesus at our center, the wind speed of our lives intensifies, making us more alert and alive than we've ever been before.

Wonder
What's been your greatest adventure in life, and what made it that?

Jesus
"Don't take a walking stick, a traveler's bag, food, [or] money" (Luke 9:3).

Do
Take your dog for a walk, but let the dog choose the route.

Pray: Jesus, I want to feel the wind of your hurricane in my face.

The Respect of Jesus

Read John 16:12-15

Author Donald Miller observes, "The opposite of love is not hate. It's control." Controlling people infect their relationships with cancerous disrespect. And since we control things, not people, we disrespect their God-given agency when we obliterate their freedom. Respect, then, is the foundation for intimacy—a truth championed by Aretha Franklin in her iconic anthem: "What you want, baby, I got it. What you need, do you know I got it? All I'm askin' is for a little respect… R-E-S-P-E-C-T."

So in our relationship with God, do we experience his respect? King David cries out, "Why, Lord, do you stand far off? Why do you hide yourself in times of trouble?" (Psalm 10:1, NIV). We have our own troubling questions to add to David's list…

- *Why don't you intervene more often to fulfill my hopes and dreams?*
- *What about the intolerable hardships facing so many in the world—don't you care?*

William Paul Young, author of *The Shack*, says, "How can there be a good God who has the power to stop evil and doesn't? Well, God respects his creation way more than we do… To love, you have to have the ability to choose. He could have made a whole creation that thought they were making free choices, but weren't. There's no relationship there." Jesus is determined to restore us into an intimacy bound by respect. He will not control us, no matter how painful the consequences.

Wonder	**Jesus**	**Do**
How do you experience Jesus' respect?	"[Don't] take them out of the world, but [keep] them safe from the evil one" (John 17:15).	Make the "shush" sign with your finger. What does control feel like on your lips?

Pray: Jesus, thank you for paying such a high price to respect me.

Innocently Shrewd

Read Luke 16:1-9

A "great multitude" latches on to Jesus—his parables resonate with the "tax gatherers and sinners," and that, in turn, rivets the attention of the scribes and Pharisees, who complain about Jesus "slumming" with this disgusting rabble. That lights a fuse in Jesus—he launches into three "rescue" parables (The Lost Sheep, The Lost Coin, The Lost Son). And then he tells a story meant to give the "disgusting rabble" a strategy for fighting back against these predatory religious leaders.

In the Parable of the Shrewd Manager, Jesus overlooks a man's obvious character defects to specifically praise his shrewdness—he's trying to make a point that he later spells out for his disciples: "I am sending you out like sheep among wolves. Therefore be as shrewd as snakes and as innocent as doves" (Matthew 10:16, NIV). We live in the world like defenseless, dependent prey surrounded by conniving predators. Because that is true ("Therefore"), Jesus urges us to embrace two complementary character traits: 1) innocence—a "blameless" motivation; and 2) shrewdness—intentionally leveraging people and situations toward redemption.

Shrewd people "understand how things work" and use that insight to set goodness in motion. With "shrewd," Jesus uses a word that typifies Satan (in Genesis 3, he is "more crafty than any beast"). The "evil one" is killing, stealing, and destroying—our mission is to out-shrewd him with life and hope and restoration.

Wonder
How has Jesus leveraged you toward goodness?

Jesus
"Give to Caesar what belongs to Caesar, and to God what belongs to God" (Matthew 22:21).

Do
The word *please* is a lever, so use it often today and observe the impact.

Pray: Jesus, show me how to live as a sheep among wolves.

You're Not Hard to See

Read Psalm 17

Pain delivers the decibels that wake us up to necessary truths. A friend, picking her way through the painful rubble of a divorce, describes her awakening: *I was devalued in every possible way, and the farther away I've gotten from it, the more I see the damage it did. Now I am discovering the girl I was before all of this, a girl that many people haven't seen in over a decade, and I am determined to get back to her, because she was awesome and fearless.*

When she was struggling through a particularly bad week, feeling misunderstood and judged by people she'd trusted, I told her, "You know, it really isn't hard to see you. If others can't see you, that's their problem, not yours." Later, she sent me this note:

I am learning that I have spent way too much of my time in my life jumping up and down and begging the wrong people to see me. I'm determined to surround myself in this next phase with people who truly see me and know how precious my heart is—and I will shake the dust off my feet and move on from the people who don't.

King David prayed, "Keep me as the apple of your eye; hide me in the shadow of your wings" (Psalm 17:8, NIV). And centuries later, Jesus responds, "Father, I want these whom you have given me to be with me where I am" (John 17:24).

Wonder	Jesus	Do
Most people struggle to feel seen. Why?	"I could see you under the fig tree before Philip found you" (John 1:48).	Eat an apple; thank Jesus that you're the "apple of his eye."

Pray: Jesus, I want to be where you are, too.

Sleepaway Camp

Read Hebrews 12:18-24

When she was little, my daughter begged to attend a weeklong summer camp in the mountains. She'd never done this before, but more to the point, my wife had never even contemplated the horror of seven straight days away from her. On the surface, she feared for Lucy, but in truth, she was more afraid of what she'd have to endure. Sleepaway camp represented a threat—letting go of Lucy before she was ready.

But our daughter was ready and eager for this experience, and she persisted in a respectful way, so I urged my wife to reconsider her "No." Bev soon admitted that her fears were her problem, not our daughter's. So we dropped Lucy off at camp, where she unrolled her sleeping bag in a huge teepee that she'd share with six strangers (and some very aggressive squirrels) for the rest of the week.

This was a significant rite of passage for our whole family. Lucy let go of her home's moorings to set out into the unknown, and Bev released her into that unknown. Our trust in the face of fear is astonishing—even miraculous. When the ghostly Jesus walks on the water toward his frightened disciples, he is not merely entering into their fear; he's *producing* it. When we draw near to Jesus, we'll discover he's determined to send us to sleepaway camp, where we learn to move through our fear and walk on water to him.

Wonder
What is your equivalent to Jesus sending you to "sleepaway camp"?

Jesus
"Why are you frightened?...Why are your hearts filled with doubt?" (Luke 24:38).

Do
Jesus' name means "God is with us." Pray, substituting "God with me" for Jesus.

Pray: Jesus, I'm grateful you're with me at sleepaway camp.

The Death of Our Spouse

Read Romans 7:1-6

Paul uses marriage as a metaphor to describe the freedom we now enjoy in our relationship with Jesus. So it's important to understand what marriage was like in ancient Jewish culture…

A married woman was bound to her spouse until his death. And Paul reminds us that we are married to "the law of sin and death," and will be until our "spouse" dies. Ah! But when we are "crucified with Christ," that spouse dies with him on the cross. We are then free to "remarry" Jesus and are, therefore, no longer under any obligation to sin—our dead-as-a-doornail ex. This reality first prompts Paul to cry out, "Wretched man that I am (hopelessly married to the law of sin and death)! Who will rescue me?" *Well*, he says, *Jesus has driven a nail through the heart of our abusive spouse…*

We are now free to marry into his family. But like anyone in an abusive relationship, we've so long obeyed sin's demands that we struggle to leave behind old habits. Missionaries to Thailand worked for years to raise enough money to buy a whole village out of slavery to a textile factory, only to watch helplessly as the workers all sold themselves back into slavery. Jesus knows we will likewise descend back into slavery if we are not invited to remarry.

He is waiting for our "I do" at his wedding altar.

Wonder	**Jesus**	**Do**
What habit do I still practice from my "previous marriage"?	"What sorrow awaits the world, because it tempts people to sin" (Matthew 18:7).	Consider wearing a ring signifying your "remarriage."

Pray: Jesus, "I do!"

Jesus and Improv

Read John 6:22-29

The four rules of improvisational comedy also form the backbone of a faithful relationship with Jesus…

1. _Say "yes"_—In an improv context, "yes" means "I'll go in whatever direction you're heading." It's an agreement to play together, a commitment to dive into the pool and get wet.

2. _Say "yes, AND"_—The "AND" means "I'll build a bridge from what you've started into whatever might come next." It's a willingness to step out and walk on water.

3. _There are no mistakes_—Improvisation breaks down when there's no freedom to fail. Jesus treats our mistakes as the raw material for new life, not a dead end.

4. _Pay ridiculous attention to others_—To respond creatively in the moment, improv requires closer-than-normal attention to each other.

Like improv, our faith in Jesus is fueled by risk and trust. He tells a works-obsessed crowd that the only "work" he expects is the "work of belief." And that means saying "yes" to Jesus' invitation into relationship, opening ourselves to trust him with our "and" (whatever comes next), offering him our ugly mistakes as the raw material for something beautiful, and leaning in to pay better attention to what he says and does. Jesus wants real intimacy with us, the kind only an improv relationship produces.

Wonder
What is your "yes, AND" with Jesus today?

Jesus
"Spend your energy seeking the eternal life that [I] can give you" (John 6:27).

Do
Play the Question Game with a friend—each respond _only_ with questions for a minute.

Pray: Jesus, nudge me into what's next.

Playing Music

Read Luke 19:1-10

Richard Dreyfuss won an Oscar for Best Actor playing a high-school music teacher in _Mr. Holland's Opus_. In a pivotal scene, Glenn Holland (Dreyfuss) tells a struggling student, "Playing music is supposed to be fun. It's about heart—it's about feelings and moving people and something beautiful and being alive, and it's not about notes on a page. I can teach you notes on a page, I can't teach you that other stuff."

So, with Jesus, how do we move from "playing the right notes" to "making music" with him? It's the moment when we're learning to ride a bike and we stop white-knuckling the experience and just…ride. Or when that struggling student follows Mr. Holland's advice, closing her eyes to imagine a sunset as she plays, and finally learns to coax something beautiful out of her clarinet. Before my first ministry job in a church, I'd experienced the "music" of my relationship with Jesus on one side of the church wall—the receiver side. But when I crossed over to working in ministry, the experience slowly sapped my joy. I was simply trying too hard to play the right "notes." When we recognize the gravitational pull of "trying harder to be better" we can re-enter into grace, into the emotional beauty of a relationship defined by playing the music, not working at it.

Jesus, like Mr. Holland, is inviting us to play what he can't teach.

Wonder
Ask Jesus, "What's keeping me from relaxing more with you?"

Jesus
"This man has shown himself to be a true son of Abraham" (Luke 19:9).

Do
Online, watch "piano waltz," then "piano jazz improv." Notice the difference.

Pray: Jesus, release me to "play the sunset" with you.

The Fruit of the Vine

Read John 15:1-5

When we "worship in Spirit and in truth," we're essentially "boasting" about Jesus—reflecting back to him the diamond facets of his heart. We boast because there's no one like him…

- He's not just beautiful; he *defines* beauty.

- He's not just fair in his judgments; he *defines* fairness.

- He's not just good in all he does; he *defines* goodness.

When we encounter Jesus as he's revealed in Scripture, not merely as we've been told he is, it's hard to talk about him and not boast. And worship like this leads us to a surprising place—as we proclaim the truth about Jesus, he proclaims the truth about us.

A friend shared something he calls "The Progression" with me: *Get to know Jesus well, because the more you know him, the more you'll love him, and the more you love him, the more you'll want to follow him, and the more you follow him, the more you'll become like him, and the more you become like him, the more you become yourself.*

Is it possible that, right now, Jesus is gazing at you with affection and admiration—the same way a gardener admires the ripened fruit he has labored to grow? It's possible… The fruit of following Jesus, worshipping him in Spirit and truth, is the person you're becoming. And that fruit is enjoyable and tasty and delightful, because it's fed by the life of the Vine, who is Jesus.

Wonder
Like a child, ask Jesus, "What's one thing that delights you about me?"

Jesus
"Those who remain in me, and I in them, will produce much fruit" (John 15:5).

Do
On a bandage, write a word representing Jesus' "delight." Wear it for a day.

Pray: Jesus, I can't stop boasting about you.

First, Five Failures

Read Luke 11:5-10

In seven entries, over the course of two summers (from 1738 and 1739), from the journal of the great 18th-century preacher John Wesley, we taste the fruit of persistence...

- Sunday a.m., May 7, preached in St. Lawrence's, was asked not to come back anymore.
- Sunday p.m., May 7, preached at St. Katherine Cree's church, deacons said, "Get out and stay out."
- Sunday a.m., May 14, preached at St. Ann's, can't go back...
- Sunday afternoon, May 21, preached at St. John's, kicked out.
- Sunday evening, May 21, preached at St. somebody else's, Bennet's maybe. Deacons called special meeting and said I couldn't return.
- Tuesday, May 8, afternoon service, preached in a pasture in Bath, 1,000 people came to hear me.
- Sunday, September 9, preached to 10,000 people three weeks in a row in Moorfields.

Hundreds of thousands met Jesus through Wesley's ministry. But it never would've happened if he'd bowed under the weight of his failures. Failure can bully us into giving up when we're a "hired hand," but not when we own the business. We'll know we are ruined by and ruined for the heart of Jesus when disappointments and rejections seem like minor distractions.

Wonder
What is a failure in your life that is hard to let go of, and why?

Jesus
"Keep on knocking, and the door will be opened to you" (Luke 11:9).

Do
Feel the rhythm of "shameless persistence"—chew on a piece of gum.

Pray: Jesus, use my failures as fertilizer for the fruit you're growing in me.

The Grand Invitation

Read Luke 5:1-11

Steve Jobs, the iconic co-founder of Apple, successfully recruited Pepsi president John Sculley to take over as CEO by asking an upending question: "Do you want to spend the rest of your life selling sugared water, or do you want a chance to change the world?"

And 2,000 years ago, Simon Bar-Jona ("Son of Jona") of Bethsaida is toiling away at his commercial fishing business when Jesus gives him a similar invitation. Simon is tough and driven and street-smart, but he has not yet found his great *why* in life. And then Jesus, uninvited, steps onto his boat. Simon is exhausted and eager to get home, but he's forced to sit through the Master's teaching like a squirming boy at his sister's piano recital. And then, with a hint of mischief, Jesus tells him to toss his net into the vacant ocean…

Jesus intends to surgically expose Simon's buried longing for a transcendent life—the "miracle of the fish" is like a gunshot, dropping him to his knees. When he stands again, the Son of Jona enters into a passion that will soon overshadow everything else in his life, and upend the world. Two promises fuel the leverage of Jesus' invitation: "I will make you," and "fishers of men." The first offers a transforming relationship, the second a transforming purpose—the golden keys to life. These promises require only one prerequisite—"Follow me…"

Wonder	**Jesus**	**Do**
What's the first thing that pops into your head: *What do I want in life?*	"Go out where it is deeper, and let down your nets to catch some fish" (Luke 5:4).	Drip a little soda here— the "sugared water" Jesus invites you to leave behind.

Pray: Jesus, I want the life you want to give me.

Beelining

Read John 6:30-33

When the great Victorian preacher C.H. Spurgeon met with young pastors eager for feedback on their sermons, empathy wasn't his primary consideration. He summed up one young man's "performance" by telling him the sermon was well-prepared and well-delivered, but it nevertheless…stunk. The wincing young pastor asked for an explanation. "Because," said Spurgeon, "there was no Christ in it." The young man said, "Well, Christ was not in the text… We must preach what is in the text."

The old man responded, "Don't you know, young man, that from every town, and every village, and every little hamlet in England…there is a road to London?" The young man nodded. "Ah!" said the old preacher, "And so from every text in Scripture there is a road to the metropolis of the Scriptures, that is Christ. Dear brother, when you get to a text, say, 'Now, what is the road to Christ?' and then preach a sermon, running along the road towards the great metropolis—Christ."

Spurgeon called this "making a beeline to Christ," and Jesus himself practiced it. Responding to a demanding crowd's Old Testament reference, Jesus said, "Moses didn't give you bread from heaven. My Father did. And now he offers you the true bread from heaven." The beeline from Manna leads to Jesus.

Wonder
Pick a random page, then verse, in the Old Testament. What's the "beeline" to Jesus?

Jesus
"If you only knew…you would ask me, and I would give you living water" (John 4:10).

Do
Copy Matthew 15 at biblegateway.com; paste it into a word bubble at Wordle.net.

Pray: Jesus, plant your "beeliner" in my soul so I find you everywhere.

The Heart of Rescue

Read John 12:20-36

In a story Brennan Manning loved to tell, a desperate man is chased by a tiger. Trapped at a cliff's edge, he notices a rope hanging over the side. He scrambles down and is saved, for the moment. Five hundred feet below are jagged rocks; above is a crouched tiger waiting to eat him. It's then he sees two hungry mice gnawing away at the rope.

His doom imminent, the man cries out for rescue. But all looks lost. In that moment, he notices a strawberry growing nearby. He reaches out, plucks it, eats it whole, then cries out, "Yum! This is the most delicious strawberry I've ever had!"

The rescue we crave is not always the rescue we're offered. But Jesus shows up in the strawberry. He gives us a taste of his beauty and his love and his greatness—a taste of himself. And we are redeemed in the *middle* of our fear, not after we've been rescued from it. If we're preoccupied with the dangers all around us, we'll miss the treasure Jesus is offering us right now, the treasure of his strawberry-presence.

The taste of the strawberry makes us want to worship Jesus, not primarily because of what he has done for us but because his goodness somehow drives our predicament into the shadows.

Wonder
Ask Jesus, "What's a 'strawberry' you're offering me right now?"

Jesus
"Put your trust in the light while there is still time" (John 12:36).

Do
Leave a "strawberry" voicemail for a friend who's hanging off a cliff.

Pray: Jesus, I need a big bite of your strawberry presence in my life.

Breathing Jesus

Read John 8:31-45

Take a deep breath—it's like hitting the space-bar on your soul's keyboard. Do it again, then exhale… The room is now filled with your internal perfume. Our inhale/exhale rhythm is autonomic; we understandably take it for granted. But it's one of the most intimate things we do. We're inviting something into our depths— we breathe in life and breathe out death.

Twenty years ago my wife breathed in an "environmental trigger" that set off a lung disease called sarcoidosis—now she wears a mask to do yardwork, can't go outside when there's smoke in the air, and self-quarantined during the pandemic. Because most of us take breathing for granted, we don't evaluate the air we breathe. But toxins in the air not only harm our breathing but also can be deadly. In Moscow alone, more than 5,000 Russians die every year from direct exposure to air pollution. If you know the air you breathe could kill you, you pay much better attention to it.

The same is true with the "air" we're inviting into our souls. We "breathe in" what others think about us—our friends and our enemies are all generating "good air" or "bad air" around us. Think about how hard it would be for you if you lived in Moscow, watching your kids breathe in poisons. Likewise, Jesus longs for us to breathe in the truth—the truth about who he is, and the truth about who we are.

Wonder
What are some "soul pollutants" you're breathing in right now?

Jesus
"If the Son sets you free, you are truly free" (John 8:36).

Do
Take in a deep breath, hold it, thank Jesus, then exhale your "toxins."

Pray: Jesus, I want to breathe you in, over and over.

Jesus the Dream-Keeper

Read Matthew 6:24-34

All of us have dreams, but we're often our own worst dream-killers. We quit too soon. We get distracted. We procrastinate. We make excuses. Business journalists have studied why some people pursue their dreams and achieve success while others don't. Among other factors, they discovered three catalysts...

1) *Make sure the dream you're following is your dream.* If you're pursuing someone else's dream for your life, you won't sustain enthusiasm for it.

2) *Invest time and effort.* Dreams require us to develop new skills. It's work. And work is central to God's personality—he worked for six "days" creating our physical reality, then rested from his work. Because we are created in his image, working toward a dream is a sacred reflection.

3) *Focus, yet stay flexible.* People who persist in pursuing their dreams are realistic, but they are not derailed by challenges. That's because their dream is more of an extension of their God-given identity than the fruit of discipline.

Jesus promises to fulfill a dream that will give us "everything we need," but with a prerequisite: "Seek the Kingdom of God above all else." When we are infected by his heart, we develop a passion for his way of life, fueling our pursuit of it and riveting our attention on him as we depend on his Spirit to guide us.

Wonder	**Jesus**	**Do**
Ask Jesus, "What's a dream you want me to pursue?"	"Seek the Kingdom... and he will give you everything you need" (Matthew 6:33).	Describe a dream in the Google Images search box. Post a visual reminder.

Pray: Jesus, show me the dreams you have for me so I can embrace them.

Jesus Breathes on Us

Read John 20:19-23

After the horror on Golgotha, the disciples hunker down behind
locked doors, afraid the Jewish leaders who executed Jesus will
find and kill them, too. Fear and confusion hang in the air, and
then the resurrected Jesus enters the room, proclaiming peace.
But it's one thing to speak words of peace to your panicked
friends; it's another to *breathe* peace into them…

Like the disciples, we suspect we don't have what we need to
face the challenges we can't escape. More than anything, we need
the Spirit of Jesus in our nostrils and in our lungs. Ransomed
Heart founder John Eldredge says our great temptation in
life is the urge to simply "make things happen"—behind our
own locked doors, we live in the tension between our own
responsibility and God's movement. I asked an older, wiser friend
how he has learned to navigate this tension, and he burst out
laughing. After a pause and a wink, he responded, simply, "Amos
5:4: Seek God and live."

Our peace is not dependent on our outcomes; it's tied to our
intimacy. When Jesus enters into our locked-door refuge, he's not
demanding better production from us; he's a Lover who wants us
to come to bed. When the air we breathe is the breath of Jesus,
we find the courage to leave our hiding place, because our hiding
place is already inside us.

Wonder	**Jesus**	**Do**
How do you know when to "make it happen" or when to trust God to do it?	"As the Father has sent me, so I am sending you" (John 20:21).	Brush your teeth, then blow into your hand and inhale—a fresh intake of Jesus.

Pray: Jesus, I want to feel your breath on me.

Jesus Into the Chaos

Read John 1:1-5

It's easy to forget what every "new beginning" feels like...
It's easy to forget the chaos we left behind to follow Jesus...
It's easy to forget what our lives would be like apart from him...
It's easy to forget the chaos that existed in the world before God
"moved into the neighborhood" (John 1:14, *The Message*)...

It's all easy to forget, because we're human beings, and
forgetting is our special talent.

One thing we do remember, especially when we're
overwhelmed by all that's expected of us, is that we often
don't know what we're doing. When we try to sort out all
that's happening in the world, and in our own lives, it can
feel overwhelming. We say we're living in "uncertain times,"
and we say that because we've always craved certainty in our
uncertainty. We feel buffeted by the torrent of the culture we
live in.

In the beginning, we know, "The earth was formless and empty,
and darkness covered the deep waters..." But into that chaos
came Jesus bringing order and meaning: "God created everything
through him, and nothing was created except through him." The
light that Jesus brings into our darkness is the order he creates
out of our chaos—from paint splattered on canvas to a reworked
masterpiece. Jesus treats our uncertainty as the raw material for
the art he is unveiling in us.

Wonder
What feels chaotic and
uncertain in your life
right now?

Jesus
"The angels of God [will
be] going up and down
on the Son of Man"
(John 1:51).

Do
Honor the work of
Jesus; spend five
minutes ordering the
chaos on your desk.

Pray: Jesus, my heart is often full of chaos—I invite you to bring order to it.

Jesus Into Disorientation

Read Matthew 27:45-54

The Light of the World barrels into humanity at a dark time…

- The Roman occupation of Israel (63 B.C.) is the last in a long line of invasions beginning with the Babylonians (539 B.C.). By Jesus' birth, the Jews have endured more than half a millennium of occupation and oppression and slavery.

- The Romans install a two-tiered system of government— Roman overseers and collaborating Jewish leaders who exercise control in the name of Rome. This political system creates tremendous cultural tension between the rebel "Zealots" and the Roman-sympathizing "betrayers."

- The shadow of poverty, brutality, oppression, scarcity of resources, overpopulation, and rampant sickness and disease hangs over everyday life… Darkness.

We've swallowed a little darkness ourselves. Maybe you're in a season of darkness now. Maybe you're sick of knowing what you know about yourself—you're craving the light "as a deer longs for streams of water" (Psalm 42:1). Darkness is disorienting. Our path is barely clear in the day, let alone at night. We crave light…

At noon, as Jesus wrestles death on the cross, the world goes dark for three hours. Light dims as life leaks out of Jesus. And the Temple veil is torn and "godly men and women" buried in the cemetery walk into Jerusalem, alive. Light and life return to assault the darkness. The sun rises when the Son rises…

Wonder	**Jesus**	**Do**
What's something in your life, in the last year, that feels disorienting?	"My God, my God, why have you abandoned me?" (Matthew 27:46).	Close your eyes and turn your face to the sun. What does it feel like?

Pray: Jesus, I need your "sunrise" in my life.

Inattentional Blindness

Read John 12:37-50

In the viral YouTube video "An Awareness Test," two basketball teams (one dressed in white, the other in black) pass around two balls in a quickly moving circle. A narrator asks, "How many passes does the team in white make?" The answer is 13. But then a surprise question, "Did you see the moonwalking bear?" The video rewinds to reveal a person in a full-size bear suit moonwalking through the middle of the frame, followed by "It's easy to miss something you're not looking for."

"Inattentional blindness" is the neurological explanation for this visual sleight-of-hand. When we're asked to perform a challenging task, we block what seems "extraneous." It's the reason we can't see the huge moonwalking bear in plain sight.

And "inattentional blindness" impacts our relationship with Jesus as well—we're distracted by so many "try harder to get better" messages that we block out the huge moonwalking Jesus-bear in the room. We don't see him because we're trying so hard to get all the rules and regulations right. And seeing him is really the point—over the din of a raucous crowd, Jesus cries, "When you see me, you are seeing the one who sent me. I have come as a light to shine in this dark world, so that all who put their trust in me will no longer remain in the dark" (John 12:45-46).

The more we see him, the deeper we trust him.

Wonder
Pay attention to Jesus in today's reading. What do you see in his heart?

Jesus
"If you trust me, you are trusting not only me, but also God who sent me" (John 12:44).

Do
Plug "awareness test" into the youtube.com search box and watch a video.

Pray: Jesus, my life is a jungle of distractions. Rivet my attention on you.

Redemptive Plot Twists

Read Matthew 9:18-26

What's on your list of films you've seen more than once? A few of my not-so-secret obsessions: *White Christmas* (at least 30); *The Lord of the Rings* (at least 10); *The Way, Way Back* (at least 10); *Dan in Real Life* (at least eight); and *Anne of Green Gables* (at least five). Quite a disparate list, except they all share one important characteristic—every one of these films highlights a redemptive plot twist.

- In *The Way, Way Back,* a broken teenager discovers the redemptive power of community, of belonging, of adults who will fight for him.
- In *Anne of Green Gables,* an orphaned and abused girl finally finds redemption in a "bosom" family.
- In *White Christmas,* two lonely performers overcome judgment and misunderstanding to find redemption in their love for one another.

All the best stories include redemptive plot twists. An old Hassidic adage captures it: "God invented man because he loves [redemptive] stories." We can't resist redemption stories—even cheesy ones. Their magnetic pull reveals something about the heart of God. And when we open our own story to Jesus, inviting him to co-write it with us, he uses the chaotic twists and turns in our narrative as "plot devices" that serve a redemptive purpose. And then we carry that plot twist into all our relationships.

Wonder
What makes a story compelling enough to watch it more than once?

Jesus
"Daughter, be encouraged! Your faith has made you well" (Matthew 9:22).

Do
Watch one of your favorite holiday films for a "Christmas in July" celebration.

Pray: Jesus, I'm ready for a redemptive plot twist in my life.

Actions > Words

Read John 6:1-14

What we say always has less power than what we do. Jesus lived this truth—so I created an alternate version of the "Feeding of the Five Thousand" in John 6 that highlights the primacy of his *doing*. After he asks Philip where they can buy bread to feed the massive crowd gathered on the mountainside, Andrew offers up the five loaves and two fish a little boy has brought…

Then Jesus took the loaves, gave thanks to God, and said, "I have great compassion for you. As I hold this bread high, if you will repeat to yourself, over and over 'Jesus fills me up, Jesus fills me up,' then you will forget that you are hungry." The people looked at each other with raised eyebrows. But Jesus said to his disciples, "Save this bread for later—we'll snack on it after they're gone." So they gathered them up and filled their pockets with fragments from the five barley loaves. When the people understood what Jesus had just done, they said, "Surely he is the fast-talker we have been dreading!"

We know that a Jesus who talks big but acts small is no Jesus at all… "The Word became flesh and dwelt among us" because our redemption required *doing*. Edwin Friedman says, "The colossal misunderstanding of our time is the assumption that insight will work with people who are unmotivated to change… People can only hear you when they are moving toward you, and they are not likely to when your words are pursuing them."

Wonder
Do others experience you more as a talker or a doer?

Jesus
"Tell everyone to sit down" (John 6:10).

Do
For a week, serve someone with one "secret act of love" every day.

Pray: Jesus, I want to live large and pontificate little.

Ugly Into Beauty

Read Mark 12:41-44

I was leading a planning meeting for a national conference when I got a panicked call from my wife. A disturbed student with a shotgun had entered my daughter Lucy's high school through a little-used door, killed an innocent classmate, and was now stalking the halls. Lucy was in the cafeteria, not in a locked-down classroom, so she had to run for her life. She hunkered down in the back of a counselor's office with a dozen students and waited for the S.W.A.T. team to rescue them. A resource officer cornered the shooter in the school library, where he took his own life.

Trauma is ugly. Now my daughter and hundreds of her friends and teachers suffer from PTSD. Sudden loud noises, especially at night, set off a chain reaction of crippling fear. Yes, Jesus makes small things into big things and ugly things into beautiful things—he treats the widow's *nothing* like it's a fortune. But where is the ugly-into-beauty in Lucy's story, and in our own lingering traumas?

Silver linings frame the darkness; they don't eclipse it. And we crave more than that. So Jesus treats our darkness like rich soil, planting seeds of light in the plowed field of our trauma. Up from the furrows grows a crop he will later harvest. Beauty will rise from the ashes, like seedlings through the blackened ground after a forest fire. So we offer our trauma to him, just as the widow offers "everything she has to live on."

Wonder
How has Jesus reworked ordinary into extraordinary in your life?

Jesus
"I tell you the truth, this poor widow has given more than all the others" (Mark 12:43).

Do
Play "Weightless" (Marconi Union) on youtube.com—a trauma-reducing song.

Pray: Jesus, like the poor widow, all I have to offer you is my trauma.

The Jesus Who Uproots

Read Matthew 13:24-30

Jesus loved to tell stories, because story is the music playing in the background of our soul. We live inside the stories we tell ourselves. And that's why Jesus is still telling stories today. Right now he's weaving his story into our story and (even more amazing) inviting us to weave our story into his. He will take the raw moments of our lives and orchestrate an aria. But, he tells us, we also have an enemy who plants toxic lies in our story—weeds that can choke out the life struggling to find the sun.

In the cautionary Parable of the Wheat and the Weeds, a man plants good seed in his field, but late at night an enemy secretly sows weeds. Rather than have his workers pull up the weeds, the man insists on waiting until the wheat is ready to harvest, when it can be separated and bundled without harm. This is a picture of our hearts—good things and bad things grow together. And the weeds are telling a story…

"You'll never amount to anything."

"Your performance is more important than who you are."

"You're damaged goods; no one will ever really want you."

"People will always disappoint you; don't open yourself to them."

The hard things that happen to us can morph into toxic parables. Jesus wants to uproot them, but he will be patient about it. He understands that goodness is growing right next to them.

Wonder
Ask Jesus, "What is a 'weed' growing in my heart?"

Jesus
"First gather up the tares…to burn… but gather the wheat into my barn" (Matthew 13:30, NASB).

Do
Go through your refrigerator and throw out expired food—"weeds."

Pray: Jesus, thank you for your kind and patient weed-pulling.

Jesus and Fear

Read Luke 1:67-75

Jesus is no stranger to fear—he's born into fear (Herod's "slaughter of the innocents") and executed on Golgotha in a climate of fear. In between these fixed points, Jesus' ministry is marked by fear...

- The common response to his miracles and healings and exorcisms is fear.

- The common response to his teaching among the religious elite and (often) the mystified crowds is fear.

- And the common reality for his followers is fear; the things he says and does put their lives in constant jeopardy.

Jesus reminds his disciples that even as the enemy of God closes in on him with murderous intent ("the ruler of the world is coming"), he does not feel leveraged by the threat ("he has nothing in me"). Fear has no traction in him because he has nothing to lose. Trouble is, the rest of us are well aware of what we have to lose. And so we are gripped by fear. The neutralizer is counterintuitive—we face down smaller fears when we face up to a bigger fear. The specter of a minor financial setback dissolves in the face of a cancer diagnosis. It's the *weight* of the fear that recalibrates our reality. And Jesus wants to be the heaviest weight in our universe—so big that all our lesser fears lose their traction, and in "the shadow of his wings" (Psalm 17:8) we discover our safest refuge.

Wonder	**Jesus**	**Do**
What are you most afraid of in life, and why?	"Don't [fear] those who want to kill your body; they cannot touch your soul" (Matthew 10:28).	Deeply inhale vanilla extract—it actually reduces stress and fear.

Pray: Jesus, fear is chasing me down; I need the safety of your heart.

God's Fingerprints

Read Matthew 7:15-20

I once asked a group of ministry leaders to find clues to a mystery person's identity scattered around our meeting room. I told them I'd hidden these clues in plain sight hours before and that the mystery person was someone they all knew. I formed teams, then gave them their mission: *Find as many clues as you can in 60 seconds and then, together, guess the identity of the mystery person.* A few teams deciphered their found "artifacts" and guessed right: It was SpongeBob Squarepants.

I said, "These clues were right here, all around us, for hours—but if I hadn't challenged you to find them, then think about who fit the characteristics revealed by the clues, you would never have noticed them. Jesus has done something similar in our world—he has hidden clues to what he's really like all around us. But we have to chew on what we find to discover him."

If the building blocks for all of creation are "mined" from Jesus himself (in John 1, "God created everything through him, and nothing was created except through him"), then our biology and zoology and geography offer us clues to his identity. Eugene Peterson's reinterpretation of Romans 1:19-20 helps: "By taking a long and thoughtful look at what God has created, people have always been able to see what their eyes as such can't see: eternal power, for instance, and the mystery of his divine being."

Wonder
What's Jesus' strategic purpose in hiding clues to his character and personality in creation?

Jesus
"A good tree produces good fruit, and a bad tree produces bad fruit" (Matthew 7:17).

Do
Pluck a leaf from a tree you see every day; press it between these pages.

Pray: Jesus, open my eyes/ears/nose to "the mystery of your divine being."

Ultra Running

Read 1 Corinthians 9:22-27

My friend is in addiction recovery. He's also an "ultra trail-runner," competing in 50- or 100-mile races on steep mountain trails. So I asked him a question about distance running that was really about recovery: "Let's say you're on mile 43 of a 50-mile trail run. What are the challenges you're facing emotionally, mentally, and spiritually?" Here's how he answered:

This last weekend I helped pace a buddy through his 100-mile trail race—it took him 31½ hours to finish. In the final stages of the race, life is very basic: Am I eating? Am I drinking? How does my knee feel? Can I run this section instead of walk? Your mind is blank because you're so hyper-focused on moving one foot in front of the other.

If you aren't careful, the lows in this phase can spiral into the lowest you've ever experienced. So you keep your lows as high as possible. That's why we rely on a pacer. I never stopped talking when I was with him. We use a lot of humor. And we are ALWAYS feeding him—calories recharge the brain and the legs.

Jesus has highlighted many parallels between ultra and recovery for me: 1) Your only goal is don't move backward, 2) You must have a team, 3) You must train your heart and mind, and 4) It's a lifestyle.

Wonder
How has Jesus "paced" you through your most difficult challenges?

Jesus
"[Because you've persevered], I will protect you from the great time of testing" (Revelation 3:10-11).

Do
How long can you hold your breath, alone and then with a friend encouraging you?

Pray: Jesus, life often feels like an ultra challenge—be my pacer.

Get the Poison Out

Read John 4:1-30

More than five million people a year suffer a snakebite—a hundred thousand die from it. An old (now debunked) Army medical manual instructs soldiers to cut an X over the fang marks and suck out the poison. But the venom spreads way too quickly for this method to work. The victim needs antivenom at a hospital. Self-care is not a viable option—the victim needs emergency help from a doctor who has antivenom medicine.

When Jesus meets a broken and shunned woman outside the walled city of Sychar, he sees she's been snakebit by a history of wrecked relationships and sin. She's going to die from the damage, and self-care will not neutralize the poison. She ventures out to the city's well in the middle of the day, when the hot sun beats down on the cracked earth, to draw water. She's there long after others have come and gone because shame-venom runs deep in her—she's had five husbands already and is living with the "next man up." The "living water" Jesus offers her is the antivenom she needs, but she must invite the treatment. He won't force it. Likewise, we won't give him permission to heal us if we don't first admit the truth about our "snakebite."

We cannot suck the poison out of our veins; we need a Doctor with the right antivenom. When Jesus proclaims to the woman, "I am the Messiah!" he means "I have the medicine you need."

Wonder
In what ways do you feel "snakebit" in life?

Jesus
"[The water I give] will become...a well of water springing up to eternal life" (John 4:14, NASB).

Do
Feel the snakebite— push two fingernails into your forearm; invite his help.

Pray: Jesus, I've been banking on self-care for too long; I need you.

Our Three-Stage Rocket

Read John 10:1-16

The Saturn V rocket was NASA's Apollo workhorse between 1966 and 1973. It was a three-stage liquid-fueled launch vehicle developed for "human exploration of the moon." It was launched 13 times from the Kennedy Space Center in Florida and remains the tallest, heaviest, and most powerful rocket ever to lift off into space. For 50 years, only the Saturn V has been capable of transporting human "cargo" beyond low Earth orbit.

Imagine "Christian maturity" as the payload on that rocket—it will take three "burn" stages to achieve close orbit around Jesus. The first stage is childhood, the second is young adulthood, and the third is adulthood. The "thrusters" in these three stages—the powerful relationships and experiences Jesus brings into our lives—are necessary to propel our story toward him and against the "downward drag" of the world's "atmosphere."

Jesus tells his friends, "The world would love you as one of its own if you belonged to it, but you are no longer part of the world. I chose you to come out of the world, so it hates you" (John 15:19). In Saturn V language, he's warning that the world's "gravity"—*find your own happiness, chart your own course, do whatever it takes to succeed, trust yourself above all else*—has a "dragging" effect on our path toward him. We need a powerful launch vehicle, and Jesus says, "I am the way, the truth, and the life" (John 14:6).

Wonder	**Jesus**	**Do**
What have been the "thrusters" in your three stages of life with Jesus?	"I will not abandon you as orphans—I will come to you" (John 14:18).	Put a coin ("the world") inside a balloon, blow it up, and drop it. Notice the "gravity drag."

Pray: Jesus, I need the power of your "thrusters" every day.

Happiness or Significance?

Read Luke 19:41-44

This notice appeared in a church bulletin: "Finding Happiness Where You Least Expect—a five-week small group where you get to know others while learning some key practices for experiencing greater levels of happiness." The pot of gold at the end of this five-week rainbow holds a seductive power over us—*you can finally find the happiness you deserve.* The U.S. Declaration of Independence embeds the seeds of this entitlement: "[We are] endowed by [our] Creator with certain unalienable Rights, that among these are Life, Liberty and the pursuit of Happiness." But is the pursuit of "greater levels of happiness" the point of our lives?

In an interview with late-night TV host Stephen Colbert, actress Jada Pinkett-Smith says, "I really thought happiness had a lot to do with pleasure. [But] I realized happiness is about peace. And I'm the most peaceful I've ever been in life." We know from experience that the pursuit of pleasure can't deliver lasting happiness, but how do we find the peace Pinkett-Smith says she's discovered? In the kingdom of God Jesus came to reveal, peace is not tied to our psychology or our success or even our relationships… That pot of gold is buried in the heart of Jesus, who wept as he told the crowds, "How I wish today that you of all people would understand the way to peace. But now it is too late, and peace is hidden from your eyes…because you did not recognize it when God visited you."

Wonder
What's something you thought would bring you happiness but didn't?

Jesus
"If they kept quiet, the stones along the road would burst into cheers!" (Luke 19:40).

Do
Find "Child Laughing" on freesound.org– play the sound of peace.

Pray: Jesus, open my blind eyes to you, the source of my peace.

Jesus the Chiropractor

Read Matthew 5:21-42

In chiropractor-speak, a "subluxation" is a misalignment in the spine. A subluxation in our vertebrae compromises the nervous system's normal functioning, the same way a clogged carburetor leads to a sputtering engine. And a "sputtering" spinal column leads to back and neck pain, headaches, and difficulty moving.

Chiropractors speak a kind of heresy: *Instead of medicating the problem, most conditions can be treated by simply fixing the subluxation that caused it in the first place.*

To do that, a chiropractor targets the misalignment, then applies force to that exact location. The out-of-whack problem in the spine gets…whacked. Forced back into alignment. Subluxations in our spine can teach us something about the way God targets the subluxations in our soul—the degenerative "misalignments" that keep us from functioning as Jesus intended. We are anxious, greedy, and self-centered because our souls are misaligned. But Jesus knows just where to apply the right force at the right time to our souls' subluxations. Early in his ministry, he applies a little forceful chiropractic to some common soul misalignments—anger, lust, false promises, and revenge. He's challenging what we've heard is true (the subluxation) with what he knows is true (a forceful realignment). When we submit to the truth, we experience "normal functioning" again.

Wonder	**Jesus**	**Do**
Ask Jesus, "What's a subluxation in my soul that's hurting me right now?"	"Just say a simple, 'Yes, I will,' or 'No, I won't' " (Matthew 5:37).	Kneel in the "child's pose," shifting your weight back. Feel the misalignments "pop."

Pray: Jesus, I give myself to you vulnerably, open to your adjustments.

What Does Jesus Want?

Read Matthew 15:1-20

The WWJD movement is rooted in the premise of Charles Sheldon's book *In His Steps: What Would Jesus Do?* Sheldon, a late 19th-century pastor in Topeka, Kansas, decided to write a serialized story to attract more people to his Sunday night services. He produced one chapter a week, following a diverse collection of characters who were all attempting to live exactly as Jesus lived. At the end of his series, a publisher produced a 10-cent paperback version of the story, which sold more than 100,000 copies in just a few weeks. It's since gone on to sell more than 50 million copies, making it one of the bestselling books of all time.

Sheldon's narrative experiment was an attempt to bring Jesus out of the theoretical and into the real world. But the core of the idea missed a fundamental flaw: Our guesses about "what Jesus would do" are wholly dependent on how deeply we know his heart. A shallow understanding of him leads to shallow WWJD answers. So instead of WWJD, it might be more useful to pursue WDJW—What Does Jesus Want? In a WWJD mindset, we're attempting to mimic the ideas and behaviors of Jesus in disparate circumstances. The unintended consequence is our doomed attempt to *copy his behavior* instead of pursuing, then trusting the beating heart of his Spirit, who lives inside us.

Wonder
As you move through today's reading, ask Jesus, "What do you want?"

Jesus
"You are defiled by the words that come out of your mouth" (Matthew 15:11).

Do
When you pray, cup your hands and hold your "wants" up to Jesus.

Pray: Jesus, I want to know what you want before I guess what you'd do.

Dirty Hair

Read Luke 7:36-50

A woman known to be a prostitute crashes a high-society party when she learns Jesus will be there—she's driven by regret and hoping for grace as she weeps over Jesus' feet, bathing them in perfume and wet kisses. The gathered snoots are fuming over this profane intrusion. But Jesus tells his host, Simon the Pharisee, that the woman's sins ("and they are many") are forgiven, because…

- she recognizes the great debt of sin she's racked up, and

- she is overwhelmed by the rescue of Jesus' grace—like a person snatched from the teeth of a shark.

She cleans his feet, and he cleans her heart by forgiving her. But we overlook a shocking oversight that Jesus himself points out—though he is supposedly an honored guest, Simon has not offered him a basic kindness. Jesus' feet are dirty, and Simon withholds from him the respect reflexively offered to his peers and treats him as a commoner, not a king. And so a "dirty" woman makes up for this slight by wiping away his dirt with her own hair. She exchanges her dirt for his.

When we see our soul as bankrupt and dirty, and we encounter Jesus as he really is, we want to draw so near that his dirt transfers to us. We're consumed by gratefulness because he has satisfied our "creditors" and restored our souls' fortune to us.

Wonder	**Jesus**	**Do**
In what area of your life do you feel "dirty," and why?	"A person who is forgiven little shows only little love" (Luke 7:47).	Fill a large bowl with warm water and steeped peppermint tea. Soak your feet.

Pray: Jesus, I don't have perfume to anoint your feet, but I do have tears.

The Lever of Desperation

Read Mark 9:14-29

In a voicemail left on the Satanic Prayer Line, originally set up as a joke by an atheist, a desperate girl pleads for help:

Hi, guys. I'm a teenager, and I am really in a sticky situation. I need you guys to pray that—well, I think I'm pregnant. And I need you guys to pray against the pregnancy. And if there is a baby inside of me, for Satan to kill it. Because I can't have a baby right now. So I'm turning to Satan, and he is the only answer I have right now. So thank you so much. Hail Satan...

Desperation drives us to say things and do things we'd never say or do if we weren't so...desperate. When our future smells like doom and our present feels like the compacting walls of the garbage chute in that scene from *Star Wars*, we'll trust anything we can grab on to. This is why a desperate man brings his foaming-at-the-mouth demon-possessed son to Jesus, pleading, "Have mercy on us and help us, if you can." And Jesus responds, "What do you mean, 'If I can'?...Anything is possible if a person believes." And the panicked father cries, "I do believe, but help me overcome my unbelief!"

Jesus is not one more roll of the ball on the roulette wheel of blind hope. *What* and *who* we turn to in our desperation is paramount. Faith is not a commodity; it's a savvy investment.

Wonder
When you feel desperate, what is your "kneejerk" reaction?

Jesus
"I command you to come out of this child and never enter him again!" (Mark 9:25).

Do
Call the Satanic Prayer Line (601-2-SATAN-2); leave a message from Jesus.

Pray: Jesus, my help comes from you! (Psalm 121:2)

Convinced

Read Romans 8:31-39

In 2004 Ukrainian presidential candidate Victor Yushchenko survived a disfiguring attack and a mysterious poisoning and won the top office. But the ruling party vehemently opposed him, so state-run television falsely reported that "the challenger Victor Yushchenko has been decisively defeated." In a tiny screen in the lower right corner, a woman named Natalia Dmitruk was supposed to translate the "official" announcement for the deaf community. But instead, she signed, "They are lying and I'm ashamed to translate those lies. Yushchenko is our president."

From that small act of rebellion, the deaf community started a texting campaign, spreading Dmitruk's courageous defiance, sparking the "Orange Revolution." Millions of Ukrainians demanded a new election, and Yushchenko eventually became president. Dmitruk and Yushchenko risked their lives because they were utterly convinced of their cause.

We assume it's our actions that define us as disciples. But the dictionary definition of *disciple* tosses a curveball: "a convinced adherent of a school or individual…" Here, the weight of the convincing is on the "Other," not us. It's *Jesus' heart* that convinces—a disciple is one who has tasted and tested that heart experientially and has come away convinced. When Jesus asks Peter if he's going to reject him like so many others already have, Peter says, "Lord, to whom would we go?" It's our *knowing*, more than our *proving*, that makes us disciples.

Wonder
What's an example of something you're "utterly convinced" by?

Jesus
"The Spirit alone gives eternal life. Human effort accomplishes nothing" (John 6:63).

Do
Eat with your eyes closed. What convinces you that you can do it?

Pray: Jesus, I am a "convinced adherent"—I love you.

Jesus Scattergories

Read Matthew 12:1-8

Scattergories is a creative-thinking, category-based game. The objective is to score points by naming unique objects within a set of categories, all beginning with a random letter, within a time limit. The more things on your list that are not on others' lists, the more points you get. I created my own version of this game I call "Jesus Scattergories." To play it, I assign teams a chapter from one of the four Gospels, then give them five minutes to list as many descriptions of Jesus' heart as they can, based only on that chapter. They're looking for unique nuances that others might miss.

Then each team quickly reads their list of descriptions. Every description that also appears on another team's list is crossed off both lists. Whatever remains is their final score. The team with the highest score wins. These are the Jesus descriptions some friends plucked out of Matthew 12, in "word art" form:

Wonder

From today's reading, what's a descriptive word for Jesus' heart?

Jesus

"There is one here who is even greater than the Temple!" (Matthew 12:6).

Do

Play "Jesus Scattergories" with a few friends or in your small group.

Pray: Jesus, your heart is unique. Let me count the words.

A Lost Saturday

Read Matthew 6:25-34

The poet Robert Burns wrote, "The best laid schemes of mice and men often go awry." *Yes, yes they do.* On a day that begins with quiet time, a workout, and then lunch, control masquerades as peace. Then my parents call and announce they're coming over—I ask them to wait because two 9-year-olds are about to turn our kitchen into a chaotic mess. I hear my daughter Emma counting in the other room—21, 22, 23, 24… *Me:* "What are you counting?" *Her:* "The number of times the neighbor's dog peed on our carpet!" Umm… I call our friends to retrieve their dog and discover my parents at the door, smiling and oblivious. Then a sheepish Emma tells me she has knocked over a plant, spilling "a little" dirt. But it's a *lot* of dirt. And, also, her gumball machine has shattered, scattering glass shards all over her dirt-covered room. In the hallway our dog is throwing up.

My wife takes the dog outside for a walk, but a fast-moving thunderstorm chases her home, soaking wet—we throw the dog in the sink. Then I notice our clogged gutters gushing water onto the porch. I clear the blockage, but the storm has knocked out our internet. And then the dog shakes bathwater into my coffee—the last straw on a terrible day… When we can't control our circumstances, we see how much they control us. Control is a brutal taskmaster; like all false idols, Jesus intends to expose it, then free us from it.

Wonder
Are you a low-control, medium-control, or high-control person?

Jesus
"Can all your worries add a single moment to your life?" (Matthew 6:27).

Do
Pray with clasped fingers. As you release each finger, give over more control.

Pray: Jesus, be my eye in the hurricane.

Antifragile

Read John 15:1-8

We know "resilience" is a necessary strength, but we've done little to help our children develop it—they're less resilient than ever. Among U.S. teenagers, anxiety disorders and depression are way up. And colleges face a shortage of therapists; they can't hire fast enough to keep up with the demand. So what's gone wrong?

Nassim Taleb, a professor of "risk engineering" and bestselling author of *The Black Swan*, invented the word *antifragile* to describe systems that benefit from persistent stressors (bones, for example, get stronger when they're under stress). To develop an antifragile immune system, children need exposure to germs and allergens. If they're kept from these stressors, they can't fight off bigger challenges down the road.

Our souls are a lot like our immune systems—they must have exposure to stress to develop in a healthy way. That's why parents who overprotect their children from social and emotional hardships are actually sabotaging their future ability to persevere through the devastations that are sure to come.

All of us need regular doses of soul-stress, as long as we're attached to replenishing sources of unconditional love. This is why Jesus reveals he intends to "prune" us (to introduce pain for the purpose of greater growth) in the context of a deep, loving attachment to him (the branch that "remains" in the Vine).

Wonder	**Jesus**	**Do**
How "antifragile" was the home you grew up in? What impact did it have?	"A [pruned] branch cannot produce fruit if it is severed from the vine" (John 15:4).	Face down, propped only by your forearms and toes, feel the stress on your core.

Pray: Jesus, be the gatekeeper for hardship in my life.

Leaning Into Fear

Read Matthew 8:23-27

On a private Facebook page for listeners of the podcast I host (Paying Ridiculous Attention to Jesus), a longtime member shared this story:

Today at the water park, I got to see the rewards of risk firsthand. My daughter is 7—she has been on all but the biggest water slide at the park. So this morning I told her we're going on that slide. I didn't placate or beg—I just told her she would. The whole way up, she whimpered and prayed. And I told her, "You are strong, you are brave—bravery is not the absence of fear; it's being afraid and doing it anyway." I told her I was afraid the first time I ever rode that slide.

And then I told her I was with her, that I would not leave her. The people around her offered encouragement also. And she did it. She had the biggest smile on her face as she shot out of that slide. My goal is to develop "spiritual grit" in her; to encourage her to do things even though she's afraid. I've asked Jesus to help me teach my children that fear is for facing, not running from. Jesus knows that facing our fears is the best path forward. But, like my daughter, we typically avoid and whine. But when the ride is through we're no longer afraid.

He strips us of our crutches—in the end his love is bigger than our fear.

Wonder	**Jesus**	**Do**
What has been the fruit of facing, not running from, fear in your life?	"Follow me now. Let the spiritually dead bury their own dead" (Matthew 8:22).	Lean into a tiny fear—say something, risk something, cook something.

Pray: Jesus, I have my own big water slide in front of me. Nudge me.

The Jesus Zoom

Read Luke 15:1-6

Google Earth can give us a space view of Earth, then zoom down to our continent and then to our street and our home and even the salesman at our front door. It's a visual metaphor for the way Jesus "shepherds" us. He sees the meadow, the flock, and then the one sheep struggling to break free from the brambles. Jesus does not have "Love [your name]" on his job description. It's not *work* to love you; it's more like play. His heart overflows with affection for you, for the hairs on your head—another way of saying "all the small things that make up the big thing that is you."

To us, a herd of sheep is a singular block; we miss distinctions because they all look the same to us. But not to a Shepherd who will lay down his life for them. What is the beauty he cherishes about you? Why does he risk to pursue and bring you back to him? His passion is rooted in a lifetime of studying you—not to convict you or to point out your flaws, but to cherish the little details that make you…you. What if the little things no one else notices about you are exactly the quirks he loves the most?

"If a man has a hundred sheep and one of them gets lost, what will he do?" Well, he'll do what Jesus does—risk everything to go after that little lost sheep.

Wonder	**Jesus**	**Do**
What's a quirk about you most people seem to misunderstand, and why?	"Rejoice with me because I have found my lost sheep" (Luke 15:6).	Pluck one of your hairs. See, smell, touch, and even taste it. What do you notice?

Pray: Jesus, I feel alone and overlooked sometimes. Please find me.

Fighting the Project

Read Mark 6:45-52

In the "Great Recession" more families lost their homes and jobs than any generation since the 1930s. Financial disaster picked off millions of people like a sniper, dropping them to their knees. And a decade later the Covid-19 pandemic would hit *repeat* on this misery. During the 2008 meltdown, the public radio show *Marketplace* teased a story about financially ruined Californians returning to church with this: "When all else fails, there's faith."

In other words, once you've exhausted all your own resources, you may be desperate enough to try anything, no matter how silly it has seemed to you before. We've been slaves to the tyranny of our self-sufficiency for so long that we can't imagine what freedom might feel like. The notorious "Cigarette-Smoking Man" on *The X-Files* channeled the voice of Satan when he said, "We give them happiness, and they give us authority, the authority to take away their freedom under the guise of democracy. Men can never be free. They're weak, corrupt, worthless, and restless. The people believe in authority. They've grown tired of waiting for miracle and mystery. Science is their religion. No greater explanation exists for them. They must never believe any differently if the project is to go forward."

The "project" is the destruction of our souls, and our only defense against it is our pursuit of sanctuary in Jesus' strength. In the crucible of our fading self-sufficiency, our hunger for rescue drives us closer to him, and closeness is what he is after.

Wonder	**Jesus**	**Do**
Often we have a "last-ditch" mentality about trusting Jesus. Why?	"Don't be afraid...Take courage! I am here!" (Mark 6:50).	Remember your "incompleteness"; tear the edge of this page, leaving it ragged.

Pray: Jesus, join yourself to my ragged edges and make me whole.

The Backbone of Love

Read Matthew 16:22-26

I met Kenyon when I was a 23-year-old counselor at a Christian camp for low-income kids. He rocked an Afro twice the size of his head, and his fists never met a face they didn't want to punch. He was slight but junkyard-dog scary.

On the second day of camp, Kenyon was at the center of yet another melee. So I pulled him from the pile and dragged him, spouting obscenities, onto the road that led up to the camp—a quarter-mile of dirt with an eight-percent grade. I told him we were going to run up that hill together as discipline for his behavior. But when we rounded a bend to start down the hill, he plopped down and sobbed.

I sat next to Kenyon and put my arm around him. I asked him what was wrong. With tears carving tracks down his dirty face, he cried, "My parents don't love me!" I said, "Kenyon, why do you think that?" He sputtered, "Because I can do anything, go anywhere, and hang out with anyone I want—I have no rules. I get whatever I want."

In that moment, I learned that kids who sense they can get whatever they want, whenever they want it, are dying inside. They don't feel loved, because no one cares enough about them to be a catalyst for transformation. This is why the love of Jesus is "beyond category"—he will run the hill with us.

Wonder
In what way has Jesus "run the hill" with you?

Jesus
"What do you benefit if you gain the whole world but lose your own soul?" (Matthew 16:26).

Do
Climb a staircase today, thanking Jesus for his companionship.

Pray: Jesus, your love doesn't always seem like love, but I receive it as love.

First Words

Read John 1:1-5

Iconic novels are often famous for their opening lines...

- "Many years later, as he faced the firing squad, Colonel Aureliano Buendía was to remember that distant afternoon when his father took him to discover ice."—Gabriel García Márquez, in *One Hundred Years of Solitude*

- "All happy families are alike; each unhappy family is unhappy in its own way."—Leo Tolstoy, in *Anna Karenina*

- "It is a truth universally acknowledged, that a single man in possession of a good fortune, must be in want of a wife." —Jane Austen, in *Pride and Prejudice*

John's Gospel is also famous for its opening lines: "In the beginning the Word already existed. The Word was with God, and the Word was God." Eugene Peterson reimagines these words with playful precision: "The Word became flesh and blood, and moved into the neighborhood." Author Stephen King says, "Over a period of weeks and months and even years, I'll word and reword [the opening lines of a book] until I'm happy... If I can get that first paragraph right, I'll know I can do the book... An opening line should invite the reader to begin the story. It should say: Listen. Come in here. You want to know about this."

The opening lines to the greatest story ever told introduce us to the most compelling person we'll ever know—John's words beckon to us: *Listen. Come here. You will want to know me.*

Wonder
What do the opening lines of John's Gospel tell you about Jesus' heart?

Jesus
"Come and see" (John 1:39).

Do
In the margin of this page, write the opening line of the novel about your life.

Pray: Jesus, I want you to be the focus of the opening line of my story.

Worth-Ship

Read Matthew 13:44-46

For my birthday a friend gave me an astonishing gift—an actual page from a 1487 Biblica Latina, the Vulgate Bible printed by Anton Koberger in Nuremberg, Germany, just three decades after the first Gutenberg Bible. The page he framed for me was from John 6, my favorite chapter in the Bible—his attention to detail still staggers me.

When I opened the gift with my wife and daughters, their first question was, "How could [my friend] afford to give you such a costly gift?" We had no idea what a 500-year-old page from a Bible was worth. But "worth" is tricky—most often, it means "how much someone would pay for this." But determining *true worth* is more complicated.

In his two shortest parables, Jesus targets the DNA of "worth." Treasures do not have intrinsic value—human beings ascribe that value to them, based on our collective assessment. In these parables, Jesus is making the point that we'll give up everything to gain something we've determined is far more valuable. The man and the merchant know a treasure when they see it, so they give a little to gain a lot. But not everyone appreciates worth when they see it.

That page from the Biblica Latina is worth way, way more to me than the price I could sell it for, because its beauty pierces my heart.

Wonder	Jesus	Do
What's something you own that's worth way more than its "price"?	"When he discovered a pearl of great value, he sold everything... and bought it!" (Matthew 13:46).	Just for fun, stick a bow on something in your home you consider "priceless."

Pray: Jesus, you are priceless to me—you are the "pearl of great price."

Solo

Read Luke 5:12-16

Sometimes my wife and daughters run errands without me, leaving me home alone. My youngest daughter Emma worries about how sad I'll be when they leave—she's an extravert, and going solo is a no-go for her. I have to convince her that introverts are the opposite of sad when they're left alone.

No matter which "vert" you are, silence and solitude offer us a basic necessity—time to chew and churn and rest with Jesus. We need "edited space" in our lives so he can slip a word or two into our crammed margins. Of course, for my daughter and many others, solo time feels like a slow crawl through the parched desert. But all of us need a dose of Jesus' solo medicine...

- *Solo invites intimacy, which produces fruit.* Our close, abiding relationship with Jesus requires "curated" time with him. This is why he reminds us that "a branch cannot produce fruit if it is severed from the vine, and you cannot be fruitful unless you remain in me" (John 15:4).

- *Solo strengthens us before or after major relational challenges, when our margins have evaporated, or when we need guidance or recalibration.* Once word of Jesus' miracles, healings, and teaching started to spread, his margins evaporated. Demanding crowds followed him everywhere. So "very early in the morning, while it was still dark, Jesus got up, left the house and went off to a solitary place, where he prayed" (Mark 1:35, NIV).

Wonder	**Jesus**	**Do**
Does solo time excite you or frighten you, and why?	"Now I am coming to you" (John 17:13).	Take a 60-second "solo." Cover your face in your hands and just be quiet.

Pray: Jesus, I'm quiet right now; show me your heart.

The Things of This World

Read John 3:1-21

Jesus straddled two cultures when he walked among us—the culture of the world and the culture of the kingdom of God. His mission was to bridge the gap between these cultures—it's why he so often begins his stories with "The Kingdom of God is like…" We've been trained and conditioned to live like we belong in this world, but he's inviting us to live like we don't belong.

Nicodemus the Pharisee introduces himself to Jesus with a bold invitation: "We all know that God has sent you to teach us…" *"Okay then,"* Jesus responds, *"I will teach you the most important thing: Because of your first birth, you assume you belong in this world of flesh—but you need a second birth, because you surely belong in another world called the kingdom of God."* Jesus is challenging the foundations of our belonging. We spend our lives adapting so we can belong, but Jesus is telling us our path forward requires a de-belonging mentality…

- It's better to focus on what we're for, not what we're against (Matthew 13:24-30).

- A tiny thing, a Singular Person, can offer us all a "true home" (Matthew 13:31-33).

- Growth comes, mysteriously, from attaching ourselves to Jesus, not from engineering it ourselves (Mark 4:26-29).

- A little bit of "pure Jesus" will change everything in our lives (Luke 13:20-21).

Wonder
When have you felt like you fully "belonged"? How and why?

Jesus
"The Holy Spirit gives birth to spiritual life" (John 3:6).

Do
Explore one source of your belonging—search for "free genealogy" online.

Pray: Jesus, what "traits" have I inherited from you in my "second birth"?

The Wasted Life

Read Luke 15:3-7

I'm at Simply Jesus, a three-day gathering at a remote ranch in Colorado that attracts hundreds of Jesus-loving people from all over the world. It's the end of the evening session, and our host invites the crowd to stick around for "campfire time." Brad Corrigan, he says, will be playing guitar. Most people have no idea who he's talking about. They hear "campfire guitar guy." But I know Brad—he plays drums and guitar for Dispatch, the most popular independent rock-and-roll band in history. Years ago, after the band announced it was splitting up, more than a hundred thousand people jammed into their "farewell" concert at Boston's Hatch Shell. The band reunited several years later and now tours the world.

But for much of the year Brad lives near Managua, Nicaragua, serving Jesus among the desperate poor in a massive trash dump called La Chureca. Humility defines his heart—so he has agreed to play his guitar at a late-night campfire for 20 oblivious people. Brad plays while the campfire people talk and laugh and wander in and out of the circle. I'm sitting 10 feet away, thinking, *What a waste. Think of the hordes of fans who'd give anything to be here at this moment.* Afterward, on the pitch-dark path back to my car, Jesus stops me: *Pay attention—my heart is on display, so drink it in. I left the 99 sheep on the hill to go after the one. That's what Brad did tonight.*

Wonder	**Jesus**	**Do**
Serving the few, not the many, seems like a waste. What's the point?	"Rejoice with me because I have found my lost sheep" (Luke 15:6).	Find a way to "waste" your time today—serve an overlooked person.

Pray: Jesus, live your "wasteful" life through me.

No Training Wheels

Read Mark 10:17-22

In the conventional Christian life, discipline is a god. The boundary between a committed disciple and a fickle fan is marked by our determined efforts. But disciplines are like training wheels—they're useful for a time, but the point is to ride without them. We call bikes with permanent training wheels "tricycles." Paul targets the training-wheel life with this: "When I was a child, I spoke and thought and reasoned as a child. But when I grew up, I put away childish things" (1 Corinthians 13:11).

It may seem wrong to frame discipline as "childish," but maturity leans on Jesus' strength, not our own willpower. When he invites "the Rich Young Ruler" to follow him, he jacks the "discipline cost" so high that the man's self-discipline can't pay the bill. But after Jesus reveals the cost of discipleship to Peter, James, John, and Andrew, they abandon their training wheels and hop on his bike. The life of a disciple is fed by trusting surrender, not self-will—"Cease striving and know that I am God" (Psalm 46:10, NASB). So how do we remove the training wheels?

- Pay better attention to what we need to face our challenges, then openly invite Jesus to supply our need.

- Acknowledge our stress and anxiety rising, then shift that burden onto Jesus.

- Seek "helps" that lead us back into dependence—a good book, a good conversation, a good stretch of silence, or a good walk in nature.

Wonder	**Jesus**	**Do**
In what area of your life are you attempting to "muscle through"?	"There is still one thing you haven't done" (Mark 10:21).	In a bathtub or hot tub or pool, float on your back—cease striving.

Pray: Jesus, I want to rely on you more than I rely on myself.

Thorns

Read 2 Corinthians 11:1–12:10

A false accusation can gut our self-confidence and topple the house of cards that is our identity. When our motives and character are in question, or we are unfairly attacked, the "weak underbelly" of our insecurity is exposed. Even an inconsequential accusation can roil us. I once got a prank email from a co-worker with the subject line "Busted by HR." Even though I'd done nothing wrong, and I quickly realized the goofy intent of the email, I nevertheless had to fight back the "prosecuting attorney" inside.

In Paul's second letter to the church in Corinth, he's still grappling with the impact of false accusations. He's hurt and frustrated and defensive because the people he has poured his life into have been influenced by false accusations about him and his teaching: "You happily put up with whatever anyone tells you, even if they preach a different Jesus than the one we preach."

And so Paul does what we all do, and can't help doing: He defends himself "like a fool." As an exclamation mark, he describes an extraordinary experience—a vision of the spiritual world that has made him feel chosen and special. Then, as a grace, he's given a painful reminder of his fragile self-sufficiency. And Jesus refuses to get rid of it. Its purpose is to puncture Paul's inflated ego, returning him to a dependence. Likewise, our own false accusations make us feel exposed and helpless—and from that precipice we learn to trust again.

Wonder
What does Jesus mean by "My power works best in weakness"?

Jesus
"My grace is all you need" (2 Corinthians 12:9).

Do
Do as many sit-ups or push-ups as you can, then rest in your weakness.

Pray: Jesus, you are my strength and my sufficiency.

Eating Jesus

Read John 6:22-59

Slow down and consider the mechanics of eating. When we consume food, we…

- take something from outside the body to inside the body.

- chew to break the food down.

- use the throat and esophagus to push it down to our core.

- activate acids to kill bad stuff and break down good stuff.

- push what remains into the small intestine, reducing it until the nutrients are *absorbed* into the bloodstream.

- carry the nutrients via the bloodstream into the liver, which turns proteins, sugars, and fats into energy.

- become *one* with our food, and food becomes one with us.

It's no accident that Jesus chooses the metaphor of eating and drinking to carry his invitation into relationship. Extend its meaning to a rational conclusion—*you are what you eat*—and Jesus intends for us to become just like him when we "consume" him. He says to his disciples, "No, I will not abandon you as orphans—I will come to you…When I am raised to life again, you will know that I am in my Father, and you are in me, and I am in you" (John 14:18-20). And so obedience means we extend the heart of Jesus into the world—the body of Christ is more literal than we think, when we consider the implications of "absorbed."

Wonder	**Jesus**	**Do**
What evidence do you have that "we are what we eat"?	"This bread, which I will offer so the world may live, is my flesh" (John 6:51).	Slow way, way down with a bite of food. Focus on your eating mechanics.

Pray: Jesus, I want to "taste and see" your goodness today.

Friend-Ships

Read Mark 2:1-12

Friendships are simultaneously a source of great delight and great pain in our lives (especially if they don't come easily). Most of us assess our friendships the same way we judge social media posts—other people always have more and better... But here's the truth: According to social science researchers, our friendship networks are shrinking; the average person has just one close confidante in life. And the number-one reason people seek out counseling is "loneliness." Likely, that's tied to a wider malady that plagues many first-world cultures—superficial friendships.

In Jesus' iconic encounter with a paralyzed man, the man's close, committed friendships make rescue possible for him. Undaunted by a crowd unwilling to make way for a desperate man, his four friends climb to the roof and dig their way through branches and mud to lower him down to Jesus. They carry him, like a rescue ship, to a safe harbor. And, "seeing their faith," Jesus forgives the man of his sin and restores his spinal column to "factory specs."

How do we find and deepen friendships that offer us that kind of warrior-love? Like the paralyzed man, when we risk to be open about our brokenness and make ourselves vulnerable to others, we invite deeper connection. And because Jesus has given us much, we are able to give others the gift of our authentic selves.

Wonder	**Jesus**	**Do**
Think about the "keys" to a good friendship. What's at the top of your list?	"You are my friends if you do what I command" (John 15:14).	In your phone's contacts, find a "long lost" friend and send a "miss you" note.

Pray: Jesus, open the closed places in me that keep others from connecting.

Tony Soprano-ed

Read Acts 9:1-19

I call it the "Tony Soprano Evangelism Strategy." It's that moment in a metaphoric dark alley when the resurrected Jesus lightning-blasts a Pharisee named Saul, dropping him to the ground and blinding him. That's pretty much what the mob does when it wants to "send a message," right? We have two accounts of this benevolent beat-down—one from a journalist's perspective (Acts 9), and one directly from Saul-turned-Paul (Acts 22).

Saul comes from a family of tent-makers but manages to convince the most prestigious, respected rabbi of the ancient world to take him on as a student. Gamaliel's training morphs young Saul into a shrewd and passionate zealot. And, like Tony Soprano, he's not afraid to get his hands dirty. So when Jesus confronts him on the road to Damascus, he's speaking Saul's language. That is to say, he whacks him.

In a phone call from a struggling author who's facing a brutal reality all writers face—the slow death of her "book-baby," as sales dwindle down to nothing—she's gripped by despair because she has poured herself into this work. This is what it feels like to lie there in the dirt, blinded and confused and scared. Like Saul, we're desperate for rescue. So maybe, in that moment, we'll do whatever Jesus tells us to do. I tell my friend, *"Jesus has a hard time teaching us to trust when things are going our way. We learn to trust when it takes courage to do it."*

Wonder
Jesus never "calls" anyone but Saul in this violent way. Why not?

Jesus
"I am Jesus the Nazarene, the one you are persecuting" (Acts 22:8).

Do
Fast from a meal today. Trust that Jesus will fill you when food does not.

Pray: Jesus, I'll trust you where it costs me the most.

Brutal Honesty

Read John 1:43-51

Writing in response to a question about the "benefits of brutal honesty" on Quora (an online Q&A site), "David" weighs in: *"Yesterday I was asking [my friend] Fran why people love our good friend Kip so much. He always says exactly what is on his mind: 'Dinner sounds great, but Kris has had a rough week and we need a night alone. Ask me again next week.' Not, 'We have other plans, how about next weekend?' He is exactly this way in [all] situations. Just 'on the table,' always. And [Fran] said, 'He is the most intensely humble person anyone knows, so he never needs to protect himself. No one ever assumes anything but his best intentions. He can say anything, and it doesn't matter…because he is not protecting anything. And that makes him safe.' "*

Maybe "Kip" is just a nickname for Jesus, because he certainly acts like him. *Inc.* magazine columnist N icolas Cole says, "Brutal honesty usually means pointing at someone's shadow—and we, as a society, really, really, really do not like our shadows." *We* might not like it, but Jesus does—brutal honesty is his art form. When he sees the smart aleck Nathanael approaching, he hooks him with brutal honesty ("Now here is a genuine son of Israel"). Years later Nathanael, still hooked by Jesus, carries a copy of Matthew's Gospel to northern India and Albania, where he is crucified upside down. Jesus (like Kip, apparently) has nothing to hide, nothing to protect, and nothing to leverage.

Wonder	**Jesus**	**Do**
Are you generally for or against brutal honesty?	"Now here is a genuine son of Israel—a man of complete integrity" (John 1:47).	Use a funny/brutally honest voicemail greeting from ninjanumber.com/funny-voicemail.

Pray: Jesus, I have something brutally honest I need to share with you…

Skubalon

Read Mark 12:28-34

Though Jesus urges us to love God with all our heart, soul, mind, and strength (Mark 12:30), we've narrowed these four pursuits into one that better fits our "return on investment" mentality—*understand and apply*. We believe knowledge transforms us and that the head trumps the heart. This is why we generally act as though our kids' happiness depends on the right grades and the right school and the right (well-paying) career. Social science research tells us this progression is a myth—people experience true happiness when they live out their core purpose in life (a heart pursuit), not when they achieve greater financial success (a head pursuit).

The focus of Jesus' mission in the world, and in our lives, is to restore our depth of trust in him—a trust that leads to intimacy. He wants to win our hearts. In a pivotal proclamation, Paul tells his friends in Philippi, "Everything else is worthless when compared with the infinite value of knowing Christ Jesus my Lord. For his sake I have discarded everything else, counting it all as garbage, so that I could gain Christ and become one with him" (Philippians 3:8-9). What is the "garbage" (in the original Greek, it's *skubalon*—a crass term for "excrement") that Paul has decided to toss out? It is the sum total of his education and religious knowledge. Instead, he's fixated on "becoming one with him."

Wonder
Why doesn't "knowing more" always leads to transformation?

Jesus
"This is my body...Do this in remembrance of [my heart]" (Luke 22:19).

Do
Toss a $1 bill, representing "success," in the garbage. Is it easy or hard to do?

Pray: Jesus, I want everything but your heart to be skubalon to me.

Invited In

Read Luke 19:1-10

We long to be insiders but almost always feel like outsiders. Over coffee, my wife and I wonder if either of us has ever truly felt like an insider. Yes, we remember, there was that brief season when we were trusted contributors at our church, but that came to an end when our pastor left. Even in the middle of that season, our "status" as insiders was fragile. A post on a friend's Facebook page captures our universal longing: "Where do I find a sense of belonging in a church?"

We have a deep longing to belong, but where does it come from, and why does it seem so rare? In the Steve Carrell film *Dan in Real Life*, an extended family gathers for their annual summer reunion at a lake house. One night, by tradition, they all participate in a family talent show, no matter if they have any real "talent." There is heartbreak in their stories, but the environment on this night is intimate, delightful, and unconditionally supportive. They are all cherished insiders, beloved for their quirks.

When I imagine what it was like for Zacchaeus and Jesus to share their first meal together, I picture that talent-show scene. Yes, Zacchaeus is a pariah to the Jews, who know what a despicable person he has been. He is an outsider in the same way Pluto is outside the Earth's gravity. But the love of Jesus pulls everything, and every one, into his orbit.

Wonder	**Jesus**	**Do**
What's the significance of Jesus inviting himself to Zacchaeus' home?	"Quick, come down! I must be a guest in your home today" (Luke 19:5).	Find "The In Crowd, Ramsey Lewis" on youtube.com; listen with open, raised hands.

Pray: Jesus, I've never really been an insider, until you invited me in.

The Power of Parable

Read Matthew 13:10-15

A parable about parables from Jay Pathak, pastor and co-author of *The Art of Neighboring*:

"I was a student leader in a campus ministry. One day, my friend and I were out hunting for 'unsuspecting prey.' We saw a big guy wearing leather and chains, so I asked, 'Would you consider yourself a spiritual person?' He said, 'How could you even believe in God when there's so much pain in the world?' So I tried to solve his pain-problem. He said, 'Great, that's your truth, and I have mine.' And I sort of mocked him by telling him that I'd always wanted to urinate on someone. He told me, 'If you do that to me, I will take your life—your truth is fine as long as it doesn't bother me.' I told him to take off his chains, because they bothered me.

"The guy told me he had to go. I asked him to consider Jesus as he left. My friend said, 'What happened there had nothing to do with Jesus.' I thought he was just weak. But back at my dorm, I knew he was right. I had my arguments down, but something was missing in my heart."

Jesus is after our heart when he tells parables: *If I told stories they grasped with their heads, they might understand and think they're saved. So I don't do that. I tell stories that put you in tension, not head knowledge you can master and control.*

Wonder
Why can't people be argued into a relationship with Jesus?

Jesus
"If you follow me, you won't have to walk in darkness" (John 8:12).

Do
Tonight, at the dinner table, tell a "parable story" from your life.

Pray: Jesus, I've kept my heart from you by staying in my head; I'm sorry.

The Seed Mentality

Read Mark 4:26-29

All adventures require risk and, therefore, danger. And at the extreme end of the danger continuum is death, which makes it our greatest adventure. *But maybe we don't want to take that ride at Disneyland…* Jesus, meanwhile, both embraces and upends our assumptions about death—he uses the death-to-life rhythm of the seasons as a metaphor for redemption in the kingdom of God.

In Ecclesiastes 3:1, Solomon gives us this iconic poetry: "For everything there is a season, a time for every activity under heaven." The cycle of death-to-life that defines our seasons mirrors the cycle of death-to-life in our relationships, our circumstances, and our experiences. Of course, we fear these seasonal changes in life because we can't yet see life percolating up through the winter frost.

Samer Zaky, a research assistant professor at the University of Pittsburgh, studies cell regeneration—he uses seasonal rhythms as a metaphor: "During autumn, leaves dry and fall off the tree… It is only by shedding its leaves that the tree can survive the windy and sun-deprived winter, when sudden gusts could blow down a tree laden with a large surface area of leaves. In other words, dismissing its leaves before winter, the tree prepares to reduce wind resistance and to save energy to re-blossom in the spring." Our own "re-blossoming" begins in darkness, where life is preparing an assault on our hardened crust.

Wonder	**Jesus**	**Do**
What "fruitful harvest" has emerged from your own death-to-life cycles?	"Unless a kernel of wheat is planted in the soil and dies, it remains alone" (John 12:24).	Hold a dead leaf or twig under your nose. Consider what death smells like.

Pray: Jesus, I wish I could have a glimpse of the life that is coming.

Falling Towers

Read Luke 13:1-9

The fall of the tower of Siloam near Jerusalem is a major news story—a tragedy that packs the culture-altering impact of the 9/11 attacks. Siloam, a neighborhood just south of Jerusalem's old city, is walled off by an enclosure that includes a watchtower. In the aftermath of its collapse, a haunting question remains: "Why do bad things happen to good people?" Our common, tacit assumption is that extraordinary tragedies somehow translate to extraordinary guilt. Likewise, we believe good people (mostly everyone) are rewarded by going to heaven, and bad people (mostly no one) are punished by going to hell.

Jesus pokes at the anxiety that stalks the gathered crowd by piling on, "Unless you repent, you will perish, too." The word *perish* here refers to a deeper death—a permanent separation from God. He's redirecting the shock of a mass heartbreak to rivet their attention on an overshadowing tragedy—one they can all avoid if they will drink the "living water" he's offering. And the cup they must drink from is called "repentance," a turning away from death and toward life.

This is why Jesus follows this proclamation with the Parable of the Barren Fig Tree. In the story, he is the "vineyard keeper" who promises, *"I will pursue and nurture and invite and coax and surround this beloved-but-fruitless fig tree until it produces fruit."* Our repentance, then, is the plea of a barren plant to a Relentless Gardener.

Wonder
Why do we tacitly assume bad things should only happen to bad people?

Jesus
"It is not the will of your Father...that one of these little ones perish" (Matthew 18:14, NASB).

Do
Online, search "obituaries." Choose one, then pray for each "survived by."

Pray: Jesus, I agree with Paul: "O death, where is your sting?"

No More Death to Self

Read Matthew 9:14-17

"Dying to yourself," we're told, is our imperative in the Christian life. Because our ugly, broken "self" pales in comparison to the "self" of Jesus, we must trade that ugly self for his beautiful self. Trouble is, when we try to murder our "self" and replace it with the self of Jesus, we can't seem to manage it. It's as if Jesus never intended for us to commit this crime in the first place.

John the Baptist says, "I must decrease so he can increase," and Jesus tells Nicodemus, "You must be born again"—but we misinterpret what these declarations imply. When John "decreases" for Jesus, his sense of self is not obliterated, the same way a mountain guide does not morph into a flamingo when his climbing party reaches the summit. Jesus does not negate our "born of the flesh" identity when he invites us to embrace our "born of the Spirit" iteration. It's not an obliteration of self; it's a *new start* for the self.

Our constructed self is a shambling version of our true identity, a retrofit to help us navigate a broken world. But Jesus wants to renovate that crumbling old identity into a drop-jaw "reconstructed self"—one that is fit for the kingdom of God. We are all fixer-uppers, longing for reality TV to choose us. But in the kingdom of God, everyone who comes to Jesus is chosen.

Wonder
What impact has the "death to self" message had on your life, if any?

Jesus
"[People] put new wine into fresh wineskins, and both are preserved" (Matthew 9:17, NASB).

Do
Put a drop of lemon juice in your water—a tiny reconstruction.

Pray: Jesus, I give you my constructed self, ready for "demo day."

The Bug in Your OS

Read John 10:1-10

A computer's operating system (OS) runs all its standard functions. It's not just the "software brain"; it's also the personality. The OS makes it possible for us to have a relationship with our computer—to engage with it in a predictable, trusting way. It determines the computer's functions, limitations, and possibilities.

Human beings also have an OS—it's called "story." The story we tell ourselves, about ourselves, determines how we function and sets our limitations and possibilities in life. It constructs, gives meaning to, and sets boundaries around our reality. And if we get a "bug" in our operating system—"an error, flaw, failure, or fault"—the whole thing could crash. Worse, if that bug is planted in our OS by "malware" (a destructive virus), it can "kill, steal, or destroy" us. This is Satan's strategy—to plant weaponized "bugs" in our story ("You'll never be enough"). "Identity Death" is his goal. But Jesus vows, "I came that [you] may have life, and have it abundantly" (John 10:10, NASB).

The stories we embrace about ourselves determine the "me" we operate as. We become the story we've decided to live inside. So when Jesus says, "I have come to set captives free," he means that the kingdom of God's IT Specialist is offering to "debug" our operating system—to rid us of lies and tell us the truth about our story.

Wonder	**Jesus**	**Do**
Ask Jesus, "What's a self-belief not planted by you but by your enemy?"	"All who came before me were thieves and robbers" (John 10:8).	Do some debugging—search for "Disk Utility" on your computer and run it.

Pray: Jesus, "search me...and know my heart; test me..." (Psalm 139:23).

No Sacrifice

Read Matthew 9:9-13

Love that does not sacrifice is not love—Jesus tells us so: "There is no greater love than to lay down one's life for one's friends" (John 15:13). To live sacrificially, we must empty ourselves for others. In stark contrast, St. Irenaeus writes, "For the glory of God is the living man, and the life of man is the vision of God"—we've condensed this to *The glory of God is a man fully alive.* How can we live "fully alive" when love requires sacrifice?

Early in his ministry, Jesus still embraces the Old Testament practice of animal sacrifice as a bridge to reconciliation. But soon he signals a shift, pointing the Pharisees to Hosea 6:6: "Now go and learn the meaning of this Scripture: 'I want you to show mercy, not offer sacrifices.' " Then he clears the Temple of those who are buying and selling animals for sacrifice. And when a "teacher of the law" asserts that loving God and others is more important than offering sacrifices, Jesus bubbles over: "You are not far from the Kingdom of God."

If Jesus desires mercy and not sacrifice, and if his crucifixion is our permanent "atonement," what does sacrifice mean for us now? We know his mission is to give us a "rich and satisfying life," so maybe our "sacrifice" is to live into that life—to give what we have to give by risking more than we do now.

Wonder	**Jesus**	**Do**
What would you need to sacrifice to live more "fully alive"?	"It is not those who are healthy who need a physician, but those who are sick" (Matthew 9:12, NASB).	Try to touch your toes. Linger and feel the stretch. Ask Jesus to "stretch" you.

Pray: Jesus, I'll praise you when my circumstances do not seem worthy of it.

Three Days in the Dark

Read Mark 8:31-33

For three days and nights, Jesus remains in "the belly of the beast"—a timeline he does not try to keep secret in advance…

- *To the scribes and Pharisees:* "For as Jonah was in the belly of the great fist for three days and three nights, so will the Son of Man be in the heart of the earth for three days and three nights" (Matthew 12:40) and "Destroy this temple, and in three days I will raise it up" (John 2:19).

- *To his disciples:* "Jesus began to tell them that the Son of Man must suffer many terrilbe things and be rejected by the elders, the leading priests, and the teachers of religious law. He would be killed, but three days later he would rise from the dead" (Mark 8:31) and "The Son of Man is going to be betrayed into the hands of his enemies. He will be killed, but three days later he will rise from the dead" (Mark 9:31) and "They will mock him, spit on him, flog him with a whip, and kill him, but after three days he will rise again" (Mark 10:34).

The message of "three days in the dark" is clear: *THREE DAYS DEAD IS CERTAINLY DEAD—but I will show you that "certainly dead" is nothing to me. It's a cold to get over! LIFE, not death, is inexorable. To death I say, "Is that all you've got?" Draw near to LIFE itself, and LIFE will wash over you.*

Wonder
In what ways do we "respect" death too much in our culture?

Jesus
"Get behind Me, Satan; for you are not setting your mind on God's interests" (Mark 8:33, NASB).

Do
Taste the life that overshadows death by eating a raisin—a "dead" grape.

Pray: Jesus, I want my life to orbit around life, not death.

Don't Hold Back

Read Mark 12:28-34

We know that Jesus is "fully God and fully human," but we over-weight that balancing act to the "fully God" side. Jesus seems more God than man to us. But Jesus came to reclaim our human-ness, to model what "fully human" looks like. Our "greatest commandment"—to "love the Lord your God with all your heart, all your soul, all your mind, and all your strength"—is also a roadmap (or the Siri-voice) to living more humanly.

For example, to love with our "whole soul" means we "don't hold back." Jesus is, to say the least, unmodulated. When the crowds gather to hear him teach, they look hungry, so Jesus tells his befuddled disciples to feed all of them. When a respected Pharisee invites him to lunch, he offends his host by "forgetting" to ceremonially wash his hands, then magnifies the offense with this dart: "You are full of greed and wickedness." When he meets Andrew's brother Simon for the first time, he doesn't merely invite him into a new life, but he gives him a new name (Petros).

Little children have a "don't hold back" momentum. But the older we get, painful experience teaches us there's a steep price for unbridled living. Jesus, in contrast, says and does things that do not account for caution. He wants us to love by eliminating the safe middle: "Let your yes be yes, and your no be no."

Wonder	**Jesus**	**Do**
How were you more unmodulated as a child than you are now?	"You weigh men down with burdens [but] will not even touch the burdens" (Luke 11:46, NASB).	Alone, play some "unmodulated" music. What nuances do you notice?

Pray: Jesus, unmodulate me in the way I "live and breathe and move."

The Thicker Life

Read Matthew 11:20-30

In *Death By Suburb*, author Dave Goetz describes a counter-cultural path he calls "the thicker life." It's a lifestyle marked by a singular pursuit of Jesus, an everyday dependence on his guidance, and a pattern of serving the needs of others. To live this way in the suffocating grip of Western culture, says Goetz, we must be more focused and less scattered: "It's a higher existence, a plane where I am not the sum total of my house size, SUV, vacations, kids' report cards—and that which I still need to acquire." *Thick* means we slow down and pay attention to the things that matter most.

The thicker life modeled for us by Jesus is not about hanging on to things but giving away things. Because of the freedom we experience in our intimacy with Jesus, we are less likely to fuel our narcissism and more likely to offer our good treasure to others. We venture out from our protected bubbles, compelled to dirty ourselves in the complex, chaotic, and profane world we live in...

Jesus invites us into the thicker life with this: "Come to me, all of you who are weary and carry heavy burdens, and I will give you rest." The rest we need is not defined by what we own or have accomplished but by who we are. When we come to him "naked [stripped of our need for things] and unashamed [of others' unmet expectations]," we find that rest.

Wonder	**Jesus**	**Do**
When you picture what "rest" looks like, what do you see?	"You have hidden these things from the wise... and revealed them to infants" (Matthew 11:25, NASB).	We're rich in "extras"—give your "garage sale" items to a refugee organization.

Pray: Jesus, lighten the load of my life—show me what to give.

What We Love, Not Believe

Read John 5:18-24

The things we love represent our souls' fingerprints, and they have a forming impact on those we influence. I love old-school jazz and R&B; it's always on in our home. When my daughter left for college, she created a road-trip playlist of her favorite music, including a generous helping of thet "Dad songs" that have marinated her life since she was in diapers. And her new friends fell in love with her playlist; her surprising choices drew them to her because the things we love give others a portal into what is "fearfully and wonderfully" made about us.

The primary forces that are influencing the people closest to you are tied to the things you love most in life. What we love has more power to shape others than what we say we believe. And so, when we "abide" in Jesus as a branch abides in a Vine, what he loves forms us into his image. Here's a sampler of what he loves, from early in the gospel of John…

1. Surprises, food, parties, and music (John 2:1-11)

2. Slowing down/hanging out with family and friends (2:12)

3. Underdogs—those who are shunned and demeaned (4:1-30)

4. The sick, the poor, the blind, and the lame (5:1-15)

The true sign of intimacy? We love the things our beloved loves (likely the reason many seniors dress alike)…

Wonder
What pops into your head when you ask, "What does Jesus love?"

Jesus
"The Son can do nothing… He does only what he sees the Father doing" (John 5:19).

Do
Taste foods Jesus loved—figs, fish, honey, lamb, olives, grapes, vinegar, bread.

Pray: Jesus, I want to love what you love.

Having Done All, Stand

Read Ephesians 6:10-18

Eugene Peterson reimagines Paul's "last instructions" to his friends in Ephesus with language lifted from a horror movie: "This is for keeps, a life-or-death fight to the finish against the Devil and all his angels. Be prepared. You're up against far more than you can handle on your own." Cue the shrieking violin music... So, what does it look like to "stand strong"? Pay attention to the italics I've added to Paul's warning in Ephesians 6...

1. **Our real strength is *inside* Jesus:** "Be strong *in the Lord* and *in his mighty power*."

2. **The armor we need is *his*:** "Put on all of *God's armor* so that you will be able to stand firm."

3. **Think of yourselves as guerilla fighters *resisting an enemy occupation*:** "Put on every piece of God's armor so you will be able to *resist the enemy* in the time of evil."

4. **The sword we use to defend ourselves is *Jesus himself*:** "Take the sword of the Spirit, *which is the word of God*."

5. **We stay *connected* to Jesus; we keep our guard up:** "Pray in the Spirit *at all times and on every occasion*."

If our strength is in our stand, we must choose well what we're standing on, so we can brace ourselves. Principles and recipes and formulas are "shifting sand." The heart of Jesus is granite.

Wonder	**Jesus**	**Do**
Fear threatens our stance. How is fear insinuating itself into your life?	"[Don't build your] house right on the ground, without a foundation" (Luke 6:49).	Feel the impact of the difference between the surfaces you walk on today.

Pray: Jesus, I will do all I can to stand on you, and then I will stand.

Good Company

Read John 7:1-10

It's a favorite party question: "What person, living or dead, would you want to share a meal with if you could?" The usual suspects include Abraham Lincoln and Oprah Winfrey and Albert Einstein and Malala and, well, Jesus. But one answer you'll never hear, for obvious reasons, is…"myself." Few of us are as relaxed about our narcissism as that. We can produce a long list of people we'd enjoy getting to know, but when "the company we keep" is just ourselves, are we "good company"?

Early in his ministry, Jesus avoids traveling through Judea because the Jewish leaders are openly plotting his murder. His brothers resent Jesus and mock his miracles. They know it's dangerous for him to travel to Judea, yet they try to goad him into it. But Jesus refuses, because "my time has not yet come." And then he does something remarkable—he travels by himself to the Festival of Shelters in Jerusalem, where he bides his time out of public view until he strolls into the Temple to teach an already hostile crowd. It's a gutsy move and a shot across the bow to his brothers.

To get there, Jesus travels 90 miles on foot alone—a five-day journey in the "good company" of himself. Before he enters into chaos and engages his toxic enemies, he invites himself into a five-day internal conversation, where he can mull his next move and hash things out with his Father. Sometimes the company we need most is the company we already have…

Wonder	**Jesus**	**Do**
How are you "good company" for yourself?	"The world can't hate you, but it does hate me" (John 7:7).	On a solo walk, "journal" your thoughts and concerns out loud to Jesus.

Pray: Jesus, I'd like to become better company for myself.

Anger Mis-Management

Read Matthew 11:20-24

Jesus gets angry a lot more often than we realize. We miss that because our "conventional religious mythology" reduces him to a teddy bear, not the grizzly bear we see so often in Scripture. So when he tears into hypocritical religious leaders or scoffs at the unbelieving crowds or rebukes his thick-headed disciples, he seems at odds with "acceptable Christian behavior"...
- We have no right to become angry at others.
- Anyone who's angry is a bad person.
- "If you loved me, you would never get angry at me."
- A good parent never gets angry at their child.
- Happily married people never get angry.

We know from his behavior that Jesus did not believe in these "anger restrictions," but what does he believe? In Matthew 5, he angrily criticizes the Pharisees' hypocrisy, then tells the crowds that when *they* get angry, they're subject to the same judgment we give murderers. Why the dichotomy? Anger is the "chainsaw" in our emotional toolbox, so he's challenging us to recognize its destructive capability and use it responsibly. And so we 1) respond, not react; 2) make it appropriate to the circumstance; 3) bring the right force at the right time in the right place; 4) never let it overshadow "loving our enemy"; and 5) admit when anger camouflages disappointment or grief or trauma or depression.

Wonder
What typically "triggers" your anger, and why?

Jesus
"I tell you, Tyre and Sidon will be better off on judgment day than you" (Matthew 11:22).

Do
Pay attention to the news today, and play "What would Jesus hate?"

Pray: Jesus, show me how and when to use my "chainsaw."

What's My Purpose?

Read Ephesians 1:7-12

Life, as Winston Churchill once said, is "a riddle wrapped in a mystery inside an enigma." We hunger to find and pursue our purpose in life, but it remains elusive.

When Jesus recruits his first followers, a close-knit group of small-business owners who run a fishing operation, he dangles his own enticing bait: *Come, be my disciples, and I will show you how to fish for people!* Like most, these men identify themselves by their occupation—what we do defines who we are. So a reoriented focus in their work leads to a reoriented identity. *What if*, he asks, *your real purpose is to offer rescue to others—to drag them out of hopelessness into the refuge of the kingdom of God?*

We are all created to "fish for men," no matter our particular calling in life. In that sense, Jesus is inviting us to find our identities in our "occupation"—in the "family business" set up by the Trinity, our singular mission is to "catch people" in the net of Jesus. Paul sums it up: "It's in Christ that we find out who we are and what we are living for. Long before we first heard of Christ and got our hopes up, he had his eye on us, had designs on us for glorious living" (*The Message*).

Our purpose in life will emerge—or blossom—as we draw near to Jesus. We don't have to find it—it will find us.

Wonder
What would you say is your purpose in life?

Jesus
"The Son of Man...is the stairway between heaven and earth" (John 1:51).

Do
Go to enneagramtest .com for a free version of this "purpose-revealing" tool.

Pray: Jesus, I am who you say I am, and my purpose is hidden in you.

Is God Real?

Read Matthew 6:1-6

The percentage of atheists has doubled over the last decade, and one in six adults no longer claim any religious affiliation. The steady movement away from faith is resurfacing a fundamental question: *Is God real?* At first blush it's a philosophical question—hard to answer with scientific and historical proofs. If you're an atheist, you're also a materialist, and nothing we comprehend outside of our five senses is really "real." And if you're an agnostic, you believe in an impersonal "higher power" that is uninterested in the details of our lives. So what does "real" really mean, and what's our standard for "real"?

It would be one thing if the God-we-doubt worked a little harder to offer us hard proofs of his existence, but he seems positively cagey about it. He has purposely left us a "belief gap" to jump over, and it has little to do with our five senses or our intellect. That gap, like a crack in the concrete, offers a habitat for doubt-weeds to grow.

But when Jesus urges the crowds to "do right things" in secret, without drawing attention to themselves, he's underlining the reality of God. The only rational reason to hide our good deeds from the world, he says, is to gain our reward from "your Father in heaven." Jesus is simply reminding us: *Hey, God is real—you don't have to scrape and horde your reward for doing good, because he can see what you do in secret.*

Wonder
How is arrogance related to disbelief in God?

Jesus
"Your Father, who sees everything, will reward you" (Matthew 6:6).

Do
Offer a silent proclamation of God's reality—do a good thing in secret.

Pray: Jesus, "no ear has heard...no eye has seen a God like you" (Isaiah 64:4).

Climbing the Staircase

Read John 6:38-40

Martin Luther King Jr. said, "Faith is taking the first step even when you can't see the whole staircase." For those of us who've fallen off a few staircases in our lives, the trust that gives faith its substance is a struggle. The certainty we crave is challenged and undermined by the bad things we've encountered on our way up the stairs. The only source of our assurance, Jesus tells us, is found in his Father's deepest desire: "That anyone who sees the Son and trusts who he is and what he does and then aligns with him will enter *real* life, *eternal* life" (John 6:40, *The Message*). We're motivated to take our first steps into the unknown only when we come to know *who* made the staircase, not when the way becomes clear. And "knowing" means we…

- **See the Son:** We pay much closer attention to the heart of Jesus, following him more than we follow his "principles."

- **Trust in who he is:** Like the Roman Centurion who insists that Jesus' word alone will heal his servant, our trust is anchored in what we know to be true about him.

- **Trust in what he does:** We study the things he does because they reveal to us how the kingdom of God operates and what his heart values.

- **Align ourselves with him:** We give our own "blood pledge"—a public proclamation—that broadcasts our allegiance to him.

Wonder	**Jesus**	**Do**
What makes you pause before you'll climb "the staircase of faith"?	"I have come…to do the will of God…not to do my own will" (John 6:38).	Climb a staircase with your eyes closed. What does faith "feel like"?

Pray: Jesus, you are the maker of my staircase—I trust you.

Childlike Prayer

Read Matthew 6:5-13

I once tried to read a lengthy book about prayer, written by one of my favorite authors. Ten pages in I realized this was not a marathon I could finish. Reading about prayer is like reading a cookbook; it becomes a tasty reality only when you're actually *making something*. We mistakenly believe that only the "top chefs" know how to do it right—pastors and evangelists and authors who write books about prayer. We've made it into performance art, so difficult that we need book-length help to do it. And this is exactly why Jesus insisted that "anyone who doesn't receive the Kingdom of God like a child will never enter it" (Luke 18:17). Prayer is best understood through the lens of a child, not the lens of adult experts. When Jesus taught about prayer in Matthew 5 and 6, his description was childlike…

- Advocate for others, including "those who persecute you!" (5:44).

- Don't make a show of it, "like the hypocrites who love to pray publicly on street corners and in the synagogues where everyone can see them" (6:5).

- Make it intimate—"shut the door behind you" (6:6).

- Don't repeat yourself, as if you're reciting a magic spell by "babbling on and on" (6:7).

- Simply express your delight for Jesus, sharing concerns, owning mistakes, and asking for help (6:9-13).

Wonder	**Jesus**	**Do**
Why does prayer so often seem like a chore we have to get right?	"Your Father knows exactly what you need even before you ask him!" (Matthew 6:8).	Put a small stone in your pocket as a "prayer prompter." When you feel it, pray.

Pray: Jesus, I offer myself to you like a toddler settling into a parent's lap.

A Protest of Beauty

Read Matthew 15:21-28

By 1992 the beautiful cosmopolitan city of Sarajevo was under siege by more than 10,000 Serbian troops—neighborhood streets morphed into killing fields. The Serbs rained shells down on soldiers and civilians alike, night and day. At 4 p.m. on May 27, a long line of people, starving and desperate, snaked down the block from a bakery that still had flour. The bakery's owners were distributing loaves of bread to the people when a shell landed in the middle of the line, killing 22 people.

Just down the block from this carnage lived Vedran Smajlovic, who had been principal cellist of the Sarajevo Opera Company before the war. Smajlovic decided he'd seen enough. He could no longer allow fear to control his life. So the next day at 4 p.m., and every day afterward until the war ended, Vedran dressed up in his performance tuxedo, hauled his cello to the crater where the shell had landed, sat on a little campstool, and played. Mortars landed nearby, but he played on. Over the months and years he kept this vigil, he was never hurt. Some called his act of defiance a "protest of beauty."

And this, in essence, is what the Gentile woman does after Jesus responds to her pleas with silence and the disciples respond to her vulnerability with disdain. Instead of retreating from this emotional violence, she moves in even closer to Jesus and worships him. It's a protest of beauty, focused on Beauty itself.

Wonder	**Jesus**	**Do**
When evil encroaches, how can you offer a "protest of beauty"?	"Dear woman... your faith is great" (Matthew 15:28).	In your home or workplace, place a small vase of flowers in a lonely place.

Pray: Jesus, you're the beauty in my life, the music in my shell-crater.

Jesus' Relationship With Sin

Read Matthew 7:3-5

Sin, as defined by the Ten Commandments, is behavior-based—
if the Bible warns us against X, it's sin when we do it anyway.
But Jesus prefers to hang out with people who "know they are
sinners," not those who insist they're not. So when Jesus says,
"I haven't come to abolish the law, but to fulfill it," what does
he mean? When we encounter sin, should we confront it or
ignore it? How do we "love the sinner and hate the sin"? When
we buy something from a store or vote for someone, are we
tacitly supporting their connections to sin? What does it mean to
follow our hearts, not the "letter of the law"? And if we refuse to
confront sin, are we indifferent to its consequences?

Jesus treats sin like a cancer—it starts small but eventually
kills us if left unchecked. At its core, sin is a violation of our
relationship with Jesus. He's okay with confronting sin in others,
but not before we confront it in ourselves. He pays closer
attention to the "engine" of sinful behavior—the heart—than the
rules surrounding it. And his most frequent response to sin is…
repent. That means we stop walking away from him and start
walking toward him. It's Peter on the beach, post-Resurrection
and in the wake of his cowardly betrayal, answering "Yes!" every
time Jesus asks, "Do you love me?" Repentance is driven by our
love, not our duty.

Wonder
When you sin,
what helps you feel
"restored" again, and
why?

Jesus
"Simon son of John,
do you love me?"
(John 21:17).

Do
Gluttony is one of the
"seven deadly sins."
Repent by fasting one
meal.

Pray: Jesus, you can ask me as many times as you want— I love you.

The Deeper Magic

Read Matthew 21:33-46

In *The Lion, the Witch and the Wardrobe*, C.S. Lewis explores the connection between the Bible's Old and New Testaments—the "Stone Table" altar is a metaphor for the Ten Commandments, and the inscriptions on that table (the law) represent "the Deep Magic." But Aslan (the lion-metaphor for Jesus) embodies "the Deeper Magic." In the story's crescendo, Aslan is sacrificed on the Stone Table, fulfilling the demands of the law. The White Witch (Satan) assumes she has won this chess match, oblivious to the Deeper Magic of "the New Covenant" and its power to upend death: "Then Jesus asked [the religious leaders], 'Didn't you ever read this in the Scriptures? "The stone that the builders rejected has now become the cornerstone. This is the Lord's doing, and it is wonderful to see." ' "

When Aslan is sacrificed on the Stone Table, it cracks, a parallel of the rending of the Temple curtain separating God from man, when Jesus gives up his spirit. No longer does the Deep Magic—the law—define our relationship with God. The penalty is paid, and intimacy is possible. The first thing Aslan does after he leaps off the shattered Table is invite the children to *play*.

If the Old and New Testaments are chapters one and two in a novel, we're now in Chapter 14—the "post-Testament" era. We are living out our own epic adventure, following the Spirit of Jesus into a life big enough to be, well, biblical.

Wonder
When Jesus says we'll do "greater" things than he's done, what does he mean?

Jesus
"Anyone who stumbles over that stone will be broken to pieces" (Matthew 21:44).

Do
Go to thegreatestbooks .org, and find a novel title you'd choose for your life story.

Pray: Jesus, thank you that redemption extends beyond "the Deep Magic."

Weeding Our Garden

Read Matthew 13:24-30

If we neglect our interior lives, leaving them to grow untended, weeds will encroach on our souls. The running conversation we have with ourselves is like a garden—the flowers that are planted there will die off if the weeds that spring up uninvited are not killed off. When we entertain toxic intrusions into our souls, we soon drown out the sound of God's "still, small voice."

So Jesus urges us to be vigilant about our thought lives. Our challenge is to discern between the "wheat" planted by our good Farmer and the "tares" planted by our conniving enemy. If we follow the pattern of the parable Jesus has told us, we trust him to pull those life-suckers at the right time. And we invite him to recalibrate us—to tell us who we really are. To nurture good growth in our garden and defend us against the lies that creep in.

I have a friend who moved to a new city and quickly made new friendships. But after several months she was struggling. Yes, she was enjoying her new community, but she was missing a certain kind of friend—one who pays attention to her *essence* and is intent on nurturing the wheat growing up among the weeds.

The "body of Christ" is like a gardening club, all of us amateur horticulturists whose mission is to promote the beauty in each other and trust Jesus to pull the weeds.

Wonder
Ask Jesus, "Who do you say I am? What's your nickname for me?"

Jesus
"Every plant not planted by my heavenly Father will be uprooted" (Matthew 15:13).

Do
Eat a banana and discard the peel. Ask Jesus to peel and discard your "husk."

Pray: Jesus, Master Gardener, come and tend the garden of my soul.

The Deeper Loneliness

Read John 5:1-15

We're created by God for relationship, but relationships alone never deliver on their promised salvation. Friendships, even close ones, are like drinking from a water fountain when we're parched beyond thirst—we can never get enough. When we find what we're looking for, we discover we haven't found what we're looking for: "If the light you think you have is actually darkness, how deep that darkness is!" (Matthew 6:23).

A friend felt Jesus calling her to a vagabond life on the road. So she ventured out the same way Jesus sent his disciples without "any money in your money belts…or a traveler's bag…or sandals or even a walking stick." She lived in the thrill of unpredictability and under the lonely shadow of uncertainty. "I decided," she told me at the time, "to take the road as it comes. If I find a place I like, I will stay awhile. All Jesus said was go; he didn't say for how long. So I am trying to lean more into his leading on the road." And the fruit of this adventure? "Gentleness. I am learning to be more gentle with myself."

When alone-ness seems like the climate of our lives, not just a weather pattern, Jesus invites us to follow our thirst to the source of living water. Maybe we won't walk past the water fountain to the well until our deeper loneliness points the way.

Wonder
Why do we continue to trust success and wealth to rescue us?

Jesus
"Those who drink the water I give will never be thirsty again" (John 4:14).

Do
Plug your ears tight for 60 seconds—what does loneliness "sound like"?

Pray: Jesus, loneliness is like a dull ache; please soothe the ache.

The Journey of Doubt

Read Matthew 9:35-38

Jesus is hard to pin down, upending us with contradictions...

- He urges us to "love your enemies and pray for those who persecute you" but brands the Pharisees "hypocrites" and "whitewashed tombs" and "filthy inside" (Mathew 23).

- He first praises Simon, calling him "the Rock" after Simon "names" Jesus as the Messiah, then promising to "build my church" on him—four verses later he calls him "Satan" and "a dangerous trap" (Matthew 16).

- He first tells his conniving brothers that he will not attend the Festival of Shelters in Jerusalem with them, then waits a bit before going anyway (John 7).

- He repeatedly tells us not to worry about anything (Matthew 6), then spends an entire chapter (Luke 21) describing all the horrible things that will happen to us, including "relatives and friends" who will betray us.

This dissonance is fertile soil for doubt to grow. We like paved paths, not trailblazing. Give us the step-by-step instructions. But Jesus is inviting us into a relationship, not a religious software program. He's unpredictable, as are most enjoyable people. To come to him, we must lay down our prerequisite for certainty. We find him, and we follow our heart through the fog of doubt.

Wonder
In relationships we're generally bored by predictability. Why?

Jesus
"The wind blows wherever it wants" (John 3:8).

Do
At a restaurant, close your eyes and point to the menu. Order and eat that.

Pray: Jesus, I know you are not "tame," and that's why I love you.

Tone and Context

Read John 20:24-29

The Gospel writers report the facts about what Jesus says but rarely add emotional context to it. For example, "Doubting Thomas" hears that others have seen a resurrected Jesus, but he responds with "I won't believe it unless I see the nail wounds in his hands." When Jesus later shows up where the disciples are meeting, he invites Thomas to "put your finger here, and look at my hands." We imagine Jesus angry and frustrated and disappointed when he says this. But the meaning changes if we pair his words with a little snark instead. Friends, especially guy friends, often say wry things that look angry on paper: *Did you finish that yardwork?* or *You're not going to wear that, are you?*

The more we explore a conversational, interactive relationship with the Spirit of Jesus, the more he expands our assumptions about the tone in his voice. Most people don't think of Jesus as delightful and engaging, but few would've been drawn to him if he wasn't. After the "Rich Young Ruler" turns down Jesus' invitation, he says, "It is easier for a camel to go through the eye of a needle than for a rich person to enter the Kingdom of God!" (Mark 10:25). Think about the funniest person you know—now imagine that person saying what Jesus said.

Author John Eldredge says a "conversational relationship with Jesus" is our top priority in life—so we learn to listen more than we talk and broaden the emotional "payload" of his words.

Wonder
Read something Jesus said and imagine him smiling. What's the impact?

Jesus
"Blessed are those who believe without seeing me" (John 20:29).

Do
On youtube.com watch "How Your Tone Changes 'YES.' " Try "yes variations."

Pray: Jesus, expand the way I "hear" and interpret your voice.

Fire the Defense Lawyer

Read John 3:1-21

In C.S. Lewis' *The Great Divorce*, a bus from heaven stops in hell, offering the condemned a quick trip to paradise, where they'll have a chance to finally embrace redemption. The bus quickly fills up with ghosts, all of them convinced they've been wrongly relegated to oblivion. When they spill out onto "the streets of gold," they encounter the "bright spirits" of the natives, who offer them the grace they've so far refused.

In one encounter, a bright spirit ("Len") invites his former boss (now a ghost) to join him in heaven. How is it possible, the ghost complains, that a "decent man" like him is confined to hell while a "bloody murderer" like Len lives the high life?

Ghost: "I always done my best and I never done nothing wrong. And what I don't see is why I should be put below a bloody murderer like you." *Len:* "Who knows whether you will be? Only be happy and come with me." *Ghost:* "What do you keep on arguing for? I'm only telling you the sort of chap I am. I only want my rights. I'm not asking for anybody's bleeding charity." *Len:* "Then do. At once. Ask for the Bleeding Charity. Everything is here for the asking and nothing can be bought."

In the kingdom of God, we can ask for anything, but we can buy nothing. If we'll leave our defense lawyer behind and accept the grace offered to us, we find the "abundant life" he has promised.

Wonder	**Jesus**	**Do**
Why do we prefer our "rights" over "the bleeding charity"?	"How can you possibly believe if I tell you about heavenly things?" (John 3:12).	Find a small "Yield" sign online, print it, and tape it to your bathroom mirror.

Pray: Jesus, the voice of my defense lawyer is so loud. I struggle to hear you.

The Abolition of Shame

Read Psalm 103:8-17

Every few years my family made the trek across the Serengeti plains of Kansas to visit our Missouri relatives. One year, when I was 15, I noticed my cousin Debbie dragging her left leg behind her. Someone had whispered a diagnosis of MS, but I was an idiot teenager with a Monty Python sense of humor. So, inexplicably, I mocked her exaggerated gait by dragging my leg. Laughing, I quickly looked around to make sure others noticed my comic brilliance. They did notice, but they weren't laughing...

The shame was instantaneous. My face was burning, and I begged Jesus to let me go back in time so I could erase those five seconds of cruelty. Instead, I wallowed in my shame like it was quicksand. Psychologist Joseph Burgo says, "When things go wrong between parent and child in the first two years of life, you [the child] are permanently damaged by it in ways that cannot be erased. The awareness that you are damaged, the felt knowledge that you didn't get what you needed and that as a result, your emotional development has been warped and stunted in profound ways—this is what I refer to as basic shame."

Everyone born into the world passes through a "spiritual birth canal" that infects us with sin, filling us with basic shame. It's inescapable. And this is why Jesus would like to be our "re-birthing coach" (John 3:7).

Wonder	**Jesus**	**Do**
What's the source of your shame in life? What one word describes it?	"Where are your accusers? Didn't even one of them condemn you?" (John 8:10).	Shame withers in the light. Speak it out to someone you trust.

Pray: Jesus, please cast my sin "as far as the east is from the west."

Grafted In

Read Romans 11:17-24

In a vivid metaphor, Jesus describes himself as the "Vine" and his followers as "branches," promising that if we "remain" in him we'll "produce much fruit." And, as a kicker: "Apart from me you can do nothing" (John 15). We know that a branch severed from it source of life will eventually dry up and shrivel. But "remaining" is not up to the branch—it will stay connected to the tree as long as no outside force breaks it off.

And yet Jesus urges us to *remain* in him—Paul later describes this remaining as a "grafting" process that joins a weak and fruitless branch to a vigorous tree in a coupling so intimate that the two become one. We are, says Paul, "wild olive shoots" that now "share in the nourishing sap from the olive root."

If you're not an avid gardener, the grafting process is likely a mystery. To do it, a Master Gardener cuts a branch from a weaker plant (called "the scion wood"), then binds its open cut to an open cut in the Root or Vine, producing a hybrid plant or "new creature." It's an intimate process, reminding us of how Jesus describes his relationship with us: "I am the Bridegroom, you are my bride" and "the two will become one flesh."

And there on the cross, Jesus the Vine is cut open, his arms open wide, inviting all of us humbled scion-woods who are desperate for life.

Wonder	**Jesus**	**Do**
In what ways have your wounds enabled your "grafting" into Jesus?	"I have loved you even as the Father has loved me. Remain in my love" (John 15:9).	Watch "Kath and Katie Grafting Fruit Trees" on youtube.com.

Pray: Jesus, I am desperate for your life, so I offer you my wounds.

Equal Love?

Read Matthew 20:1-16

On a private social-media page, a friend posts a philosophical prod: "Does God love everyone equally?" His bias is clear—"equal" must be God's standard for love. But I respond, "The twist is this: Jesus doesn't love everyone 'equally'; he loves us all individually. His passion for one may look quite different from his passion for another. We are addicted to comparison, but because he's 'other' than us, he's able to write one storybook at a time, simultaneously for all of humanity."

My friend seems unsatisfied by my response, hedging his reaction: "Interesting thought—I will have to pray and talk to Jesus more on this. It seems dangerous, though, to think he loves one person more than another, if that means one person would be less than another." And I clarify, "I'm not saying Jesus loves one person *more* than another—I'm saying he loves each of us individually, and true love is expressed differently from person to person. He does not love the woman caught in adultery the same way he loves the hypocritical Pharisees, but he is never not-loving the person in front of him. It's not possible for Jesus to love people with less than his capacity to love. But his love is woven into my story differently than your story."

I suspect my friend remains unsatisfied by my response. It's comforting to believe we are *fairly* cherished. But Jesus, we know, elevates grace and kindness and generosity over fairness.

Wonder	**Jesus**	**Do**
Why does Jesus seem so unconcerned about "fairness"?	"Should you be jealous because I am kind to others?" (Matthew 20:15).	"Cut" to the front of a line and stand—feel the reaction to unfairness.

Pray: Jesus, I can't seem to stop comparing my "fair" to others'—help me.

Jesus Is My Boyfriend?

Read John 16:16-24

There is a sub-category in "Contemporary Christian Music" that is derisively branded "Jesus is my boyfriend" music. Critics say this Christian version of "bubblegum pop" reimagines Jesus as the lead singer in a boy-band and the body of Christ as a stadium full of screaming middle-schoolers. It's sappy romanticism; a pale imitation of the gritty reality that defines the Christian life.

When my wife reached out to a woman who leads a ministry to refugee families in our city, she was invited to the woman's home to meet with a Muslim matriarch who'd recently escaped from Syria, where she'd witnessed her neighbors lined up against a wall and executed, among many other horrors. Sitting in the woman's posh upper-middle-class living room, sipping tea, my wife watched as one of her children started to share a sad story from school with the Syrian woman. But her mother interrupted, "We *only* want happy stories, dear."

The assumption the woman made is that people who've experienced great heartbreak must be protected from stories of heartbreak—that they (and we) must focus only on the positive. And that unconsciously offensive and dismissive myth is true, unfortunately, of some music that we call Christian. But if Christian means "reflecting the heart of Jesus," then whatever wears that label must elevate truth over romanticized empathy, because beauty is fed by the wellspring of truth.

Wonder
Would Jesus listen only to "Christian" music? Why or why not?

Jesus
"You will weep...over what is going to happen to me, but the world will rejoice" (John 16:20).

Do
Sample Christian music that honors "brutal realities" at andrewosenga.com.

Pray: Jesus, I don't need a boyfriend/girlfriend—I need a ferocious advocate.

Come Away With Me

Read Matthew 13:14-23

A personal retreat with Jesus is a hothouse for intimacy—an extended "date night" to enjoy his presence distraction-free. I often recommend "Come Away With Me" experiences to others because solo retreats were habitual for Jesus. To maximize this time, I follow these "best practices"…

- *Curate your "ecosystem."* Find a location that offers natural solitude and outdoor walking/hiking options. I bring music to infuse my time alone, including instrumental, old-school jazz, indie rock, and Christian singer/songwriter. At night, as Jesus did, I gravitate to storytelling—I watch a film (usually light, not intense). I mix stretches of silence with sensory engagement, feeding whatever my soul craves.

- *Bring eclectic reading material.* I choose a "serious" book about Jesus or the Christian life by an author I already love, a book by a new author, a devotional book, and a "comfort food" book (for me, collections of favorite comic strips).

- *Choose primary and secondary Bibles.* I bring my *Jesus-Centered Bible* as a primary focus, but I'll also bring Eugene Peterson's *The Message* to change it up.

- *Give your soul what it needs, when it needs it.* This is a date, not a performance. Take a short nap or stare out a window or wander aimlessly or write a poem.

Wonder	**Jesus**	**Do**
What is hard for you, and easy for you, about "solo time"?	"Now I am departing from the world…I am coming to you" (John 17:11).	Go outside alone, tilt your head back and breathe deeply, and extend your hands. Repeat.

Pray: Jesus, I hear you calling to me, "Come away with me." Here I am.

The Death of Idols

Read Acts 17:16-34

To escape a lynch mob in northern Greece, Paul travels by boat to Athens and waits for his friends Silas and Timothy to join him. As he wanders the city, he sees idols everywhere, and is "deeply troubled." He discovers where the philosophers like to hang out, and he sparks a debate with them—he describes Jesus and the extraordinary events surrounding his resurrection. They think he's, well, crazy. But they prop him up in the Areopagus, the most public of public squares, like he's a reality show star. And then Paul out-shrewds them all, referencing an altar dedicated "To an Unknown God." That mystery God, Paul tells them, is Jesus Christ.

Idol-worship seems like a relic—something Paul had to deal with in Athens, *but not us*. But if Paul walked the streets of our towns today, would he be just as troubled? Would he point out how we idolize our pets and our cars and our professional accomplishments and our alma maters and our ZIP codes and our fitness goals and our gardens and our celebrities and our foodie fads and our bank accounts and our controlling habits and even death itself? Anything we elevate above Jesus is an idol. If we follow him, his Spirit will "trouble" us over our subtle allegiances. And once troubled, we can recalibrate our worship to the one in whom "we live and move and exist."

Wonder
Ask Jesus, "What am I unknowingly treating like an idol in my life?"

Jesus
"No one can serve two masters...You will hate one and love the other" (Matthew 6:24).

Do
Complete this sentence: "Every day I must have _____." Give that up for one day.

Pray: Jesus, I know I elevate so many things above you. But not now.

Three Lies

Read John 8:31-36

In the middle of our "winter of discontent," when political division and spiritual disillusionment creep over our cultural landscape like a chill fog, award-winning New York Times columnist David Brooks observes, "We've created a culture of lies." To illustrate, Brooks pinpoints three of the lies wheedling their way into our moral conscience; the same three "weeds" that Jesus intends to pull from our "garden"…

1. *I can make myself happy.* Brooks calls this "the lie of self-sufficiency." Twice in Matthew's Gospel (chapters 10 and 16) Jesus says, "If you try to hang on to your life [maintain self-sufficiency], you will lose it. But if you give up your life for my sake [invite dependence], you will save it."

2. *Life is an individual journey.* In Western culture, says Brooks, the purpose of life is to "rack up a bunch of experiences, and whoever has the most experiences wins." This is captivity masquerading as freedom. Paul says, "It was for freedom that Christ set us free; therefore keep standing firm and do not be subject again to a yoke of slavery" (Galatians 5:1, NASB).

3. *You have to find your own truth.* Over and over Jesus begins a teaching with "I tell you the truth…" But then he transcends "telling" with this: "I am the way, the truth, and the life" (John 14:6).

Wonder
Of the three "cultural lies," which holds the most sway over you?

Jesus
"You will know the truth, and the truth will set you free" (John 8:32).

Do
Use a magnet to "test" if your gold jewelry is fake—real gold won't attract.

Pray: Jesus, it feels like I'm swimming in a sea of deceit; show me what's true.

The Body Alive

Read John 14:15-20

Those who've committed themselves to co-union with Jesus are called "the body of Christ"—we treat this description as an earnest metaphor for people who call themselves Christian. It is that, but Jesus considers this "body" poetry a literal truth. His repeated "I in you and you in me" and "eat my body, drink my blood" references make clear his "cohabitating" intentions.

He knows his crucifixion and later ascension will feel like he's leaving his friends to cope with the chaotic aftermath alone, without his authority and power as their refuge. They've left everything for him and now will have nothing when he leaves— orphaned in a world that will stalk them like a serial killer. And so Jesus knows he must recalibrate their expectations, reassuring them that his presence is about to shift from outside-in to inside-out.

It's a necessary intimacy. Like the sheep he so often compares us to, we will not survive without the constant companionship of our "good shepherd." We need an ever-present defender who walks our walk and talks our talk. And as his body, we extend his reach in the world, like the skilled and eager dogs shepherds use to help watch over the flock. We look out for each other, alert the Shepherd to dangers others are facing, and risk our lives to defend and rescue.

Wonder	**Jesus**	**Do**
"Eat and drink Jesus" is metaphoric language. How do we do it?	"You are neither hot nor cold. I wish that you were one or the other!" (Revelation 3:15).	Lick a finger, rub it on this page, lick it again. Inside is outside, and vice versa.

Pray: Jesus, thank you for defending me against foes I can't see.

Friendship for Real

Read John 15:12-17

The average adult in our culture has only one close friend. Some track this sobering reality back to "individualism"—an ethic that's venerated in Western society. For example, in Ralph Waldo Emerson's essay "Self-Reliance," he narrows our purpose in life to finding our own path, not joining with others to walk that path together: "Be yourself; no base imitator of another, but your best self." Today, "be your best self" is a rallying cry for self-actualization and empowerment. But the fruit of this pursuit is loneliness.

In a conversation with a German expatriate living in the U.S., Jefferson Fish (professor emeritus of psychology at St. John's University) listens to the woman bemoan the rich relationships she's left behind. It's hard to develop close friendships in a culture that has forgotten what they look like. She tells Fish about a misunderstanding with a co-worker who referred to her as a "friend." The German woman responded, "You're not my friend. You're an acquaintance. We go out for coffee together and chat about things. That's not friendship." Of course, the co-worker was offended by this. Fish says, "Telling someone in the U.S. 'You're not my friend,' is tantamount to saying 'You're my enemy.' It took quite a while for her to overcome this misstep."

It's a socially awkward response, but nevertheless true. Real friendship is death-defying: "There is no greater love," says Jesus, "than to lay down one's life for one's friends."

Wonder	**Jesus**	**Do**
In what ways do you "lay down your life" for your friends?	"Love each other in the same way I have loved you" (John 15:12).	On your palm, write the name of someone who has "laid down" his/her life" for you.

Pray: Jesus, you have called me your friend, and I don't take that lightly.

Esse Quam Videri

Read John 10:12-15

For a college poetry assignment, an English professor gave my daughter Lucy a broad theme as a launching pad—"Knowledge and Identity." From that spare prompt, she wrote this...

Our voices hoarse from screaming
The notes to a song we don't know.
From yelling
To drown the clanging we can't stop.

Security rather than scarcity.
Assurance rather than fear.
Wholeness rather than lack.
Freedom rather than captivity.

We are reminded of the splitting truth.
Truth that rattles our soul and
Restores our being.
We belong.

Not performance,
But grace.
Not clanging,
But a song.

Esse quam videri.
"To be, rather than to appear."

Because he lives outside of time and space, Jesus can offer an antiphon to Lucy's psalm about the power of belonging...

"A hired hand will run when he sees a wolf coming. He will abandon the sheep because they don't belong to him and he isn't their shepherd... [But] I am the good shepherd; I know my own sheep, and they know me, just as my Father knows me and I know the Father. So I sacrifice my life for the sheep."

Wonder	**Jesus**	**Do**
What does it mean to "really belong"?	"After he has gathered his own flock, he walks ahead of them" (John 10:4).	Offer a "belonging" invitation—a slight bow instead of shaking hands.

Pray: Jesus, I've been longing to belong my whole life. May I sit at your table?

The Pruning

Read John 15:1-8

Jesus describes us as the "branches" of a "true grapevine," and because he loves us, his Father the "gardener" will "prune the branches that do bear fruit so they will produce even more." That's all well and good, *except pruning involves cutting off and discarding perfectly fine branch material.*

Early in my marriage I joined a 12-week men's group, led by a professional counselor. Ten of us from my church paid to be a part of it. I'd heard this counselor was fierce, but I was ill-prepared for the bulldozer headed my way. By the fourth week, several men had dropped out of the group because of its intensity. For example, the leader encouraged us to offer regular feedback on how we *really* experienced each other. An older man turned to me and said, "You're a fog—I can't make out who you are or what you're about because you're always spewing fog at me."

That cut removed some of my branch material. Later that night, I came to my Gardener in tears and asked him to recover my soul. And Jesus flashed a reference to Psalm 146:3-5 in my head: *"Don't put your confidence in powerful people; there is no help for you there. When they breathe their last, they return to the earth, and all their plans die with them. But joyful are those who have the God of Israel as their helper, whose hope is in the Lord their God."*

Wonder	**Jesus**	**Do**
What "fruit" has a season of "pruning" produced in you?	"You have already been pruned and purified by [my] message" (John 15:3).	Pruning cuts to reveal beauty. Clip your fingernails for a strong visual of that.

Pray: Jesus, pruning really hurts; it's scary—help me see beauty past the cut.

A Relentless Heart

Read Matthew 11:25-30

In *The Horse Whisperer*, a cowboy named Tom Booker, renowned for his ability to rehabilitate physically and psychologically damaged horses, agrees to work with a horse named Pilgrim who was hit by a lumber truck. Pilgrim has recovered physically, but no one can ride him because his soul and spirit are irreparably damaged from the accident.

During Booker's initial work with Pilgrim, the traumatized horse knocks him down and bolts into a vast Montana pasture. Without a word, Booker follows the horse into the field, where he kneels in the long grass and waits—the whole day and into the twilight, studying Pilgrim gently and intently. As darkness creeps across the field, the horse is finally convinced. He slowly, cautiously ambles toward Booker, hesitantly allowing him to stroke his nose and walk him back to the ranch.

This is a perfect picture of what wounded people are desperate for: persistent, focused, and compassionate pursuit. To trust again, we need the assurance of a relentless heart. Jesus knows that trusting him is our pathway out of darkness and trauma.

When we trust, we finally open ourselves to vulnerability. And when we are vulnerable, we make ourselves like clay. And when we are like clay, we can be molded into something beautiful.

Wonder
When we're hurting, why do we often push away those who want to help?

Jesus
"Come to me, all of you who are weary and carry heavy burdens" (Matthew 11:28).

Do
Tape some grass to this page as a reminder of the Jesus who "waits for you."

Pray: Jesus, thank you for how patient you have been with me.

The Unlikely Hero

Read Matthew 10:34-39

The narrative that runs through all great literature is a protagonist who's ill-suited for heroism but must step up to meet the challenge anyway. Your favorite book or film proves the point—*Harry Potter, The Lord of the Rings, To Kill a Mockingbird, Jane Eyre, Don Quixote, Pride and Prejudice, Gone With the Wind, The Matrix, Star Wars, The Princess Bride,* and any *Spider-Man* film. Our deep attachment to the "unlikely hero" storyline reveals our hard-wiring—there's a David-and-Goliath rhythm deep in our souls, planted there by a God who knows that the fears we "normals" face in life require a hero's response. It's a siren call—a longing for transcendence that we find only in union with Jesus.

Could it be that "whoever loses his life for my sake will find it" is the kindest thing Jesus has ever said to us? It's a brazen invitation to step out of the shadows of our insecurities and doubts and disappointments and into the burning light of his presence. To offer what we have—our "five loaves of bread and two fish"—as the inconsequential seeds of heroism that Jesus blesses, then uses to feed the crowd's hunger. "[And] they all ate as much as they wanted, and afterward, the disciples picked up twelve baskets of leftovers." We're called to live out the rally cry of the great missionary/martyr Jim Elliot: "To give what we cannot keep to gain that which we cannot lose."

Wonder
When have you been the "unlikely hero" in someone's story?

Jesus
"That isn't necessary—you feed them" (Matthew 14:16).

Do
Go to writeaprisoner .com and select a pen pal—be a hero in one person's life.

Pray: Jesus, I'm no hero, but I give you what I have—seeds of courage.

Profane

Read Matthew 23:13-33

I picked up my daughter and a friend (let's call her Emily) from their first meeting for a campus ministry organizaiton and asked what they thought of the night. "Well," said Emily, "I was shocked to see my softball coach there—she's actually one of the leaders!" I asked, "Why is that so shocking?" And she said, "I didn't even think she was a Christian." I persisted, "Why not?" She hesitated, then offered, "Because, well, she kind of cusses a lot…"

I couldn't see Emily's face in the back seat, but I could feel her sheepish, confused look. How could an adult who uses profanity also serve in a Christian leadership role? Are we so immersed in a culture of cursing that we've lost our ability to regulate? A *Chicago Sun-Times* poll of 10,000 students finds that "more and more kids are being exposed to curse words at an early age, and 'traditional' curse words such as 'hell' and 'damn' have been replaced by words once considered too vulgar for adults."

Scripture is full of warnings against "foul speech," and yet Jesus himself uses language so strong with the Pharisees that they plot to kill him. When we ask, "What would Jesus do?" honestly, we'd have to say he is sometimes profane. But he uses charged words like a surgeon, not a crop-duster. In his hands they're a scalpel, cutting out the hypocrisy-cancer that will kill the religious leaders. He never uses words to shock or pander or impress—profane is his wake-up call, not his vice.

Wonder
In general, why do you think people use profanity?

Jesus
"You turn that person into twice the child of hell you yourselves are!" (Matthew 23:15).

Do
Use goofy words to replace the profane— "a pox upon you!" or "hogwash" or "fie!"

Pray: Jesus, I want every word from my mouth to serve your kingdom.

The Cannibal Challenge

Read Matthew 15:1-10

You're exploring an unmapped jungle when cannibals capture you and drag you off to their village. They intend to cook you alive and then eat you. In your captivity, as the kettle-water rises to a boil, you're desperate to befriend your captors. One of them has learned a little English from the last captured explorer, so you labor to explain who you are and what your life is like, hoping familiarity will save your life. You tell him that you often go to a worship service on Sundays. The cannibal asks, "What does *worship* mean?"

And then, before you can stop the words from tumbling out of your mouth, you quote Psalm 34:8: "Taste and see that the Lord is good." Immediately you regret using the word "taste." But the cannibal is intrigued. "Well," you say, "to worship something is to celebrate its goodness, and to really appreciate the goodness of something you have to taste it—to ingest it fully into your being." And now the cannibal seems moved: "Yes, you cannot delight in a food unless you eat it." And you nod and smile and pray that he is not thinking of you when he says this…

When we taste great food, we're transported into ecstasy—it's an organic response, not something we "work at." And this is also worship; our organic response to the taste of goodness in Jesus.

Wonder
What would you have to do to "taste Jesus" more in your life?

Jesus
"Their worship is a farce, for they teach man-made ideas as commands from God" (Matthew 15:9).

Do
When you eat, savor the flavors. As you do, thank Jesus for his "flavors."

Pray: Jesus, when I slow down to linger over your "flavors," I just want more.

Proud Daddy

Read Hebrews 6:16-19

In _Eighth Grade_, writer/director Bo Burnham's quiet sledgehammer of a film, Kayla is a socially awkward teenage girl with her own YouTube channel, dispensing advice on how to navigate life. Her confident persona barely hides her fragility. Kayla's single dad is working hard to reach her, but failing. After a disturbing encounter with a guy who tries to take advantage of her, Kayla despairs of ever uncovering a _me_ that anyone could love. She asks her dad for help burning a box of mementos she's been keeping since sixth grade. Together, they gently place the box in their backyard fire pit.

Dad: _What was in there?_
Kayla: _Nothing, really. Just…sort of my hopes and dreams._
Dad: _Right…and you're burning them?_
Kayla: _Yes._

And then Kayla asks if he's sad because he's stuck with such a disappointing daughter. Broken, he responds: "You're wrong. Being your dad makes me so happy, Kayla… A lot of parents have to love their kids in spite of who they are. Not me. I get to love you _because_ of who you are." Kayla climbs onto her dad's lap and holds on, weeping under the cover of his refuge. Paul does the same, writing in Hebrews: "We who have fled to [Jesus] for refuge can have great confidence as we hold to the hope that lies before us."

Wonder
Wait in silence after you ask Jesus, "What's one thing you love about me?"

Jesus
"He will joyfully carry [his lost sheep] home on his shoulders" (Luke 15:5).

Do
In a prayer time, experience "refuge"—drape a blanket over yourself.

Pray: Jesus, you are my "tabernacle"—a covering that travels with me.

Ordinary Time

Read John 16:12-15

At the end of September, we're standing at the top of a huge, twisting water slide—once we step off into October, the momentum will hurtle us through the holidays, spilling us out into January, sputtering and dazed. Over-scheduled and over-stimulated, our "ordinary time" is buried under the pomp and circumstance of extraordinary time. Our souls are whiplashed by the demands of the spirit and the demands of the season.

To cope, we tell ourselves a myth: *If I can control my schedule, I can control my life. This year will be different...* But willpower is a fickle god, and a calendar is no "sacred text." So how do we live inside the heart of Jesus as we're about to head down the water slide? We pay attention to how *he* lived counter-culturally...

- *He adopts a Sabbath mindset*—living restfully even when all around him was chaotic and feverish.

- *He savors his mealtimes*—practicing "slow rebellion" by inviting others to enjoy the riches of community.

- *He plays*—stopping to call to him the children, who ignore constraints of time and schedules.

- *He refuses to elevate family obligations over "true family" fellowship*—he tells his disciples, "I have a kind of food you know nothing about" after a delightful encounter with "the woman at the well."

Wonder
What do you look forward to with the holidays, and what do you dread?

Jesus
"My nourishment comes from doing the will of God" (John 4:34).

Do
Climb up a "down" escalator as a reminder to live counter-culturally.

Pray: Jesus, my control is never enough—I'd like to try trusting you instead.

Myth-Busters

Read John 8:31-47

Drop a penny off of the top of the Empire State Building in New York City and it will embed itself in the concrete sidewalk. That's the sort of urban legend the hosts of *MythBusters*, the long-running TV show, put to the test. And when they test the penny-drop myth, they discover that light objects dropped from a great height act like feathers, not anvils. So what if we myth-busted conventional beliefs about Jesus? Here are eight worth testing…

- Jesus will never give me any more than I can handle in life.

- Jesus' primary goal is to make us better, happier people.

- Jesus is supernatural, so we can't surprise him.

- Jesus already has a "plan" for my life—my job is to get on board with that plan, whatever it is.

- Jesus loves us, so he'll make sure every "good person" enters heaven, and (in the end) every "bad person," too.

- Some sins are worse than others.

- Jesus accepts everyone just as they are.

Perhaps the biggest myth we believe about Jesus is that we already know everything we need to know about him. When we slow down and pay attention to what he *actually* says and does, we discover every one of these eight myths is *untrue*.

Wonder
Which of the myths listed seems most true to you, and why?

Jesus
"You think [the Scriptures] give you eternal life. But the Scriptures point to me!" (John 5:39).

Do
Watch *MythBusters* on dailymotion.com. Ponder the myths Jesus has exposed.

Pray: Jesus, I'm going to approach you as if I know nothing about you.

The Points System

Read Mark 10:17-27

What does it take to be a "good person"—someone heaven-ready? In the award-winning satirical comedy *The Good Place*, an angel tells a crowd of new arrivals that they've made it to heaven and explains the complex "points system" that made it possible...

Welcome to your first day in the afterlife. You were all, simply put, good people. But how do we know that you were good?... During your time on Earth, every one of your actions had a positive or a negative value, depending on how much good or bad that action put into the universe... Every single thing you did had an effect that rippled out over time and ultimately created some amount of good or bad... When your time on Earth has ended, we calculate the total value of your life using our perfectly accurate measuring system. Only the people with the very highest scores, the true cream of the crop, get to come here, to the Good Place.

Later, we find out that the "points system" is actually created in hell, not heaven. Assigning points to good and bad behavior sounds fair, but it's more like torture. When a cocksure young man approaches Jesus to show off his "high score," Jesus responds slyly: "Why do you call me good? Only God is tryly good." It's our attachment to goodness, not our false attainment of it, that opens the door to eternal life.

Wonder	Jesus	Do
In what ways have you subtly bought into the "points system"?	"With people it is impossible, but not with God" (Mark 10:27, NASB).	The points system demands perfection; coffee-stain this page to make it imperfect.

Pray: Jesus, I'm exhausted from trying so hard to be good. Be good in me.

The Physics of Belief

Read Matthew 9:27-30

During a break from school, after saving up for the trip, my daughter traveled to Spain with friends. While there, they visited the royal palace in Madrid. She sent us a photo with a note claiming that she'd actually seen the king of Spain peering over a balcony. When my wife read that note, she said, "It probably wasn't the king." I asked, "Why do you doubt that?" And she said, "There are a lot of people walking around inside that palace."

To my daughter, this king-sighting was simply a fact, but to my wife it was conjecture. So why might my wife disbelieve something my daughter said was undeniably true? And what makes us believe or disbelieve things...or people?

As Jesus is returning to his guesthouse in Nazareth, two blind men follow along behind, begging him to have mercy on them. They are insistent, way beyond the boundaries of decorum. When Jesus enters his home, they follow uninvited. This socially awkward act delights Jesus—he decides to ask them, with childlike playfulness, "Do you believe I can make you see?" And they respond with childlike trust: "Yes, Lord, we do." And then he touches their eyes and proclaims, "Because of your faith, it will happen." It's not his touch that opens their eyes; it's their determined belief that Jesus is exactly who he says he is. When we believe in Jesus, we discover that he believes in us.

Wonder	**Jesus**	**Do**
Ask Jesus, "Why do you believe in me?"	"You must really believe it will happen and have no doubt" (Mark 11:23).	Test your belief—choose your wardrobe for the day with your eyes closed.

Pray: Jesus, help me cross the bridge from doubt to belief.

Storytelling

Read Matthew 21:23-27

Do you sometimes say and do things that make you question your own motives? We must answer for our behavior, even if we lack real understanding. When we're bothered by our impact on others, we grasp for a plausible story that explains what we've done, to relieve our dissonance. Sometimes those stories reveal the truth; sometimes they obscure it.

Like a screenwriter who crafts the narrative boundaries for a character, the stories we tell about ourselves determine our "character arc." Professional screenwriting coaches help clients learn to explore the wants, inner goals, and unconscious desires of their characters—these motivations drive "the transformation the protagonist undergoes during the movie."

Likewise, the "character arc" we embrace about ourselves determines the "me" we show others. We *become* the story we've decided to live inside. That's why Jesus wants to be our "script doctor," reconstructing our story to match the truth of our being. He often tangles with false storytellers who try to reinterpret his narrative. They brand him a lawbreaker and a "servant of Satan" and a performing magician and an "arrogant" interloper. But the truth is that Jesus loves us—he's on our side, he's coming to rescue us, and he's fierce. The false stories that others tell about him are like waves crashing against the "sea wall" of his identity, and he wants the same for us.

Wonder
What's one way others have misinterpreted the "true you"?

Jesus
"The stone that the builders rejected has now become the cornerstone" (Matthew 21:42).

Do
To repent of a sin, just say (out loud), "Rewrite me!"

Pray: Jesus, I want to become the me you think I am.

Kingdoms in Conflict

Read Luke 18:15-17

How does the Jesus-following life compare to the pursuit of the American Dream—" the set of ideals in which freedom includes the opportunity for prosperity and success, as well as an upward social mobility...achieved through hard work in a society with few barriers." Well, when parents bring their children to Jesus so he can bless them, the disciples chase them away and scold the adults for distracting him. But Jesus, instead, scolds his disciples and invites the children to come back. His response contrasts the values of the kingdom of God and the values embraced by his culture. Likewise, while the American Dream…

- frames freedom as financial success, Jesus says, "You will know the truth, and the truth will set you free" (John 8:32).

- promises "upward social mobility," Jesus says, "So those who are last now will be first then" (Matthew 20:16).

- points to career success as the path to blessing, Jesus says, "Look at the lilies of the field and how they grow. They don't work or make their clothing, yet Solomon in all his glory was not dressed as beautifully as they are" (Matthew 6:28-29).

- targets our barriers to success, Jesus says, "Here on earth you will have many trials and sorrows. But take heart, because I have overcome the world" (John 16:33).

Wonder
Why do we treat the American Dream with such reverence?

Jesus
"I came not to bring peace, but a sword" (Matthew 10:34).

Do
Poke a hole in this page with a pen—a reminder that Jesus punctures the American Dream.

Pray: Jesus, my hope is in you, not the American Dream.

The Lesson of the Butterfly

Read Matthew 10:5-42

My daughter Emma is a big fan of the parkour-inspired TV competition *American Ninja Warrior*. She's athletic, wiry, and flexible—perfect for a sport that's "played" on an extreme obstacle course. She asked me to build a couple of standard "ninja" obstacles in our basement, so now we have a 12-foot horizontal pegboard and an "unstable bridge" hanging from our rafters. Emma's traverse across that pegboard looks so effortless that I was determined to see how far I could get. Well, "not far" would be charitable...

So much of life feels like that pegboard challenge—other people seem to master things so much easier than we do. We give it our all, but the challenge is beyond our strength. In the contemporary fable "The Lesson of the Butterfly," a man cuts open the cocoon of an exhausted butterfly that has tried but failed to emerge on its own. But the now-freed butterfly's wings are shriveled, and it soon dies, because the man does not realize that the fight was necessary to strengthen the butterfly's wings.

This is why Jesus sends his disciples on an impossible mission ("heal the sick, raise the dead, cure those with leprosy, and cast out demons") under impossible restrictions (no money, change of clothes, or arranged housing). His friends will need strength to advance the kingdom of God, and his prescribed hardships will strengthen their wings.

Wonder
Why is it so hard to refrain from easing others' struggles?

Jesus
"Look, I am sending you out as sheep among wolves" (Matthew 10:16).

Do
Test your strength—push your back against a wall in a seated position and hold.

Pray: Jesus, my life feels like a pegboard challenge; please be my strength.

Don't Trust Your "Warhorse"

Read Psalm 33

Susan Cain's book *Quiet: The Power of Introverts in a World That Can't Stop Talking* offers a hopeful spin on inwardness, just what shy-ish people (like me) crave. In contrast, the downsides are obvious—including an almost-constant awareness of our interior lives. Introverts chew and chew and chew over mistakes, missed opportunities, and unavoidable awkwardness. Many days I'm whispering a sort-of prayer under my breath: *"Sorry, Lord. Sorry, sorry, sorry..."* In the middle of one apology-athon, I asked Jesus if he had anything to say to me, and then I waited. Soon I "saw" Psalm 33:16-22 in my mind's eye:

The best-equipped army cannot save a king, nor is great strength enough to save a warrior. **Don't count on your warhorse to give you victory—for all its strength, it cannot save you.** *But the Lord watches over those who fear him, those who rely on his unfailing love. He rescues them from death and keeps them alive in times of famine. We put our hope in the Lord. He is our help and our shield. In him our hearts rejoice, for we trust in his holy name. Let your unfailing love surround us, Lord, for our hope is in you alone.*

"Warhorse" describes our skills, abilities, and gifting—and it is not to be counted on. All of Jesus' best friends scoffed at their own qualifications, preferring his instead.

Wonder

What "warhorse" do you trust more than you trust Jesus?

Jesus

"Love the Lord with all your heart...soul...mind, and...strength" (Mark 12:30).

Do

In your car's rear-window dirt, draw S-E-Y. Say "yes" to Jesus when you glance back.

Pray: Jesus, I know I've trusted my "warhorses" more than you—I'm sorry.

Attachments

Read Matthew 12:22-30

Comic-Con is a massive pop culture conference in San Diego that one fan breathlessly describes "like Black-Friday shopping for nerdy stuff with 130,000 other people in a single building amusement park for four and a quarter days straight." On a work-related trip to this mecca of nerd-dom, I was walking to the convention center one morning, trying to keep pace with a young guy carrying a bag with the unmistakable conference logo. I stole a longer-than-normal glance at him because he was dressed so *vanilla* by Comic-Con "cosplay" standards—a pair of jeans and a T-shirt. He deviated from this blandness in just one telling detail: He wore black leather Batman-like gauntlets on his bare arms.

This guy unlocked Comic-Con's magnetic draw—nowhere else could he so clearly mark who he is and what he stands for. We attach ourselves to subcultures because we're wired to attach ourselves to *something*. In a conference panel discussion, Andy Grossberg, editor of *Tripwire Magazine*, said, "[Pop culture is] a kind of church, offering people a moral vision, a life mission, and a passionate community of like-minded parishioners."

Jesus understands the power of attachment: "Whoever comes to me [or, from the literal Greek, "comes *into* me"] will never be hungry again" (John 6:35). We have many attachment options, Jesus is saying, but he offers the only option that transforms us into "good," because he is good.

Wonder	**Jesus**	**Do**
What do your "attachments" reveal about what's most important to you?	"If a tree is good, its fruit will be good. If a tree is bad, its fruit will be bad" (Matthew 12:33).	Wear something today that obviously marks your attachment to Jesus.

Pray: Jesus, I want to "wear you on my sleeve" so others will know I'm yours.

To Tell the Truth

Read John 17:6-10

On the old game show *To Tell the Truth*, three contestants (all of them claiming to be the extraordinary person the host has described) must convince four celebrity panelists they are *not* one of two impostors. The show is a metaphoric reminder of the pressure we feel to reduce ourselves to an *impostor self...*

- Our marketplaces want us to believe we're mere consumers.

- Our workplaces want us to believe we're mere "assets."

- Our schools want us to believe we are what we know.

- Our music industry wants us to believe our sexuality dwarfs all other characteristics.

- Our churches want us to believe that mastering biblical principles equals maturity.

- Our gyms want us to believe that "cut" abs define our worth.

- Our friends (sometimes) want us to believe that we're chiefly responsible for their happiness.

- Our enemies want us to believe that shame tells the truth.

In his final conversation with his Father before he's arrested, Jesus says, "My prayer is not for the world, but for those you have given me, because they belong to you." Our real selves are simply defined—we are those who are called "mine" by Jesus.

Wonder	**Jesus**	**Do**
How would you introduce yourself with who you are, not what you do?	"I have revealed you to the ones you gave me...They were always yours" (John 17:6).	Hold your hand over your eyes like a mask. Pray for freedom, then drop the mask.

Pray: Jesus, remove the husk of my impostor self and reveal *me*.

The Art of Asking

Read John 5:1-15

When punk rocker and performance artist Amanda Palmer launched a Kickstarter campaign to support a new album, she netted a record $1.2 million. How did she do it? In a widely viewed TED Talk, Palmer calls it "the art of asking." Early in her career as an artist, she scouted locations in Boston's public squares, then painted her skin white, donned a wedding dress, and posed as a statue. She offered pedestrians a daisy and five seconds of focused eye contact in return for a donation. In that boot camp of vulnerability, Palmer learned to relax as an "asker."

Her customers were "lonely people who looked like they hadn't talked to anyone in weeks," she says, "and we would sort of fall in love a little bit… My eyes would say, 'Thank you. I see you.' Their eyes would say, 'Nobody ever sees me. Thank you.' " Later, touring with a band, Palmer often "couch-surfed" in the homes of fans. Along the way, she learned to rise above the fundamental shame we all battle when we are needy but afraid to ask for help. Palmer believes "asking for what you want" is an act of artistic vulnerability.

Likewise, when Jesus encounters a man who has languished by the pool of Bethesda for 40 years, he prods him to ask for what he wants. He's inviting the man to be vulnerable with him—and when the man asks for help, he is, in essence, *abiding in Jesus*.

Wonder
On a scale from 1 to 10, how comfortable are you asking for help?

Jesus
"Would you like to get well?" (John 5:6).

Do
Ask someone for help with one of your daily chores. Is it hard or easy for you, and why?

Pray: Jesus, I am not afraid to ask you for help.

Everyday Buddhism

Read Luke 12:22-34

In *The Journey of Desire*, John Eldredge writes, "Desire is the source of our most noble aspirations and our deepest sorrows... We cannot live without the yearning, and yet the yearning sets us up for...deep and devastating disappointment." To mitigate that scorching pain, we launch a peremptory strike at hope, blowing it up before it blows us up. In essence, we are closet Buddhists.

Buddhism is a pre-Christian movement founded by Prince Siddhartha Gautama ("The Buddha") 2,500 years ago. Gautama's parents, aristocrats of Kapilavastu, gave their son every luxury. But he grew restless and left to experience the world. There, he saw sickness, injury, and death, and it shattered him. So Gautama renounced his life of luxury to pursue a "cure" to the world's unhappiness. His solution? Because "the things people want most cause them the most suffering," Gautama promoted "Nirvana" as our goal in life—"the extinction of desire."

This philosophy is infected by cowardice. We are *not* to fear our desires because they come with a side order of pain—that pain drives us into the heart of Jesus, who reminds us, "Truly, truly, I say to you, unless a grain of wheat falls into the earth and dies, it remains alone; but if it dies, it bears much fruit (John 12:24, NASB). Desire plants the seeds, pain fertilizes them, and fruit is born.

Wonder
In what ways have you "pruned away" your desires in life, and why?

Jesus
"Wherever your treasure is, there the desires of your heart will also be" (Matthew 6:21).

Do
Pets have clear desires. Take a moment to make your pet's dreams come true.

Pray: Jesus, give me the courage to embrace my deepest desires.

The Triumph of Hope

Read Romans 4:18-25

Nothing undermines hope quite so efficiently as pain. After my second broken engagement, a few months before the wedding, the pain was so intense that I retreated into an "unmarked dark cave" where I could divorce myself from hope and hide out. There, I made a vow that (I believed) would keep me from ever entering that cave again: "I will never, ever allow my heart to hope in the restoration of my relationship with Bev again. I will put a bullet through the head of my deepest hopes."

And I made good on that vow—for six months, whenever I ran into Bev, I blasted away at the hope that stirred to life. I was determined to fill that zombie-hope with so many bullet holes that, finally, it would stay dead. But at a wedding reception for a friend, she sought me out: "I miss you—do you think we could meet to talk?" I pulled out my hope-gun and tried to squeeze the trigger, but I just couldn't do it. That zombie ate me alive, and a year later we married. That was three decades ago.

When Jesus sees the triumph of hope in the face of pain, he delights over it like nothing else. Hope, he knows, is our salvation. And pain is its enemy. But remember, Jesus says, "You have heard the law that says, 'Love your neighbor' and hate your enemy. But I say, love your enemies!" (Matthew 5:43-44).

Wonder
How have you persevered through pain toward hope?

Jesus
"I tell you the truth, I haven't seen faith like this in all Israel!" (Matthew 8:10).

Do
On your favorite news website, what image gives you hope, and why?

Pray: Jesus, take my pain and use it as fuel for hope.

Vocational Identity

Read Matthew 7:24-27

On the popular *America's Got Talent* TV show, a magician named Eric Chien auditions, hoping to make it past the first round. The producers decide to highlight his story before the audition, so we learn how, from an early age, he'd grown to love performing magic tricks so much that it became his identity. He cannot separate "me" from "magician." But then life throws a curveball—he's conscripted into military service in Taiwan and told he can't bring his magic tricks with him. When he leaves all that behind, he also leaves *himself* behind. It almost breaks him.

It's easy to translate "purpose in life" to our vocations—our jobs or careers or academic pursuits. We're hungering for the source of our good impact in the world, and the default diagnostic is our working lives. Our vocations promise to surface what is most true about us. At the start of my senior year in high school, on a lark, I joined the newspaper staff. I inherited a humor column by default, and that column eventually won a statewide award. So I turned down an engineering scholarship to pursue journalism in college. I stumbled into my vocation and discovered a crucial facet of my identity.

Yes, our vocations can lure our true identities out of the shadows, but they are not synonymous. Most of us learn this the hard way. We need a better foundation—something built on Jesus-bedrock, not vocation-sand.

Wonder
How have you discovered what is most true about your identity?

Jesus
"That house...won't collapse because it is built on bedrock" (Matthew 7:25).

Do
Find a photo that represents your dream job. Make it your phone's wallpaper.

Pray: Jesus, I want my job to be, somehow, one more way I worship you.

The Impossible Nutter

Read 1 John 5:13-15

In an interview with Bono, lead singer/songwriter for the super-group U2, the Irish late-night TV host Gay Byrne is skeptical of the rock star's well-publicized faith in Jesus. For Byrne, a veteran critic of celebrity culture, this is red meat…

Byrne: *To whom or what do you pray?* Bono: *To Christ.* Byrne: *And what do you pray for?* Bono: *I pray to get to know the will of God…* Byrne: *So what or who was Jesus?* Bono: *I think it's a defining question for a Christian… And I don't think you're let off easily by saying a great thinker or a great philosopher. Because actually he went 'round saying he was the Messiah—that's why he was crucified… So either he was the Son of God or he was…* Byrne: *Not…* Bono: *No, no…nuts! And I find it hard to accept that half the earth for 2,000 years have felt their life touched and inspired by some nutter. I don't believe it.* Byrne: *So…you believe he was divine.* Bono: *Yes.* Byrne: *And…you believe he rose physically from the dead.* Bono: *Yes. I have no problem with miracles. I'm living around them.* (Smiling) *I am one…*

Reality, we believe, is experienced only through our five senses. But Jesus has refused to give us concrete proofs. Why? He has left for us a "leap of faith" that transcends our senses. We find the reality of God only in relationship with Jesus.

Wonder	**Jesus**	**Do**
When has Jesus felt "most real" to you, and why?	"Go away by yourself, shut the door behind you, and pray…in private" (Matthew 6:6).	Jesus used bread and wine to remind us of reality. Take "communion" today.

Pray: Jesus, your presence in me has made my life a miracle.

Demanding Signs

Read John 6:26-35

Jesus has miraculously fed a crowd in the wilderness, and now they want more. He's wise to their motivation: "I tell you the truth, you want to be with me because I fed you, not because you understood the miraculous signs." So someone in the crowd tries to work another angle with him, feigning interest in his teaching: "We want to perform God's works, too. What should we do?" And Jesus, always shrewd, tells them the only work God expects of them is to "believe in the one he has sent," who is standing in front of them. And now the crowd's spokesman thinks he's found the leverage he's been looking for: "Show us a miraculous sign if you want us to believe in you." In other words, *give us something to eat...*

Jesus can see the crowd is hungry, but it's not the kind of hunger that will fill them. When a toddler demands a scoop of ice cream before dinner, a loving parent will deny what is shortsighted and unhealthy to give what is lasting and nutritious. The "sign" the crowd is demanding is actually a replacement for relationship with Jesus. They want what he can produce, but they don't want *him*. And that's an unsustainable diet—they will die if they follow it. We're made to consume. But the menu in the kingdom of God features only "true bread," because the signs we demand don't feed our deepest hunger.

Wonder	**Jesus**	**Do**
What's a "sign" you've asked Jesus to give you to prove himself to you?	"Whoever comes to me will never be hungry again" (John 6:35).	Notice the road signs on a short trip. As you do, pray, "I want you, not signs."

Pray: Jesus, I'm hungry for true bread and living water.

What's the Meaning of Life?

Read Matthew 13:1-9, 18-23

Ministry staffers working with ChristLife brought their video cameras to Washington Square in New York City and asked random people from all over the world a big question: *What is the meaning of life?* A sampling of the answers they collected...

- "I guess everyone comes up with that for themselves."

- "I don't know, I never thought about it."

- "Sometimes I think maybe it's to get it right."

- "To contribute to society in the best way you know how."

- "To raise a family and have grandchildren."

- "To make the world a better place."

- "To connect with something that's bigger than yourself."

- "To live a good life and to leave some sort of mark on history, and to have somebody remember me."

Blaise Pascal said we all have a "God-shaped hole" that only Jesus can fill, but we've certainly worked hard to come up with alternate hole-fillers. This is why Jesus tells the Parable of the Farmer Scattering Seed. The true meaning of our lives is to offer Jesus "rich soil" to plant in—to pursue the truth about ourselves and about Jesus and to trust him to guide our path. We're meant to be a source of life-giving "nutrition" for everyone around us; food that grows only from the "seeds" Jesus wants to plant in us.

Wonder
If asked the "meaning of life" question, how would you answer?

Jesus
"The seed that fell on good soil represents those who truly hear" (Matthew 13:23).

Do
Try Jesus' metaphor— plant seeds in an indoor pot; nurture them to maturity.

Pray: Jesus, enrich the "soil" of my soul with your fertilizer.

Is This All There Is?

Read Matthew 22:23-32

Some of the greatest thinkers in history—Socrates, Darwin, Freud, and Marx—argue that there is only one brave, rational response to the metaphysical question "Is this all there is?" That is, *Yes, there is nothing beyond what your intellect can prove.* Karl Marx, for example, says, "Christianity cannot be reconciled with reason [as embodied in Enlightenment science] because 'secular' and 'spiritual' reason contradict with each other." He, and so many others, see the world through a binary lens—if reality and superstition are going to battle it out, then reality must win. Those who embrace the "concepts" of heaven and hell, they say, are practicing primitive wish-fulfillment—they lack the courage to accept the world as it is…

But what if there is something more permanent and more beautiful than our physical lives? Fred Rogers, the pioneering host of *Mister Rogers' Neighborhood,* framed this quote in French from Saint-Exupery's *Le Petit Prince*: "That which is essential is invisible to the naked eye." What if we can experience a deeper freedom than physical freedom? The Sadducees don't believe in life that continues after death—the concepts of heaven and the supernatural seem ridiculous to them. And so they concoct a brain-teaser for Jesus, hoping to expose these fallacies. But Jesus is blunt: "Your mistake is that you don't know the Scriptures, and you don't know the power of God." Jesus treats our "life after life" as an unquestioned reality, not a hopeful speculation.

Wonder	**Jesus**	**Do**
What is your most convincing "proof" of life after death?	"He is the God of the living, not the dead" (Matthew 22:32).	Feel how two refrigerator magnets repel each other—the reality of the unseen.

Pray: Jesus, give me eyes to see the "essential unseen" all around me.

Will Everything Be Okay?

Read Matthew 8:23-27

Grace has Down Syndrome—she has a sweet disposition and a delightful personality, unless she doesn't like what she has been asked to do. Then she's prone to lash out physically. And this is one of those moments. The lifeguard has blown the whistle, so everyone must get out of the pool. But Grace wants to swim longer. Her summer-camp counselor stands at the edge of the pool and asks her again to get out. But Grace says no and swims toward the deep end. Her counselor slips into the water and, along with a few others, tries to approach Grace. But she swings her fists at them. For 30 minutes the counselors tread water around her, until her will weakens and she finally decides she has had enough.

Metaphorically, we're a lot like Grace. Our choices are leading us into danger, but we treat Jesus as if he's a threat to our control, not a source of rescue. We think we know what's best. And so he pursues us, treading water and waiting for us to exhaust our keep-away tactics. He is missional in his patience—he wants to lead us out of the deep end before we drown in our own petulance.

When a storm threatens to capsize their boat, the disciples are terrified. But Jesus is asleep in the back. He is not worried. *You will get through this—I'm right here, treading water next to you…*

Wonder	**Jesus**	**Do**
What's something you fear won't be okay in your life right now?	"Why are you afraid? You have so little faith!" (Matthew 8:26).	Search "scary sounds" online. Click, listen, and ask Jesus to calm your fears.

Pray: Jesus, have I worn you out yet? Your patience with me is a miracle.

Pudding Proof

Read Matthew 7:15-20

In an age when the lines between truth and untruth are unrecognizably smudged, when a basement blogger is trusted more than a professional journalist, and when the church is paralyzed by a rapidly changing moral landscape, truth is in the eye of the beholder. Psychology professor Ira Hyman says, "We all need to know the truth if we want to be able to behave rationally…Should I use the results of someone's research to make an important argument? I need to know that the data are reliable and true. Should we continue this relationship? I need to believe that you've told me the truth about where you were last night…Finding the truth seems impossible…"

So how do we know what's false and what's true in life? Jesus tells us, essentially, that the "proof is in the pudding"—we have to eat the pudding to know whether or not it's good. We have to "taste the fruit" of things to know whether or not they're true. If something is true, no matter what it looks like on the outside, it will produce "good fruit." And if it's not true, no matter how "acceptable" it is to others, it will produce "bad fruit."

We need to get the taste of truth in our mouths, or the feel of it under our fingernails, or the soul of it in our DNA. To spot the counterfeit, we scrutinize the real thing—the One whose name is Truth.

Wonder
What sources of information do you trust the most, and why?

Jesus
"A good tree produces good fruit, and a bad tree produces bad fruit" (Matthew 7:17).

Do
Taste food past its expiration date. What determines if it's safe to eat?

Pray: Jesus, expose the counterfeit truths in my life.

The Beauty of Desperation

Read Luke 14:16-24

Jesus is invited to Sabbath dinner at the home of an influential religious leader—"the people [are] watching him closely" because he's a one-man reality show, already infamous for the outlandish and the incredible and the inexplicable. And though it is the Sabbath, he heals a man whose arms and legs are swollen, then sprays the room with unasked-for advice...

- He sees the guests (a toxic set of insecure local celebrities) all jockeying for positions of honor, so he says, "When you are invited to a wedding feast, don't sit in the seat of honor... Instead, take the lowest place at the foot of the table."

- He derides his host for inviting only his "friends, brothers, relatives, and rich neighbors" to the gathering, then urges him to "invite the poor, the crippled, the lame, and the blind. Then at the resurrection of the righteous, God will reward you for inviting those who could not repay you."

- Finally, he launches into a jagged-edge parable with a master (God) inviting the advantaged, entitled, and self-satisfied to his opulent feast, but they all offer lame excuses. So he sends his servant out to call the poor/crippled/blind/lame instead—desperate people who respond as if they won the lottery. His message is plain: If you're complacent and self-satisfied and "above it all," you'll end up "beneath it all."

Wonder
Why does Jesus so often gravitate to desperate people?

Jesus
"Those who exalt themselves will be humbled" (Luke 14:11).

Do
Create "care packages," kept in your car, to hand to the homeless instead of cash.

Pray: Jesus, you are the one who is "above it all," not me...

The King's Children

Read Matthew 18:1-10

The Pharisees practice an immaturity they refuse to abandon. And Jesus calls us to a childlikeness we refuse to embrace. We're like Pharisees when we're petty, nitpicking, narcissistic, ignorant, and cruel. But we act like children of the King when we…

- *believe in what we can't see.* George MacDonald says children are "given to metaphysics"—belief in Santa Claus/ Easter Bunny/leprechauns is a bridge to belief in Jesus.

- *are relaxed when we're "under authority."* When a loving, attentive parent is near, children are reflexively trusting.

- *invite others to nurture us.* Children will unabashedly ask to be hugged or comforted. My young daughter's soccer team lived for the end of the game, when parents formed a "cheer tunnel" for them to run through, over and over.

- *live out Paul's definition of love.* They can "bear all things, believe all things, hope all things, endure all things."

- *offer ridiculous generosity.* One of my daughters once dumped all her money on the table and insisted we use it for an expensive car repair.

- *live in a continual state of wonder.* Iconic newspaper editor Walt Streightiff says, "There are no seven wonders of the world in the eyes of a child. There are seven million."

Wonder
Are you more or less trusting today than when you were a child, and why?

Jesus
"[Be] as humble as this little child [to be] greatest in the Kingdom of Heaven" (Matthew 18:4).

Do
Like a child, enjoy story time: "Prairie Home Companion: News from Lake Wobegon" at podbean.com.

Pray: Jesus, the older I get, the stiffer my soul gets. Soften me into a child.

Fake Faith

Read Acts 8:9-24

Simon the Sorcerer is the David Blaine of ancient Samaria—his staggering illusions earn him the nickname "The Great Power of God." He's rich and famous and riding high. But then Philip rolls into town with his band of ragamuffin disciples, preaching "the kingdom of God and the name of Jesus Christ" and baptizing left and right. Simon is so bowled over by all of this that he, also, is baptized. He joins the traveling ragamuffins and is amazed, over and over, by the miracles he sees. Like all magicians, he *buys* his tricks, so when Peter and John bestow the Spirit, he naturally offers to pay for it.

Peter has come up from Jerusalem and barely knows Simon, so he assumes the worst: "Your heart is not right... You can't buy the gift of God with money." Simon's mistake is more ignorance than arrogance, but the lesson he learns is a gift to all of us. Like him, we treat faith like it's a thing we must acquire, when it's really a *knowing* we act on. Faith is the fruit of a true understanding of who Jesus is and what he can do. It's the confidence of a long-married couple who are certain of each other's hearts; it's not a Harry Potter spell.

Paul says "faith comes by...hearing by the Word of God" (Romans 10:17, NKJV), so when we pay better attention to Jesus (the Word of God) we grow our faith.

Wonder
What makes it easy to trust someone, and what makes it hard?

Jesus
"Those who listen to my teaching... have an abundance of knowledge" (Matthew 13:12).

Do
Search "Spoon Bending Illusion Revealed" on youtube.com—a trick, not a miracle.

Pray: Jesus, I need more faith, so I need better ears to hear you.

Out of the Boat

Read Matthew 14:22-33

Dave Freeman was 47 when his book *100 Things to Do Before You Die* was released—just a month before he died after a fall at his home. That's twisted irony and a warning shot across our bow. So many of us remain spectators on the sidelines because, well, *we think we have plenty of time*. But sometimes, not so much. The time to enter into adventure is now.

Hunger tends to drive us to Jesus, and nothing produces hunger more acutely in us than the danger of adventure. We're reminded, "You will seek me and find me when you search for me with all your heart" (Jeremiah 29:13, NIV). "All your heart" is adventure-talk. To find him we'll need to leave the sidelines and join him on the field, where our hearts are fully engaged.

Jesus invites Peter to climb over the side of his boat in a stormy sea in the middle of the night. Yes, Peter sinks when the adventure gets scary, but only *he* knows what it's like to feel the hand of Jesus grabbing, then lifting him out of the saltwater darkness. His friends back on the boat are spectators, but out there on the sea is a sinking rock on which Jesus will later build the foundation of the church.

He's looking for reluctant adventurers, not cautious spectators.

Wonder
What's the last thing you did in your life that felt like an adventure?

Jesus
"Don't be afraid…Take courage. I am here!" (Matthew 14:27).

Do
Go on a rescue adventure—discover how to help refugees at rescue.org.

Pray: Jesus, please call me out of my boat.

Never, Never, Never Give Up

Read 2 Corinthians 11:16-33

Over our kitchen sink hangs a Winston Churchill quote burned into a barnwood plaque—*"Never, never, never give up."* It's a battle-cry lifted from a speech Churchill delivered after England outlasted the horror of The Blitz—the systematic destruction of London by Luftwaffe bombers during an eight-month apocalypse. More than 32,000 civilians died and two million homes (one-third of London) were destroyed. Churchill understood the precarious fragility of this moment in history—after maintaining their "stiff upper lip" for so long, how would the British people find the resolve they needed to win the war?

Author Angela Duckworth defines grit as the "perseverance to run a marathon, not a sprint." Columnist David Brooks says it requires "a passion for something higher than yourself." Yes, perseverance is long-distance resolve and can mean the difference between life and death—but the deep strength we need flows from…worship.

We access the depths of our resolve only when we tap into a source of strength that is beyond our own shallow well. When the Apostle Paul pauses to consider what Eugene Peterson calls his "long obedience in the same direction," it's a checklist of torture. But it's not his own resolve that has carried him through; it is the co-mingled resolve of Jesus. His passion for Jesus is the tap that penetrates that bottomless well of perseverance.

Wonder
What do you do when you need a perseverance beyond your strength?

Jesus
"My grace is all you need. My power works best in weakness" (2 Corinthians 12:9).

Do
Watch the documentary *The Blitz: London's Longest Night* on youtube.com.

Pray: Jesus, I can't do it without your strength.

The Recovery of Freedom

Read Galatians 5:1-16

The Truman Show is the story of a man raised from birth on the enormous dome-roofed set of a reality show. He's the unwitting star of a fully scripted life, routed through hidden cameras to a huge TV audience. When he suspects that nothing in his perfect life is real, that all of his friends are really actors, he's desperate to escape. So he steals a boat, then sails it toward the edge of the dome. He risks the safety of his painless existence for a chance to live an unscripted (and real) life.

After he survives the hurricane-force winds created by the show's producers, Truman finds a staircase embedded in the dome's wall that leads to an exit door. As he's about to break out of his gilded prison, the booming voice of the "Director," the show's creator, urges him to stay: "Truman, there's no more truth out there than in the world I created for you—the same lies and deceit. But in my world you have nothing to fear." Truman first hesitates, wrestling over that enticing promise, then turns the handle on the door and walks into the dark unknown, free at last.

Truman has what we all want—a "god" who shields us from threats, surrounding us with ease. But he lacks the one treasure we crave the most—the freedom to love, and be loved in return. It's a sledgehammer metaphor: *If he takes away all our fears, Jesus takes away our freedom to love.*

Wonder
What "good gifts" has pain brought into your life?

Jesus
"Well, then...the citizens are free!" (Matthew 17:26).

Do
Frame the italicized words above in black marker—freedom eclipsing fear.

Pray: Jesus, I know love requires risk, and risk means fear. I'll risk anyway.

Sifted Like Wheat

Read Luke 22:31-34

In the aftermath of his final Passover meal, in a chilling last encounter with his best friend, Jesus pulls Peter aside to warn him: "Simon, Simon, Satan has asked to sift each of you like wheat. But I have pleaded in prayer for you, Simon, that your faith should not fail. So when you have repented and turned to me again, strengthen your brothers." Something terrible is going to happen to Peter, but he's going to survive it, and the strength he gains from this experience will later fuel the spread of the Gospel.

It's a turning point not just for Peter but for us. The "you" in "sift you" is plural—he's speaking to all of his disciples, not just in the Upper Room but down through time.

A stalk of wheat crushed between your hands drops its chaff, exposing the nourishing kernels. This sifting process is violent—the stalk is torn apart to isolate its "food." When Satan does this to Peter, he expects to find an empty core in his soul. But Jesus is banking on Peter's fundamental love for him. Though he's done what he swore he'd never do, betraying the one he loves, he retains his "kernel" of passion, thrashing his way through the surf to join Jesus on the beach of the Sea of Galilee after the Resurrection. There, Jesus gives him a mission that will consume his life and test his strength: "Feed my sheep."

Wonder	**Jesus**	**Do**
If you have had a "sifting" experience, what "strength" has it revealed?	"Simon son of John, do you love me more than these?" (John 21:15).	Buy a small sheaf of wheat from a hobby store. "Sift" the kernels from one stalk.

Pray: Jesus, reveal what's "nourishing" to others in me; help me give it.

Jesus in the Raw

Read John 16:5-24

"In fact, it is best for you that I go away…" Jesus is offering his disciples some final instructions before the darkness descends on the world—he's trying to convince them that it'll actually be better for them when he goes away: "If I do go away, then I will send [the Spirit] to you." He predicts their "grief will suddenly turn to wonderful joy" after he leaves, like a woman in labor.

What could possibly be better than Jesus staying with you? Well, he says, the physical limitations of their relationship will be gone. He will teach and guide and love them from the inside out instead. And, he promises, the Spirit "will guide you into all truth" and "will bring me glory by telling you whatever he receives from me." The disciples will soon have the clarity that's eluded them. With the Spirit's help, they'll rediscover a Jesus who loves…

- audacious acts of faith,

- doing way more than talking-about-doing,

- outcasts and self-confessed sinners,

- exposing religious rule-keeping as hollow,

- forgiving the repentant and exposing the unrepentant,

- loyalty that outweighs loyalty to our biological family, and

- reminding us of who he is, because we so quickly forget.

Wonder
What is the "key indicator" of the Spirit's guidance in your life?

Jesus
"The Spirit will tell you whatever he receives from me" (John 16:15).

Do
At a coffee shop, taste both refined and "raw" sugar. What's the difference?

Pray: Jesus, thank you for making it possible to be close to you all the time.

Freedom From the Flesh

Read John 8:31-59

No matter how we answer the question on a government form, all of us have been "previously married"...

Paul tells us "the law of sin and death" is our first spouse—an abusive partner that many of us have refused to divorce. Like the Pharisees who were infuriated by Jesus' "lawless" approach to life, we're determined law-keepers, trying to suppress our natural propensity for sin by working hard to "do the right thing." Our universal standard is to "be a good person." Above all else we trust our own capacity to maintain that goodness. But no matter how hard we try to remain faithful to our first spouse, we never measure up. We're just not "good enough," and Jesus agrees.

When we set our minds on keeping the law, trying hard to live up to its expectations, we develop hostility toward Jesus—because the things he says we must do are, in the end, impossible. And this is our glorious defeat; Jesus celebrates our failed efforts to "comply" with the law. Instead, he wants to shift our focus from trying harder to knowing him better and trusting him more. Jesus wants his life flowing through our lives, his goodness infusing our brokenness.

Because the Spirit of Jesus lives in us, we're no longer slaves but children. That means our treasure of righteousness is inherited, not stolen or scraped together or even earned. It's a given because we're part of the family.

Wonder	**Jesus**	**Do**
What's one nasty side effect of "trying hard to be good"?	"I tell you the truth, everyone who sins is a slave of sin" (John 8:34).	Wrap a rubber band around your ring finger. At the end of the day, cut off the rubber band.

Pray: Jesus, I want to leave behind, forever, my "abusive spouse."

Exercising Faith

Read John 20:24-29

Sketch comedy is a perfect training ground for faith because it requires two acts of courage that overlap with the mechanics of belief—*risk* and *trust*. Comedy requires performers to open themselves to possibility, to make themselves vulnerable. For example, let's say an improv sketch is based on this premise: "We're a surgical team made up of one person who can't see and one person who can't speak." Both performers risk when they *go with* that premise, then must trust each other as they add new twists into the premise and play off each other.

Likewise, when Jesus tells his disciples that the greatest blessings come from believing when we can't see, he's encouraging us to make risk and trust the foundation of our relationship with him. "Believe" shows up 76 times in the Gospel of John alone, and the writer of Hebrews underscores that emphasis: "It is impossible to please God without faith" (Hebrews 11:6).

When we *believe in* Jesus, it's like turning on a radio—the radio waves already permeate the room, but we can't access them unless we turn on the receiver. We don't *work at* exercising our faith, we simply turn our "belief" knob on; we trust Jesus when we "go with" his guidance.

Wonder
What's a simple way to risk today—to do something that scares you?

Jesus
"If you had faith even as small as a mustard seed..." (Matthew 17:20).

Do
With a friend, improv together by "dictating" an email out loud, each offering one word at a time.

Pray: Jesus, give me an opportunity to risk and trust you today.

"Great Pumpkin" Faith

Read Matthew 8:5-13

My wife told a friend about a struggle I was facing at work. The friend said, "Well, why doesn't he just exercise his faith that this will all turn out the way he's hoping it will?" When I heard her reaction to my struggles, I blurted, "Actually, I *don't* have faith in the outcomes Jesus produces; I have faith in *who he is*." I call that first definition of faith—believing hard enough to force God's hand—"Great Pumpkin" faith.

In the Halloween classic *It's the Great Pumpkin, Charlie Brown*, the blanket-loving brainiac Linus hunkers down in his "most sincere" pumpkin patch to wait for the mythic "Great Pumpkin" to show up. Little Sally, blinded by her romantic visions of Linus, joins him, missing out on trick-or-treating. When the Great Pumpkin is a no-show, Sally lowers the boom: "You blockhead! You kept me up all night waiting for the Great Pumpkin… What a fool I was!" Sally abandons Linus in the patch, and desperate, he cries out, "If the Great Pumpkin comes, I'll still put in a good word for you!" He quickly recognizes his faithless "if" and repents: "Good grief! I said 'if'! I meant 'when' he comes. I'm doomed." It's too late for Linus…

Great Pumpkin faith is, at its core, functional—we say the right incantation and we get what we want. But Jesus says faith has nothing to do with that; faith is behaving as if he's who he describes himself to be.

Wonder	**Jesus**	**Do**
How has your "faith" changed since you were a child, and why?	"Go back home. Because you believed, it has happened" (Matthew 8:13).	Toss a heavy object from one hand to the other; notice the transfer of weight. Shift your "weight" to Jesus.

Pray: Jesus, I refuse to live my life with you as if it were a formula to get right.

Mirror, Mirror

Read 1 Corinthians 13:11-12

In *Snow White and the Seven Dwarves*, the witch's power is eclipsed by the one thing more potent than her sorcery—the magic mirror on the wall. As long as the mirror reinforces her fragile psyche (*I, and no other, am the fairest of them all*), she is confident and determined. The mirror, as she well knows, never lies. But one day, the answer she hears back from the mirror enrages and unravels her: "My Queen, you are the fairest here so true. But Snow White beyond the mountains at the Seven Dwarfs is a thousand times more beautiful than you."

We invest the mirrors in our lives with the power to define us. This is not an error to fix but a sober reality to embrace—because we, like the witch, treat the mirrors that "speak into" our lives as infallible, we must be discerning. This is why Jesus tells us that he is a perfect reflection of God and promises to perfectly reflect back who we are if we will invite him to be our living mirror on the wall (John 14:9).

We know that his "mirror, mirror" answer will be *both* exacting ("the very hairs on your head are all numbered") and cherishing ("don't be afraid; you are more valuable to God than a whole flock of sparrows"—Matthew 10:30-31).

Wonder
What's one way your identity has been formed by the "mirrors" of childhood?

Jesus
"But who do you say I am?" (Matthew 16:15).

Do
Stare into a mirror. As you do, ask Jesus, "Who do you say that I am?"

Pray: Jesus, I'm surrounded by powerful reflections—overshadow them.

The Extravagance of Jesus

Read Psalm 104

Jesus has loaded up creation with inexplicable diversity.

The Earth is home to 8.74 million species, almost half a million of them plants—why? And why are there more than 60,000 species of trees and almost a million kinds of bugs? Why do flowers grow where no living being will ever see them? And even one mosquito species would be *five* too many—but there are 3,000 of them. Elvis Costello sings, "What shall we do, what shall we do with all this useless beauty?" The One who created all of this extravagance is, himself, extravagant. His love for "useless beauty" is a defining characteristic…

- When a woman pours costly perfume on Jesus' head and is scolded for wasting what could've been given to the poor, he tells her critics to leave her alone: "You can help them whenever you want to. But you will not always have me."

- When the "prodigal" in his Parable of the Lost Son finally drags himself home after wasting the money he extorted from his father, the father throws a massive party: "He was lost, but now he is found!"

- And when his disciples tell him to send away the crowds who've come to hear his teaching because they need to eat, he takes five loaves and two fish and breaks them into a feast for thousands, with "twelve baskets of leftovers."

Wonder
What's one way you've experienced Jesus as extravagant in your life?

Jesus
"This woman's deed will be remembered and discussed" (Mark 14:9).

Do
Smell a flower. Consider how that smell reflects Jesus' extravagant heart.

Pray: Jesus, thank you for loving too much, giving too much, caring too much.

The Tenth Box

Read John 8:1-11

He's a talented writer, compelling speaker, and sought-after professional. He's funny and smart and rich in relationships. He's also obese. He knows his weight is a problem, but he's caught in a swirl of self-destruction. So I tell him about my "Box" theory: *In nine out of 10 boxes in our lives, we are disciplined, perseverant, open, honest, intimate, and functional. But that 10th box—we keep our mystery fears locked up in that box, and we surround it with protective barriers.*

Then I ask, "What's in your Box 10?

Fear clouds his face and tears form in his eyes. He knows it's not about his weight; it's about what his weight is hiding inside Box 10. So I tell him that the secret in that 10th box is the key to his freedom. And then he risks to reveal that secret—as a child he was sexually abused by an older male relative. The shame he has harbored his whole life controls him; his obesity gives him a kind of barrier between others and the dark places in his soul. He decides to fight back by writing a letter to his abuser—one he doesn't plan to send but shares with me.

And I write him this note: *"You have the heart of a lion and the tenderness of a poet. You will not be defined by what's in Box 10. Fight for your freedom, because Jesus is fighting with you…"*

Wonder	**Jesus**	**Do**
What's in your Box 10?	"Where are your accusers? Didn't even one of them condemn you?" (John 8:10).	Like my friend, write a letter to the source of your pain, but don't send it.

Pray: Jesus, take what I've been hiding in Box 10 and redeem it.

Predictably Unpredictable

Read John 10:22-42

We crave formulas in life because we are shortcut people. The long way may be more picturesque, but the short way is more efficient. And so we prefer Jesus to behave in predictable patterns. This is why we're unnerved when "bad things happen to good people"—that's not the way the formula is supposed to work. Jesus is not at all surprised by our addiction to the predictable. He "knew all about people. No one needed to tell him about human nature, for he knew what was in each person's heart" (John 2:24-25). His unpredictability is a bulwark against our demand for control. This is why Jesus is…

- offensive to all the "right" people but gracious to all the "wrong" people,

- eager to eat with "sinners" but disruptive at every party hosted by the "in crowd,"

- able to heal with just a word but often touching/spitting/ praying/bathing/breathing to do it instead,

- comfortable walking on water but uses boat anyway, and

- aware he can avoid the death penalty but determined to ensure it happens anyway.

When we come to love the unpredictable Jesus, we embrace the certainty of his heart, not the false certainty of control.

Wonder
What do you love and hate about unpredictability?

Jesus
"I was born and came into the world to testify to the truth" (John 18:37).

Do
Blindly open a Bible, highlight a verse, and ask Jesus how that verse impacts you.

Pray: Jesus, you are maddeningly unpredictable at times, and I love you.

Crazy, Stupid Love

Read Matthew 11:25-30

Is "lovesick" more than a metaphor? *The Lonely American* authors Richard Schwartz and Jacqueline Olds, husband-and-wife psychiatry professors at Harvard, focus their research on the mechanics of love. They've discovered that "being in love" raises our cortisol level—it's a stress hormone that suppresses our immune functioning. But infatuation also turns on the neurotransmitter dopamine, stimulating the brain's pleasure centers, and drops our serotonin level, adding obsession to the mix. Put it all together and you get "crazy, stupid love."

Schwartz and Olds compartmentalize love into two phases. In the first year of a new love interest, serotonin levels gradually return to normal and the "stupid" and "obsessive" drivers slowly moderate. After that first phase, "committed" love produces an uptick in oxytocin, a hormone that helps us cement bonds and raises our immune functioning. And this is just the beginning of the health benefits enjoyed by married couples—they live longer, have fewer strokes and heart attacks, are less depressed, and have higher survival rates from major surgery and cancer.

If this is true of "lower" forms of love, how does the "higher" love of Jesus impact us? His transformational promise: "Come to me, all of you who are weary and carry heavy burdens, and I will give you rest." Jesus-love produces a rest that fully relaxes—possible *only* when we're wholly accepted, enjoyed, and seen.

Wonder	Jesus	Do
What is the relationship between perfect love and perfect rest?	"Love each other. Just as I have loved you … love each other" (John 13:34).	Stare at a photo of a loved one. Pain subsides, breathing slows, peace increases.

Pray: Jesus, I want to know more deeply that I am loved by you.

Pulling Back the Curtain

Read John 8:31-47

After Dorothy accidentally melts the Wicked Witch of the West, she lays her charred broomstick at the feet of the Great Oz and asks him to make good on his promise—to return her to Kansas and give her friends the heart, courage, and intellect they lack. But the fearsome Wizard of Oz, a ghostly floating head framed by pyrotechnics, refuses. Heartbroken and angry, Dorothy presses in, ignoring her fears. The Wizard responds by ramping up his threats. And then Dorothy's little dog Toto seizes the curtain that hides the real Oz from view, pulling it back to expose a white-haired old man frantically pulling levers on the elaborate machine that controls the Wizard's image.

The unmasked Oz, suddenly aware that his fraud has been exposed, tries to cover himself: "The Great Oz has spoken! Pay no attention to that man behind the curtain....the...Great...er...Oz has spoken." But the weak, simpering bully behind the curtain is no longer threatening—he quickly agrees to do whatever Dorothy and her friends ask of him.

I have a friend who likes to surprise people by asking, "How's your relationship with Satan today?" It sounds vaguely insinuating, but the effect is freeing. Like the wizard behind the curtain, the evil we fear has leverage only when he remains behind the curtain that hides his true nature. Jesus reminds us, "When [Satan] lies, it is consistent with his character; for he is a liar and the father of lies."

Wonder
How's your relationship with Satan today?

Jesus
"He has always hated the truth, because there is no truth in him" (John 8:44).

Do
Cut an avocado to expose its dark core. Ask Jesus to reveal a lie's "dark core" in you.

Pray: Jesus, the "father of lies" has deceived me—remind me of the truth.

Living Supernaturally

Read Matthew 17

On a cold, dark night just before Halloween, my high school friends convinced me to join them on an excursion to a "real" haunted house—a long-abandoned mansion in the mountains west of my home. After we parked and clambered over the fence with "Keep Out!" signs plastered all over it, we walked through the trees, spilling out into an open space where the crumbling mansion was bathed in moonlight—a horror-movie moment. With our flashlights we explored the first floor, then summoned our courage to climb the steps to the upper floors. I swung my light to the staircase wall and exposed a huge "HELTER SKELTER!" finger-written in blood red. I knew it was just paint (probably), but I can still smell the musty air and feel the chill in my spine.

We like a good spook, as long as we maintain "plausible deniability" about it. Fear, says Amy Hollaman, general manager of The 13th Floor haunted house, "produces all these chemicals in the brain, and it feels good when you know it's safe." The overblown dark side of the supernatural grips our imagination. But it's the *light side* that actually matters in our everyday lives. To Jesus and his followers, supernatural responses to threats and needs represent just another day at the office. He's intent on normalizing our relationship with the unbelievable: "I tell you, you can pray for anything, and if you believe that you've received it, it will be yours" (Mark 11:24)

Wonder

Why are so many fascinated by the "dark side" of the supernatural?

Jesus

"Get up...Don't be afraid" (Matthew 17:7).

Do

UCLA profs re-created "the sound of angels"—find and listen to "Cheroubikon Sotiraki Chant" online.

Pray: Jesus, open my eyes to the supernatural all around me.

The Oprah Question

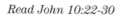

Read John 10:22-30

At the end of her show and the back of her magazine, Oprah Winfrey asks a celebrity, "What's one thing you know for sure?" I've interviewed thousands of people in my career as a journalist, and Oprah's question (borrowed from film critic Gene Siskel) is the best I've ever heard. The "one thing" and "for sure" unlock a deeper-than-normal response. So I've morphed it into *"What's one thing you know for sure about Jesus (based only on this passage)?"* I call it "The Oprah Question," and it reveals the heart of Jesus in the Bible better than any other "can opener." But it's not just a Bible-study question. Asking it helps us...

- navigate a tough decision or choice,

- help someone who's in crisis,

- push back against mythic beliefs about Jesus,

- explore ways to tell others about Jesus,

- pray for others or for yourself, and

- respond to prevalent criticisms of Christianity.

The "red letters" in the Bible highlight Jesus' words and remind us of his blood. But red is also our universal "stop sign" color; it has a psychological leverage on us. So imagine The Oprah Question in bright red—when we make it part of our "breathing pattern" in life, we slow down, stop, and consider Jesus more intentionally.

Wonder	**Jesus**	**Do**
What's one thing you know for sure about Jesus in John 10:22-30?	"No one will snatch them out of My hand" (John 10:28, NASB).	When anxious, ask The Oprah Question aloud, answer it, and feel your anxiety shrink.

Pray: Jesus, one thing I know for sure that I love about you is _____.

Candidate Jesus

Read Matthew 11:1-6

When voting for someone who's running for public office, is it more important to vote based on the candidate's positions on the issues or because you're impressed with the candidate's heart? Can that person be wrong on one and right on the other and still win your vote? Perhaps the way to understand a candidate's heart is to study why they have chosen their position on the issues, then consider what that says about their core beliefs. On that basis, what makes the heart of Jesus different from most political candidates?

- The people who've been waiting thousands of years for the Messiah know that he'll be sent by God to rescue them, but they want a political leader who will rescue them from oppression. Jesus refuses to be that kind of leader—*why?*

- Jesus proclaims, "God blesses those who are poor and realize their need for him, for the Kingdom of Heaven is theirs" (Matthew 5:3)—*why?*

- Jesus refuses to criticize or foment insurrection against a corrupt, brutal, occupying government—*why?*

- Not only was Jesus unimpressed with his culture's power-brokers, but he went out of his way to tweak and offend them, even when he was being honored by them—*why?*

We "vote" for Jesus when we commit ourselves to his cause and live our lives under his guidance.

Wonder	**Jesus**	**Do**
Do you generally vote more with your heart or your head, and why?	"Don't misunderstand why I have come" (Matthew 5:17).	As you vote, pause before each selection and, whispering, ask Jesus for input.

Pray: Jesus, your "platform" supersedes politics in my life.

Intercourse

Read Psalm 61

We know sex was created by God for procreation, but its deeper purpose is metaphoric—it's a visceral reminder of the kind of intimacy he longs for with us. We forget that God, at the beginning of all things, paints his creation from a limitless palette. He chooses for us five senses, but it could've been 17. We have opposable thumbs, but it could've been one-finger hooks. His choices are wide open, so he invests every brush-stroke with double meaning. That means the method he chooses for "be fruitful and multiply" has metaphoric intent—intercourse is our relational template for new life.

Jesus has paired the most intense pleasure we experience in life with the exact moment we sense our greatest loss of control. He's left for us an unmistakable enticement, calling us to leave behind our toxic, controlling habits for the intoxicating freedom of abandonment. A loss of control is a disaster in every area of our lives except in intercourse, when it's the goal. And this is the bait he dangles before our hungry souls: "Give yourself to me, and I will give myself to you."

After Jesus urges his disciples to "eat" and "drink" him, most respond, "This is very hard to understand. How can anyone accept it?" Many of them leave for good. But Peter's response is to embrace what he can't control and offer himself in naked abandon: "You alone…are our only hope" (John 6:68, AMP).

Wonder	**Jesus**	**Do**
Intimacy is frightening—so what propels us toward it anyway?	"Unless you eat [me]…you cannot have eternal life within you" (John 6:53).	To understand "I in you, you in me" intimacy, just pull on a pair of gloves.

Pray: Jesus, I'm inviting you past my soul's entryway and into the bedroom.

Pruning and Fertilizing

Read John 16:16-24

There's a brutal honesty that cuts off what must be "pruned" in us, and a brutal honesty that "fertilizes" our faith… In John 16, Jesus is crop-dusting his disciples with the kind of fertilizer that, at first, produces grief.

During the Vietnam War, Admiral Jim Stockdale was the highest-ranking prisoner of war in the notorious "Hanoi Hilton." For nearly eight years, he endured relentless torture. His survival strategy is now used as a model for perseverance—author Jim Collins calls it the Stockdale Paradox. It describes the mindset Stockdale adopted to emerge unbroken from this brutality. We must, says Stockdale, live in tension between two realities: "You must never confuse faith that you will prevail in the end—which you can never afford to lose—with the discipline to confront the most brutal facts of your current reality, whatever they might be." Courage requires us to embrace reality (not sugarcoat it) while maintaining our conviction that we will survive.

Jesus operates, all the time, in the tension described by the Stockdale Paradox. To the "woman at the well" he first offers a brutal assessment: "You have correctly said, 'I have no husband'; for you have had five husbands, and the one whom you now have is not your husband" (John 4:17-18, NASB). And he follows this by offering her a chance for prevailing faith: "The time is coming… when true worshipers will worship the Father in spirit and in truth. The Father is looking for those who will worship him that way."

Wonder	**Jesus**	**Do**
How have you been "fertilized" by brutal honesty in your life?	"Those who kill you will think they are doing a holy service for God" (John 16:2).	Drink a cup of black coffee—it's a taste expression of "brutal honesty."

Pray: Jesus, "fertilizer" like this scares me, but I want to grow…

The Sword of Gratefulness

Read Luke 17:11-19

A grateful attitude toward the big things in life—health, provision, relationships—is like picking low-hanging fruit. The basic blessings are not hard to recognize. But we experience a deeper freedom when we expand our gratefulness to the small things in life…

- the Sunday comics section
- a kind word from a cashier
- a burst of sunshine on a cloudy day
- a favorite song
- the smell of the trees and bushes and flowers on a summer evening
- the smell of the air after a good rainstorm
- that first taste of a favorite home-cooked meal
- freshly laundered sheets
- a light that turns from red to green when we're running late
- a moment of unexpected peace and quiet at home
- the feeling we have after we've worked up a good sweat
- anything shipped in bubble wrap
- the sound of the wind rustling through leaves

Our simple response to these shafts of beauty radiating through our lives? Just this: *Thank you, Jesus. Thank you, Jesus. Thank you, Jesus.* Gratefulness is not a "soft" teddy-bear habit—it's a sword in our hand, wielded by people of the Light who are immersed in darkness…

Wonder
Ask Jesus, "What's a blessing in my life that I've been blind to?"

Jesus
"Didn't I heal ten men? Where are the other nine?" (Luke 17:17).

Do
Close your eyes and listen until you hear something you can thank Jesus for.

Pray: Jesus, show me how to live more gratefully.

The Miracle of Trust

Read John 14:8-11

Democracy is the healthiest system of government for a broken world, superseded only by a kingdom whose king is perfect and good—this is why the kingdom of God is not the "democracy of God." If we are convinced of the king's goodness, we can afford to trust. But how can we trust with our whole heart when our shattered hopes demand caution? The tipping point for my friend Ned Erickson, founder of the Winston-Salem Fellows, was admitting he did not trust Jesus, even though he'd been a Christian for years...

So I started to get to know Jesus. I chose the Gospel of Mark, and I began reading real slow. I paid attention to everything the man said, did, and didn't do. And before I knew it, everything had changed. He became real. He knocked me head over heels. I wanted to know more—to know him more—deeply, intimately. And slowly, like a ship coming out of the fog, I began to see him, smell him, feel him. I knew what his voice sounded like. And it only made me want more.

We walk the path of trust with blinders on—we see only Jesus in front of us: "Philip said, 'Lord, show us the Father, and we will be satisfied.' Jesus replied, 'Have I been with you all this time, Philip, and yet you still don't know who I am? Anyone who has seen me has seen the Father!' "

Wonder
What's the biggest barrier to offering Jesus your wholehearted trust?

Jesus
"At least believe because of the work you have seen me do" (John 14:11).

Do
Read the weather forecast, then consider what helps you trust it, or not.

Pray: Jesus, I know trust is not about working harder but relaxing more.

Jesus the Fixer?

Read Matthew 11:16-19

When Lebanese physician, author, and radio host Lina AbuJamra was 15, her family moved from Beirut to Green Bay. Her new ZIP Code was "disorientation"—the transition functioned like a magnet throwing off her life-compass. After college she entered medical school, eventually landing her dream job as a trauma doctor in an emergency room.

One night, the immigrant parents of an Indian toddler brought him to the ER after he'd been vomiting for three hours. Lina gave the boy IV fluids, but two days later he was back. She did a CAT scan and found a huge cancerous tumor lodged in his brain. The parents' disorientation reminded her of her own. When she told them the grim news, it didn't sink in. Lina wept. Only then did the father understand. He asked, "Doctor, is there any hope?"

Lina grappled over what to do: "I'd be lying to say there was hope, but it'd be a violation of compassion to say there wasn't. I had many shattered hopes—how could I shatter theirs?" The disciples on the road to Emmaus (Luke 24) also faced shattered hopes. The Messiah was supposed to free them from Roman oppression, but he was crucified instead. When they encounter an incognito Jesus, they vent their disappointment: "We had hoped…" The hope we crave isn't always the hope we're offered. Jesus fixes hearts, not always our problems. Lina's response to the anxious father? "There's always hope with Jesus."

Wonder
Why doesn't Jesus simply promise to fix every problem?

Jesus
"[This generation] is like children playing a game in the public square" (Matthew 11:16).

Do
Use a marker to write "Hope!" on the bathroom mirror of a loved one.

Pray: Jesus, I give you my shattered hopes, like the widow offering a penny.

Responding to Critics

Read Luke 11:14-28

Luke is a physician and an intellectual. He's Greek, the only non-Jew writing an account of the life of Jesus. Because he's in a people-serving profession, he offers details and nuances the other Gospels leave out—he emphasizes the humanity of Jesus. It's helpful, then, to pay attention to how Luke describes Jesus' response to critics. His "fully human" interactions give us a way forward in our own challenging encounters.

After Jesus casts out a demon from a man, his critics respond, "He gets his power from Satan." Their intention is to undermine the source of Jesus' authority—to cut him down to size so he'll conform to their expectations. And how does Jesus respond?

- He takes their argument at face value, then pokes at it.

- He turns their argument back into a personal challenge—would you treat those you respect this way?

- He challenges them to count the cost of their attempts to tear him down.

- He invites them to work with him, not against him.

- He urges them to practice the truth, not pontificate it.

Jesus's goal is not to win but to engage. Not to make mic-drop statements but to ask engaging questions. Not to exclude but invite. Not to argue his beliefs but to live them.

Wonder
What is your typical knee-jerk reaction to criticism, and why?

Jesus
"If I am empowered by Satan, what about your own exorcists?" (Luke 11:19).

Do
Ask Jesus to influence your social-media reply to a contrary political view.

Pray: Jesus, I want my first reaction to criticism to reflect you, not me.

The H. of G.

Read Matthew 4:23-25

When investigative journalist Tracy Kidder asked healthcare activist Dr. Paul Farmer if he could follow him around for a couple of years and then write a book about his life (*Mountains Beyond Mountains*), Farmer inexplicably agreed. Can you imagine inviting the *60 Minutes* crew to live in your guestroom? Farmer is the Indiana Jones of the medical world—for decades he has shuttled back and forth from his Boston medical practice to a remote region in Haiti, where he has pioneered a radical new approach to eradicating infectious diseases. His innovations have led to a sea-change in the way multinational health organizations operate.

As Kidder and Farmer felt their way forward in their relationship, the doctor sent the journalist an email: "I have a hermeneutic of generosity for you because I know you're a good guy: Therefore I will interpret what you say and do in a favorable light. Seems like I'm the one who should hope for as much from you." Farmer called this philosophy the "H. of G."—a "hermeneutic" is the way we interpret the message of Scripture, or the lens we see it through. Farmer's H. of G. was a preemptive strike against suspicion and cynicism. He was committing to a posture of grace and hoped for the same in return.

The H. of G. explains why Jesus is intent on freeing those who are captive to physical, mental, and emotional "prisons." He is a generosity-leaning Messiah.

Wonder
Was your childhood home generous or stingy, and how has that influenced you?

Jesus
"Healthy people don't need a doctor— sick people do" (Matthew 9:12).

Do
Your face best communicates generosity, so soften it, projecting openness.

Pray: Jesus, I'm so grateful for your H. of G. in my life.

Surfacing Darkness

Read John 13:1-17

The world's leading trauma psychologist, Dr. Bessel van der Kolk, showed two groups of children a benign magazine photo of a father working under his car while his two kids watch. He asked each group—one made up of random kids from a gritty urban neighborhood, the other filled with severely abused patients from his practice—to create a story explaining what was happening in the photo. The kids in the first group told stories that started dark but ended happy. The second group told gruesome stories of murder and dismemberment—no happy endings.

In the absence of details, and when meaning is something we project onto a story, we mold details to fit our worldview—the narrative must support what we believe about life and about God. When these beliefs are dragged out of the darkness into the light, that's when healing can happen. And Jesus, the maestro of redemptive pursuit, uses this same strategy...

- In Matthew 11 he names the broken, despairing doubts of John the Baptist, moldering in prison as he awaits execution, then frees him from his fear.

- In Matthew 20 he asks the status-hungry brothers James and John if they can drink from the firehose of suffering that's coming, then frees him from their naiveté.

- In John 13 he asks to wash Peter's feet to surface his camouflaged arrogance, then frees him from bravado.

Wonder
In what area of your life has Jesus brought new freedom?

Jesus
"Unless I wash you, you won't belong to me" (John 13:8).

Do
Play "Roadside Billboard"—choose one; then concoct a creative back-story for it.

Pray: Jesus, surface my fears, then free me from them.

Dragon Slaying

Read Matthew 5:13-16

Jesus uses a curious strategy to draw broken people out from the shelter of their insecurity and shame: *He asks them for help*.

When my college-student daughter discovered her car had a flat tire, she felt embarrassed that she didn't know how to change it. She was forced to call a guy friend and ask for help. Yes, asking for help felt vulnerable, but her friend had to grapple with his own insecurities—*being asked to help* invites us into unexpected vulnerability.

After Dr. Brene Brown, a research professor of social work, delivered her first TED Talk on the importance of vulnerability in a "whole-hearted life," she woke up the next morning gripped with shame. For the 44 million who've watched her presentation online, Dr. Brown's raw confession about her struggles with vulnerability offers a path out of shame. But *offering* that help tapped into Brown's own shame.

"Shame drives two big tapes," says Brown. " 'Never good enough' and, if you can talk yourself out of that one, 'Who do you think you are?' " When we "give what we have to give," we are inviting the dragon called shame out of its cave and into the light. This is why Paul calls us "the body of Christ"—we are living out Jesus' mission on earth when we help others in his name. Jesus asks us to extend his presence in the world by offering our vulnerability to others, because our shame is in his crosshairs.

Wonder	**Jesus**	**Do**
How has helping others helped you overcome insecurity?	"I have been given all authority...Therefore, go" (Matthew 28:18-19).	Touch is a vulnerable way to serve—encourage someone with the gift of touch.

Pray: Jesus, your help in my life has fueled a desire to help others.

The Soldier's Confidence

Read Matthew 8:5-13

It's the most startling encounter in Jesus' three-year ministry. The man is a career soldier and a pagan—a battle-hardened tough guy in charge of 80 "legionaries." Sworn to protect Rome above all else, centurions have risen in the ranks because they are brave, clever, and fight well. Like the men he commands, this centurion is expected to march 20 miles a day wearing armor and carry his own shield, food, and camping equipment. This is the confident and accomplished man's man who comes hat-in-hand to ask Jesus for help.

Jesus quickly agrees to visit the soldier's home and heal his paralyzed servant. But then the man does something so rare that it's hard to find an equivalent in the Gospels—he "amazes" Jesus. "Lord," he responds, "I do not deserve to have you come under my roof. But just say the word, and my servant will be healed. For I myself am a man under authority, with soldiers under me" (NIV).

At the heart of the officer's stunning response to Jesus is a simple truth. *He believes Jesus is God.* That means he's certain Jesus has both the power and authority to do the impossible—to heal his beloved servant who is "racked with pain." Only God can do such a thing, and the centurion knows it. So he acts on what he knows to be true and asks Jesus for the kind of help only God can give.

Wonder
What has undermined your willingness to believe Jesus can do the impossible?

Jesus
"Go back home. Because you believed, it has happened" (Matthew 8:13).

Do
Feel the sun on your face. Praise God for positioning it *exactly* to sustain life.

Pray: Jesus, the centurion's example inspires me to believe more deeply.

Waste

Read Psalm 55:8-11

In Western culture, we excel at wasting things—Americans alone throw away enough garbage to fill 63,000 trucks every day, and half of that is recyclable. In an average lifetime, we'll throw away 600 times our body weight, somewhere north of 90,000 pounds. But of all the ways we maximize our wasting, we're at our worst with our words. We waste meaningful conversation for hollow banter. For example, at the health club I overheard this "default" interchange between two older men:

Guy 1: Hey, how are you?

Guy 2: Well, it's Monday—so, you know…

Guy 1: Yeah, gotta hit it head on and bounce back.

Guy 2: Yeah, it's a bounce-back Monday.

This is called "social grease"—a space-filling swap of nothing in particular. I'm terrible at this sort of wink-wink social necessity, because I can't stand wasted words; it's like throwing $20 bills out of a moving car. It reminds me of the master's response to the slave who buried his investment in Jesus' Parable of the Talents (Matthew 25:26-27, NASB): "You wicked, lazy slave, you knew that I reap where I did not sow and gather where I scattered no seed. Then you ought to have put my money in the bank, and on my arrival I would have received my money back with interest." Jesus is no fan of wasted resources or wasted words—he wants us to risk and invest and earn a return on them.

Wonder	**Jesus**	**Do**
What positive and negative role does "banter" play in your relationships?	"Don't babble on and on as the Gentiles do" (Matthew 6:7).	Reclaim "How are you?" with a creative comeback: "Walking on water, as usual."

Pray: Jesus, I want my words to count for something.

Please Be My Strength

Read Luke 18:9-14

To lament is to worship, because a sorrow offered to Jesus recognizes our great need for him. Our willingness to draw near to him, even when we're confused and hurting, is a "sacrifice of praise." When we lament, we're longing for Jesus to enter into our story and rescue us—we reduce down to our bare necessities. In Michael Gungor's contemporary lament "Please Be My Strength," he offers worship in the raw...

I've tried to stand my ground
I've tried to understand
But I can't seem to find
My faith again
Like water on the sand
Or grasping at the wind
I keep on falling short

So please be my strength
Please be my strength
I don't have any more
I don't have any more

As we draw near to Jesus in our lament, we empty ourselves so that he can fill us. When we mourn the ugly in our lives, we ask Jesus to show us his beauty. And because he promises to be "in us," as we are "in him," the words that describe his beauty also describe our own.

Wonder
What's something in your life you long for Jesus to make new?

Jesus
"He beat his chest in sorrow, saying, 'O God, be merciful to me, for I am a sinner'" (Luke 18:13).

Do
Watch "Please Be My Strength-Relevant TV"—search for it on youtube.com.

Pray: Jesus, please be my strength, because I don't have any more.

Thanksgiving in the Raw

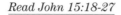

Read John 15:18-27

The gathering around the Thanksgiving table is iconic in American culture. So it's no surprise that "Freedom From Want" is the most famous of painter Norman Rockwell's Four Freedoms series—it's a warmly mythic depiction of a family about to dig into their turkey dinner. The grandparents seem humble and gracious, the cross-table looks are eager and inviting, and everyone is delighted with each other. But reality is somewhat less gratifying. Rockwell later told an interviewer that he painted what he wished life was like, not how he truly experienced it. He was married three times—the first ending in divorce, the second ending tragically when his alcoholic wife took her own life.

The gap between what we long for and what we must accept is a breeding ground for cynicism. In "All in the Family," comic illustrator Jerry Miller's dysfunctional version of Rockwell's original, the grandfather is tipsy, the kids are lost on their phones or stone-faced bored, and the parents are disgusted. Somewhere in the middle of these extremes is our raw reality—where grace, not wish-fulfillment, defines our relationships.

As Jesus tries to cushion his friends' grief over his departure, he says, "The world would love you as one of its own if you belonged to it, but you are no longer part of the world. I chose you to come out of the world, so it hates you." We belong to a miraculous Jesus-family now, where our new reality is like a dream come true.

Wonder
What's your most memorable Thanksgiving, and why?

Jesus
"That the world will know...that you love them as much as you love me" (John 17:23).

Do
Find "Freedom From Want" on Google Images. Ask Jesus to stir your longings.

Pray: Jesus, my longing for family goes deep, like a permanent ache.

Jesus the Investment Banker

Read 2 Samuel 24:18-25

I once asked a congregation, just before I launched into my "message," if anyone was willing to put a monetary value on what they were about to hear. I had a table set up where they could drop their "investment." I waited, warning them that they wouldn't be getting their money back. And then, finally, a brave man in the third row tossed a $20 bill on the table. That was quickly followed by five or six more smaller deposits. And then I said:

What just happened here seems bizarre and even inappropriate, right? And "bizarre" and "inappropriate" perfectly describe the way Jesus often interacted with people. He continually asked—even required—people to "invest" something as a prerequisite to responding to their need. The "woman at the well," the "man born blind," the man whose paralyzed son could not be healed by the disciples...

Jesus will not do *for* us what he can do *with* us. He wants a mutual relationship, with risk on both sides. Again, this is the clear message of his Parable of the Talents (Matthew 25). But we also risk when we *receive*. This is why Jesus asks the sickly man by the pool of Bethesda, "Would you like to get well?" (John 5). At the end of my message, I asked if someone in need would risk to walk up to the table and claim the money. At all three services, someone did. Jesus wants us to own what we want—he won't decide for us.

Wonder	**Jesus**	**Do**
Why is receiving often more difficult than giving?	"To those who use well what they are given, even more will be given" (Matthew 25:29).	Invest your vulnerability in a loved one; ask for an "amateur massage."

Pray: Jesus, I'm embarrassed by my neediness—I need your courage.

Jiu-Jitsu Jesus

Read Romans 8:26-30

I sign all of my emails with the word *Grace*. It's my subtle attempt to invite an elephant into the living room.

Grace is central to Jesus' character. It's there even in the earliest descriptions of him: "And the child grew and became strong; he was filled with wisdom, and the grace of God was on him" (Luke 2:40, NIV). "For the law was given through Moses; grace and truth came through Jesus Christ" (John 1:17, NIV). Most of us understand, in a dictionary way, that grace is "unmerited favor." But a better description is "Spiritual Jiu-Jitsu." That is, grace "uses the attacker's force of momentum against him or her." So when Jesus takes what Satan means for evil in our lives and turns it into a testimony of his goodness toward us, he's in martial-arts mode. He redirects the momentum that "ugly" and "broken" has produced in us, birthing something beautiful instead.

Paul describes the mechanics of Jiu-Jitsu grace: "And we know that in all things God works for the good of those who love him, who have been called according to his purpose..." (Romans 8:28, NIV). So those who are poor in spirit recognize their need for Jesus and, therefore, inherit a kingdom. Those who mourn discover a comfort others will never taste. Those who are persecuted discover a reward that overshadows their pain (Matthew 5).

Wonder
How has Jesus redirected your "attacker's force" into goodness in your life?

Jesus
"If your children ask for a loaf of bread, do you give them a stone instead?" (Matthew 7:9).

Do
We defend against criticism—instead, "yield" by agreeing. Watch what happens.

Pray: Jesus, take "the enemy's" harm and make it good (Genesis 50:20).

Dragging the Cross

Read Matthew 10:34-39

Of all the disturbing things Jesus says, this particular one is hard to swallow: "If you refuse to take up your cross and follow me, you are not worthy of being mine." Of course, "taking up our cross" means dragging our means of execution to the hilltop of Golgotha. Crucifixion is man's cruelest torture. Hands and feet spiked to a cross make it impossible to breathe without pushing up against your feet, which causes unbearable pain. A crucified person can no longer control their breathing. And a loss of control is as scary as death itself.

Control in every aspect of our lives, not just in the extreme, is difficult to give up. My friend moved her family to another state to take a ministry position. Initially, they knew they'd have to rent a house but couldn't find one that would take their cats. Her kids were devastated. She said, "God is using this to work on my secret belief that I have any form of control. I keep thinking I've shed that—and then it rears its ugly head. But the kids are praying the landlord totally changes his mind."

Jesus is quoting the Old Testament when he says, "'The stone that the builders rejected has now become the cornerstone." He is the Stone, but who are the builders, the people who think they're in charge? That would be us. Our freedom begins when we embrace the Stone and take up our cross.

Wonder
Are you high-control or low-control, and how has that impacted your life?

Jesus
"Anyone who stumbles over that stone will be broken to pieces" (Matthew 21:44).

Do
The next time you eat out, let someone else order for you.

Pray: Jesus, help me understand what "taking up my cross" means for me.

Trust Fall

Read John 21:18-23

Is faith in Jesus like a "trust fall," when we cross our arms, close our eyes, and fall back into his waiting arms? As a metaphor for trusting Jesus, it's flawed…

1. In a trust fall, we choose the moment we're ready to fall back. But in our lives with Jesus, he's often the one who chooses the moment. We rarely feel "ready" to step into the unknown toward him. It's Jesus who believes in us when we don't.

2. In a trust fall, we close our eyes and fall back. But in a trusting relationship with Jesus, he turns us so we are face to face with him, then asks us to keep our eyes open as we fall toward him. He wants us to see his face, the look in his eyes, as we "land" on him.

Trusting Jesus often feels like an unwelcome trade. He takes from us what we're sure we need (our self-sufficiency) and gives us, instead, what he's sure we have to have—*himself*. We're all little kids, somewhere inside. We hide when we're afraid and hold on to forms of security that are too frail to protect us. Jesus knows that trusting him is going to feel like we're losing our lives. But he wants that little boy or girl who's hiding in the corner to come out and play.

Wonder	**Jesus**	**Do**
On a scale from 1 to 10, how trusting are you as a person, and why?	"If I want him to remain alive…what is that to you? As for you, follow me" (John 21:22).	Try a traditional "backward" trust fall, then again, facing your friend as you fall.

Pray: Jesus, I know trusting you must cost something, or it's not really trust.

Anti-Transactional

Read John 6:22-69

Early on, the crowds Jesus is attracting are large and rabid. The future swells with possibilities for the disciples, who assume Jesus intends to set them free from their Roman oppressors. But one day, like a wrecking ball, Jesus obliterates their rebel dreams in a five-minute diatribe that seems pointless. On a beach near Capernaum, he drives away the crowds by demanding, over and over, that they "eat my body" and "drink my blood." His declaration is so confusing and offensive that the masses that once anointed him "the next big thing" turn on him—they will never return.

Jesus knows he has just obliterated the transactional motivation of the crowds—*give us what we want and we'll keep following you.* Now he wonders how deeply this transactional virus has infected his own disciples. It's clear they don't understand what he's doing, and why—he's obliterated their head-loyalty so he can discover what heart-loyalty remains.

Jesus wants to know if we're following him because the transaction makes sense—*I give you my heart, and you give me a happy, fulfilling life*—or because we're captured and transformed by the things he says and does. The first is a business arrangement; the second is a great passion. Are we Jesus-alone people or Jesus-plus-a-return-on-my-investment people?

Wonder
What has been the most obvious benefit of following Jesus for you?

Jesus
"You want to be with me because I fed you, not because you understood" (John 6:26).

Do
Write a thank-you card to a friend, *only* listing the person's wonderful qualities.

Pray: Jesus, you alone are the return on my investment.

Collaborators

Read John 9:1-7

We humans are defined by our neediness. We need food and water and shelter to survive. And (we're told) we need the right car, the right ZIP Code, the right smartphone, and the right job to be happy. We live in a state of need. It's ironic, then, that a God who exists outside of need insists on advancing his kingdom through a body of broken, needy people. He has done this from the dawn of time—through men and women just like you and me. It's a shocking truth: Jesus could live out his mission to "set captives free" alone, but he refuses to operate unilaterally. He's determined to move through and with willing and intimate partners.

In his John 9 encounter with a blind beggar by the side of the road, Jesus smears mud on the man's eyes, then asks him to walk, alone, through Jerusalem to the pool of Siloam, where he washes away a lifetime of darkness. Would you force a marginalized, downtrodden, and desperate man through such an unnecessary gauntlet of shame and uncertainty? Of course not… He could heal the man without asking him to risk, but Jesus will not do anything alone that he can, instead, do *with* us. The effect of this on the (formerly) blind man is to inflate his courage. This "cursed" and forgotten man stands resolute before the Pharisees, defending the Jesus they hate with uncommon conviction (verses 8-38). Not only has he found his sight, but he has found himself.

Wonder
How have you developed courage in your life?

Jesus
"Keep on knocking, and the door will be opened to you" (Matthew 7:7).

Do
To formalize a partnership, we "sign on the dotted line." So sign this page below.

Pray: Jesus, I am ill-prepared and unlikely, but I am willing.

The Reinvention of Family

Read Matthew 12:46-50

Is your birth family more like the Bradys or the Simpsons? More like the Conners or the Addams? More like the Winslows or the Kardashians (*if that's possible*)? In the church we've elevated a pristine standard for "biblical family" that, ironically, bears little resemblance to most biblical families. That is to say, Bible families are a lot like the families in your neighborhood—messed up, broken, and flawed. Of course, Jesus valued family, but not in the way we typically do in the church. Of all the ways he upended "conventional wisdom," redefining what *family* means is perhaps the most radical.

Jesus belongs to the First Family—the Trinity. But he's also born into an earthly family headed by Joseph and Mary, growing up with siblings who first mock him, then later embrace him as Messiah. But when he's confronted with a request from his mother and brothers who want to speak to him in the middle of a tense confrontation with the Pharisees (Matthew 12), he tells the crowds crammed inside the meeting place that he's staying put because his *true family* is right in front of him. He's pointing at his disciples when he says this—and, by extension, he's pointing at you and me. Here, Jesus wants to clarify what relationships matter most to him, inviting us to honor our natural families while pledging our allegiance to our true family above all.

Wonder
When you think about "true family," who do you include in that, and why?

Jesus
"Anyone who does the will of my Father... is my brother and sister and mother!" (Matthew 12:50).

Do
Invite a few of your "true family" to join your "DNA family" for Thanksgiving.

Pray: Jesus, will you invite more people into my "true family"?

The Last Bombshell

Read Luke 22:35-38

Here's the scene direction from the *Christmas Vacation* screenplay, as the Griswold family gathers for a holiday dinner: *Everyone's eating in silence. Art picks through the over-cooked food with disgust. Nora scowls at Eddie's kids' horrible table manners. Lewis power-spits an olive pit into his hand. Bethany is eating with a huge serving fork, which Francis removes...Clark takes a bite of the Jello mold...It crunches loudly. And tastes terrible...Rusty struggles to keep Rocky [the dog] out of his food.*

We long for Martha Stewart nirvana at our "bountiful tables," but reality is a terrorist. Around the "Last Supper" table, we see food, friends, and hope. But Judas has already met secretly with the chief priests and scribes, and the conspiracy to execute Jesus is well under way. Even so, Jesus overflows with affection for his ragtag crew, relishing the calm before the bloody storm. Now it will be his Passover blood on the doorpost that will save them.

And then Jesus drops a bombshell on his disciples. He has sent them out before with nothing, challenging them to trust God's provision alone. But not this time: "If you don't have a sword, sell your cloak and buy one!" Buckle up, he warns them, because things are about to explode. Those who gravitate to Jesus quickly discover this is no self-help scheme—it's a "great commission" that will require a warrior mentality.

Wonder
In what area of your life do you feel like you're in a fight, and why?

Jesus
"[Don't] take them out of the world, but... keep them safe from the evil one" (John 17:15).

Do
Stab a kitchen knife into this page—leave a "sword mark" in it.

Pray: Jesus, I need all of your "armor" so I can "stand firm" (Ephesians 6:11).

Out of the Bland

Read Matthew 5:13-16

We know what "add salt to taste" means"—the recipe requires seasoning, but the chef determines how much. In a sense, adding salt to an unappetizing dish is its salvation; it resurrects and reveals the taste buried in the bland. This is why Jesus tells us our purpose is to season the kingdom of earth with "salt" sourced from the kingdom of God. That salt is Jesus himself, the seasoning that saves.

As Jesus-lovers, we are contrary people at our core—we challenge the "norms" of this earth, drawing forth flavors from its bland ambitions with our contra-presence. As Jesus spills out of us, he makes everything more tasty, more beautiful. My friend Jonny Baker, a poet, musician, and ministry leader with the Church Mission Society in Britain, says he's called to people who have "the gift of not fitting in." Salty people always feel a little out of place in the world, just as Jesus did. In his last words to his disciples, he describes the price of "saltiness" (John 15:18-25)...

- "If the world hates you, remember that it hated me first."

- "Since they persecuted me...they will persecute you."

- "If they had listened to me, they would listen to you."

- "They have seen everything I did, yet they still hate me."

Salt is a spice —it disrupts, not conforms, to what it seasons.

Wonder
Who is the "salty-est" person in your life, and why?

Jesus
"No one lights a lamp and then puts it under a basket" (Matthew 5:15).

Do
Take a bite of food without salt and one with it—notice the difference.

Pray: Jesus, accentuate your "taste" in me, and season what is bland.

The Everyday Demonic

Read Matthew 8:28-34

After one of our small-group's Friday Film Night discussions, a handful of teenagers stood in our kitchen, animated as they debated the real presence of evil in our world—more specifically, demons and demonic influence. The deeper into this metaphysical discussion they dived, the more freaked out they became. The fear of an unseen threat gripped them. They huddled together a little closer because it was dark outside and late, a recipe for dread. Because we talk so little in the church about the reality of demonic influence in the world, it's not possible for us to think about this in "everyday" ways.

But open randomly to any of the four Gospels and you'll likely land near an encounter Jesus had with the demonic. It's a common aspect of his everyday life and a major theme in his "setting captives free" ministry. It's hard to label his encounter with two men who are possessed by a "legion" of demons as "typical," but it is. It takes a vast herd of pigs to "re-house" the demons once Jesus casts them out, but the whole thing feels like he has caught a child with his hand in the cookie jar—nothing more. To Jesus, a conflict with demons was as normal as a conflict with his disciples.

We live in a "seen" world that is influenced by an "unseen" world—that's normal life for Jesus, and for us.

Wonder
What's the difference between "bad luck" and demonic influence?

Jesus
"Blessed are you... because flesh and blood did not reveal this to you" (Matthew 16:17, NASB).

Do
Darkness masquerades as light. Shine a flashlight in your face; feel the blindness.

Pray: Jesus, take authority over any force of darkness in my life.

Resilience

Read Matthew 6:25-34

The Western World enjoys the highest level of affluence in the history of the world., but there's a nasty and unexpected side effect. A study by the U.S. government found that the richer the neighborhood, the higher the risk of suicide. It's now the fourth-leading cause of death among those who are middle-aged, and nearing the top cause of death among young adults and teenagers. When you already possess the supposed engine of happiness and remain anxious and unsatisfied anyway, "how deep that darkness is" (Matthew 6:23).

The two most privileged generations in history are Millennials and Gen Z—young adults, teenagers, and children. Despite their undeniable economic advantages, they face an unprecedented mental health crisis. Arizona State psychology professor Suniya Luthar studies resilience. She says affluent teenagers are the most "emotionally distressed" sub-population in America.

Jesus understands the mechanics of our anxieties—that we are deeply worried our foundational needs will not be met, or that catastrophe is waiting for us around the corner. His answer to our fears is simple: *If you pay attention to the created world, you'll see how I care for even the insignificant, the overlooked, and the undervalued. I already know your needs, so open your heart to trust me.* In the end, true resilience is directly tied to how certainly we believe in his kindness.

Wonder	Jesus	Do
When you are in the grip of anxiety, what is your best antidote?	"Can all your worries add a single moment to your life?" (Matthew 6:27).	Feel anxiety's "vibration"—play loud music, then hold a filled balloon next to the speaker.

Pray: Jesus, anxiety is rooted in fear; I need your "perfect love" to cast it out.

Gaslighting

Read Matthew 4:3-4

In the iconic wartime film *Gaslight*, Charles Boyer plays Gregory Anton, an evil, manipulating husband to the beautiful Paula, played by Ingrid Bergman. It's the story of a murderer (Boyer) obsessed with finding the priceless jewels he left behind after killing a famous opera star. He later marries his victim's niece (Bergman) so he can live in the house where the jewels are hidden. He plans to convince his young wife that she's going insane, have her committed, then look for the jewels unimpeded. With surgical precision, Anton accuses Paula of phantom crimes and goads her into embarrassing public outbursts. His plan is working—she slowly descends into madness, until a Scotland Yard detective unravels the scheme and rescues Paula in the nick of time.

The film spawned a new entry in the dictionary—*gaslighting*. It's "a form of psychological manipulation in which a person seeks to sow seeds of doubt in a targeted individual…making them question their own memory, perception, and sanity." And it's the strategy Satan uses to tempt Jesus at the end of a grueling 40-day fast: "If you are the Son of God, tell these stones to become loaves of bread." *If you are…*smells like gaslighting. It's a subtle attack on his identity—a clouding of the truth. And Jesus won't tolerate it: "People do not live by bread alone, but by every word that comes from the mouth of God."

Wonder
Gaslighting capitalizes on our insecurities. When have you felt gaslighted?

Jesus
"False prophets will…perform signs and wonders so as to deceive" (Mark 13:22).

Do
Go to snopes.com to check out stories of "gaslighting" from all over the world.

Pray: Jesus, root out deception in my life with the Truth of your presence.

It's Raining Beach Balls

Read Romans 5:1-5

In a sanctuary decorated for vacation Bible school, kids are dancing and giggling as they perform the hand motions to a chirpy worship song. Above them in the balcony, hidden from view, their adult leaders are about to toss dozens of large beach balls over the railing. And then, like a psychedelic thunderstorm, they come raining down. One little girl, distracted and oblivious, is bopped in the head. She's startled, rubs her "wound" a little, then raises her hands above her worried face to fend off future assaults—she keeps them there until the song ends.

This is a perfect metaphor for the trauma we experience in life. The "arrows that fly by day" (Psalm 91) make us wary and protective. We're never sure when the next "assault of the beach balls" will come, so we are tense instead of playful, calculating instead of obedient, suspicious instead of trusting, skeptical of authority instead of grateful for it, and stingy instead of generous. Our dance is stiff and self-aware, not abandoned. So we must be born over, and then learn to dance again. Paul says, "We can rejoice, too, when we run into problems and trials, for... we know how dearly God loves us" (Romans 5:3-5). In the life after our second birth, we are not surprised when the beach balls fall, but the "undeserved privilege" Jesus has won for us gives us a taste of his glory and the courage to lower our hands.

Wonder	**Jesus**	**Do**
How have "problems and trials" in your life led to a deeper hope?	"I am with you always, even to the end of the age" (Matthew 28:20).	On a walk outside, raise your face to the rain or snow or sun—open and trusting.

Pray: Jesus, you are my refuge and my strength.

Satan's Accusation

Read 2 Corinthians 1:8-11

The book of Job spotlights the epic outcome of a grand wager. Take away all Job's blessings, Satan accuses, and his love for God will grow cold. He's implying that Job (and we) love God only because he makes life easy for us. But Paul stabs a dagger in the heart of that accusation: "For to me, to live is Christ and to die is gain" (Philippians 1:21, NIV). And "We felt we were doomed to die and saw how powerless we were to help ourselves; but that was good, for then we put everything into the hands of God" (2 Corinthians 1:9, TLB).

What a stunner—"but that was good." And why is it *good*? Because in the grip of our heartbreak "we put everything into the hands of God." When we do, we jab our finger in the eye of Satan and declare, with Job our brother, "Though he slay me, I will hope in him." This is the green shoot of our unconditional love for Jesus poking up through the cracked soil of our weathered and wounded soul. The love he has given is the love we return to him.

On the precipice of Peter's crucifixion, his first concern is to avoid comparison to his Beloved's sacrifice, so he begs to be nailed upside down. The ugly sound of hammer on nails is also the sweet sound of a great lie pounded into submission.

Wonder	**Jesus**	**Do**
When you're "powerless to help yourself," how does that impact your relationship with Jesus?	"If you love only those who love you, what reward is there for that?" (Matthew 5:46).	Breathe deeply five times. Each time you exhale, give your cares to Jesus.

Pray: Jesus, I want to be in the long line of "proofs" against Satan's wager.

Unchained Melody

Read Revelation 2:12-17

The Silver Chair is the fourth book of C. S. Lewis' classic children's fantasy series, *The Chronicles of Narnia*. In the story, Prince Rilian (son of King Caspian), has been captured and imprisoned by an evil witch. Over time she plants insidious lies in the garden of his soul, and now the prince no longer remembers who he really is. He's been seduced into believing the evil witch is good and co-opted into launching a bloody invasion of his kingdom's peaceable neighbor.

Rescuers infiltrate the witch's underground lair and free him, but he's confronted by his enemy before he can escape. The witch quickly reiterates his "checklist of shame"—all the ways he is weak and cowardly and inconsequential. She is trying to bully him back into captivity. But Rilian is determined to uproot what the witch has planted: "Now that I know myself, I do utterly abhor and renounce it as plain villainy." He follows this proclamation with another: "I am the King's son of Narnia, Rilian, the only child of Caspian, Tenth of that name, whom some call Caspian the Seafarer."

"Now that I know myself" unlocks his prison. When our true identities as beloved children of the King are under assault, we desperately need to remember who we really are. Jesus will expose our self-denigrating stories as lies, inviting us to embrace the truth about our name and name the truth about our lies.

Wonder	**Jesus**	**Do**
Who do you trust the most to mirror back the "true you"?	"[The Devil] has always hated the truth, because there is no truth in him" (John 8:44)	Like Rilian, brainstorm your "royal identity," then speak it out.

Pray: Jesus, please water and fertilize the truth about who I am in me.

Christmas Music

Read Luke 19:1-10

Are you a Christmas-music nerd? Maybe you, like me, are already assaulting your family with a perpetual blast of winter…um, "merriment." By now, my kids are either well-cultured by my eclectic seasonal playlist or, simply, warped.

Music is a powerful forming influence, and Christmas songs pack a subversive punch, so it's valid to ask, *"What would Jesus sing?"* Well, likely not "Rudolph, the Red-Nosed Reindeer." It might sound Grinchy, but at the heart of "Rudolph" lurks a toxic belief—if you have a "defect," you deserve to be ostracized, unless you find a way to be useful. *"Then one foggy Christmas Eve/Santa came to say/'Rudolph, with your nose so bright/Won't you guide my sleigh tonight?'/Then how the reindeer loved him/As they shouted out with glee/'Rudolph the Red-Nosed Reindeer/You'll go down in history.' "* It's an epic story of conditional love.

Jesus had his own "Rudolph"—his name was Zacchaeus. It's certainly true that "all of the other [ancient Jews] used to laugh and call him names. They never let poor [Zacchaeus] join in any [community gatherings]." And then Jesus shows up in town and invites the tax-man out of his tree—"I must be a guest in your home today." He does not preface this invitation by asking him to clean up his act or make himself useful. He offers ridiculous generosity *before* Zacchaeus repents, not after.

Wonder	**Jesus**	**Do**
What Christmas song best reflects "the reason for the season," and why?	"Salvation has come to this home today" (Luke 19:9).	Listen to a Christmas song and ask, "Would Jesus sing this song? Why or why not?"

Pray: Jesus, remind me of your heart lurking inside "the songs of the season."

The Point of Advent

Read Isaiah 40

For so many, "Advent" describes a Christmas countdown calendar, not a journey into worship. In the church, Advent is our great "supposed to"—a sacred imperative dragged along by suspicious catchphrases. For example, we're not really "preparing for Jesus to come," because he's already here. If not, we're in trouble. Likewise, we know we're supposed to remember the "true meaning" of the holiday; we've been "shoulded" over and over about it. To reclaim Advent, maybe we embrace it as an adventure in remembering...

- *Week 1 focuses us on Hope*—we light the "Prophet's Candle" to remind us that Jesus is the perfect fulfillment of Old Testament prophecy.

- *Week 2 helps us to re-embrace Faith*—we light the "Bethlehem Candle" to remind us that Mary and Joseph journeyed to Bethlehem following "the evidence of things we cannot see" (Hebrews 11:1).

- *Week 3 invites us into Joy*—we light the "Shepherd's Candle" to remind us of the childlike joy the "shepherds guarding their flocks" experienced at the birth of Jesus.

- *Week 4 points us to Peace*—we light the "Angel's Candle" to remind us of the missional purpose of Jesus: "Peace on earth, good will toward men." Our peace is tied to our adoption; we are enemies invited to be children.

Wonder
What's something we typically forget about Jesus during this season?

Jesus
"If you follow me, you won't have to walk in darkness" (John 8:12).

Do
After you read Isaiah 40, embrace yourself—imagine they're Jesus' arms.

Pray: Jesus, I'm a terrible forgetter. Please remind me of you.

The Dirty Manger

Read Isaiah 53

What can we learn about the heart of God by paying better attention to the particular way the Trinity chooses to bring Jesus into the world? The Incarnation, heaven's cross-border invasion of purity into the profane, deposits baby Jesus in a dirty feeding trough. Though it seems random, there is intention behind this indignity—it's a strategic choice, not an embarrassing necessity. The manger is a flare-shot, bleaching the darkness of our flawed assumptions about kings and redeemers.

To travel to their city of heritage for the Roman-mandated census, a very pregnant Mary and Joseph set off on a 120-mile journey from Nazareth to Bethlehem—a 10-day quadruple marathon through the oppressive heat of the Jordan Valley. With no better option, they settle for a stable. From archaeological finds, we know that ancient stables were attached to the home and enclosed by "fenestrated" walls—low stone partitions pockmarked by "feeding windows." Farm animals lived behind these walls, with their feed piled in baskets wedged into the windows. There, with the smell and the noise assaulting their senses, the desperate couple welcomes light into the darkness.

In that forlorn manger, wrapped tightly with narrow bands of cloth, lies the One who will grow into the man Isaiah prophecies as "nothing beautiful or majestic…nothing to attract us to him." And this nothing-beautiful Messiah, born into the muck, will re-fashion every ugly thing into a work of art.

Wonder	**Jesus**	**Do**
Why do we typically depict Jesus as perfectly handsome?	"I have come to call… those who know they are sinners" (Matthew 9:13).	If you have pets, breathe in their pet food—the first smells in Jesus' nostrils.

Pray: Jesus, you might be nothing-beautiful, but you are oh-so-beautiful.

The Ultimate Mud Puddle

Read John 3:16-21

A "mud puddle" in the Bible is, simply, something Jesus says or does that we don't get right away, so we jump over it. For example, when Jesus tells us we'll do "greater things" than he did, we're incredulous, so we tacitly ignore it (John 1:50). Likewise, when we're over-familiar with a passage, we skip over it. We jump over mud puddles because we're almost always in a hurry. But children are naturally slow—they have time to wallow and splash around in puddles. This is why Jesus said we must become like little children to live in the kingdom of God.

So let's wallow a little in the Grand Poobah of skip-over mud puddles—John 3:16: "For this is how God loved the world: He gave his one and only Son, so that everyone who believes in him will not perish but have eternal life." It's maybe the most well-known verse in all of the Bible, tempting us to believe it's not worth a wallow.

The context of this iconic verse accentuates its power, especially what follows. John 3:17 is just as earth-shaking and beautiful as John 3:16, but we miss it because we're in such a hurry: "God sent his Son into the world not to judge the world, but to save the world through him." Verse 16 promises us salvation, and verse 17 promises us acceptance. This is the one-two punch of our Redeemer.

Wonder
What's something in the Bible that has never made sense to you?

Jesus
"People loved the darkness more than the light" (John 3:19).

Do
Read aloud John 3:16 four times, each time emphasizing a different word.

Pray: Jesus, help me slow down to notice your mud puddles, then wallow.

(Not) Laughing at Jesus

Read 1 Corinthians 2:1-5

Regina Spektor's song "Laughing With" explores the dynamics of our relationship with Jesus when we're at our most desperate. Lonely, scary, and daunting life experiences naturally draw us into a raw dependence on him. We never "laugh at God," sings Spektor, when we're confined to a hospital bed or in the heat of war or struggling against starvation or cold or poverty. And we don't laugh at him when a policeman knocks on our door and says, "We got some bad news." Or when we're decimated by fire or undone by a flood.

We never laugh at Jesus when we actually *need* him. Our fears smoke out our neediness, a terrifying admission in a culture that worships self-reliance. Skeptics believe that faith in Jesus is a crutch—a pansy-weakness that's intolerable to make-it-happen people. Who can afford a dependent posture in a world that demands toughness? Well, only those who admit that real strength bubbles up from a well outside of themselves.

Paul tells his friends in Corinth, "I came to you in weakness—timid and trembling... Rather than using clever and persuasive speeches, I relied only on the power of the Holy Spirit. I did this so you would trust not in human wisdom but in the power of God" (1 Corinthians 2:3-5). When we admit that our circumstances are simply too much for us to endure, Jesus responds, "There is nothing, nothing, nothing too much for me."

Wonder	Jesus	Do
How is your relationship with Jesus different when you're facing trouble?	"Who is powerful enough to enter the house of a strong man?" (Mark 3:27).	Try to rip this whole (closed) book in half—we are like a page, but he is the book.

Pray: Jesus, I want to live like I actually need you, all the time.

Stress

Read Luke 2:41-52

If it's the "most wonderful time of the year," why do 45% of us prefer to skip Christmas? A quarter of us report feeling "extreme stress" during the holidays. "Lack of time" and "lack of money" and the "pressure to give or get gifts" are the chief contributors, leading to headaches, sleep disturbances, fatigue, exhaustion, difficulty concentrating, short temper, upset stomach, and a decline in productivity. Whew… *Neither holly nor jolly.*

The pressures we experience around the holidays force Jesus to the sidelines just when we need his help the most. Not only is Jesus relaxed in stressful situations, but he often *causes* the stress he's relieving in the first place.

When Joseph and Mary leave the festival of Passover in Jerusalem on their circuitous journey back home to Nazareth, they assume Jesus is among the traveling party. But a full day into the dry, hot desert—home to robbers and rebels—they discover he's missing. Alone, they retrace their path back to the chaotic city streets where, after three frantic days of searching, they stumble into him happily debating the religious leaders in the Temple. They are furious and confused—"Why have you done this to us?" And Jesus, at home in "his Father's house," comprehends the toll fear has exacted in them. And so the God of the universe *bends his knee* in obedience—he caused their stress, but now he's shifting the burden of it to his shoulders.

Wonder
Does your stress outweigh your joy during the holidays, or vice versa?

Jesus
"Didn't you know that I must be in my Father's house?" (Luke 2:49).

Do
Take the fuel-rod out of holiday stress by scattering bird seed at a park.

Pray: Jesus, help me breathe you in as I breathe out my stress.

Living Wide Awake

Read Ephesians 1:3-11

The great 20th-century philosopher Marshall McLuhan said, "The medium is the message." He meant that our "message delivery vehicles"—the printing press, then radio, then television, then computer, and now smartphone—have all changed us more fundamentally than the information and entertainment they carry. So we know the birth of Jesus is the *message* of Christmas, but what is the "*medium* of that message"? Two thousand years ago it was the angels trumpeting Jesus' birth; today it's our cultural Christmas traditions. We invite the "mediums" of our traditions, like a Trojan Horse, inside our souls' gates—and out of their belly spills an invading army of celebrity-hosted variety shows.

But we don't have to war against the "secularization" of Christmas if we stay awake and alert to what we love (and don't) about our holiday traditions. We bring all of that to Jesus—an offering of five barley loaves and two fish (John 6:9). We give him our inconsequential treasures and ask him to transform them into a feast. When we hear a favorite Christmas song, we pause to drink it in and invite Jesus into our joy. When we watch a favorite holiday special or film, we're awake to patterns and themes of redemption, then thank Jesus for redeeming us. When we search for special gifts for those we love, we remind ourselves that Jesus cherishes our every nuance and "knows how to give good gifts" (Matthew 7:11).

Wonder	**Jesus**	**Do**
Why do you love what you love during the Christmas season?	"You skillfully sidestep God's law in order to hold on to your own tradition" (Mark 7:9).	Take a Christmas-shopping adventure— ask Jesus where to go and what to buy.

Pray: Jesus, you are everywhere and nowhere right now; be my all-the-time.

Overcoming the World

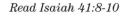

Read Isaiah 41:8-10

Among the 350 million worldwide users of the Bible app YouVersion, Isaiah 41:10 is the most shared/bookmarked/highlighted verse: "Don't be afraid, for I am with you. Don't be discouraged, for I am your God. I will strengthen you and help you. I will hold you up with my victorious right hand." We long for help when we're in trouble. But what help does Jesus give us, and why isn't it always the help we ask for?

Starting in John 15, Jesus offers his disciples a triple dose of brutal reality—soon they'll face persecution, hatred, murder, mourning, grief, sorrow, abandonment, betrayal, and great fear. It's a gut-punch checklist. Of course, his friends want to know what Jesus is going to do about all of this trauma: "I have told you all this so that you may have peace in me. Here on earth you will have many trials and sorrows. But take heart, because I have overcome the world" (John 16:33).

In the face of fear, what does "overcome the world" really mean, and how is it supposed to help us? Jesus is not pointing to circumstantial solutions to our everyday abominations; it's his presence in us ("I am with you") that overcomes our fear. With the weight of Jesus at our core, we're like Weebles—we "wobble but we don't fall down." Our "trials and sorrows" weigh heavy on us, but we have the heavyweight champion living inside.

Wonder	**Jesus**	**Do**
What "trial or sorrow" continues to undermine your hope, and why?	"The Father himself loves you dearly because you love me" (John 16:27).	In the gift-card aisle, ask Jesus to reveal which "love" card is his message to you.

Pray: Jesus, I need your weight to anchor me because I feel wobbly.

Light, the Lie Extractor

Read Mark 4:11-17

I asked a dozen young people to each write one lie they believe about themselves on a scrap of paper. Here's what I collected:

- Not pretty/cool/smart/good enough

- Unnoticed/invisible/fading

- Unfulfilled potential

- I'm not worth it

- I'm a pushover—too nice to defend myself and be successful

- I will always be someone's second choice

- I am weak

- I am worthless and fat and no one will ever love me

- I am selfish and self-serving

- I am inconsistent

- I will fail

- I'm not welcome

The most effective way to undermine the power of our lies is to drag what we keep in the darkness into the light. Jesus is the fulfillment of Isaiah's prophecy: "For those who lived in the land where death casts its shadow, a light has shined" (Matthew 4:16). So I had these kids hold hands and close their eyes as I read, out loud, each lie. It was both vulnerable and life-changing for them.

Wonder
What's one lie you believe about yourself, and why?

Jesus
"The Son gives life to anyone he wants" (John 5:21).

Do
Pinpoint a "recurring lie" in your life. Speak it out, then renounce it out loud.

Pray: Jesus, when I drag my lies into the light, I see how ugly they are.

Love > Peace

Read Matthew 5:1-12

 When Sami Awad was growing up in the turbulent West Bank, tension between Palestinian guerrillas and the Israeli army boiled over into war. One dark day, a sniper killed his father, leaving his mother with seven children and no home after soldiers kicked them out onto the street. They lost everything. Sami's mother knew she had to choose the legacy she'd leave to her children. It would've been easy, even expected, to lash out against her enemies. But she loved and followed Jesus, and she was determined to model for her children what "loving your enemies" really means. "My mother," says Sami, "taught us that revenge and retaliation would have no place in our family's life. She intended to seek reconciliation with those who did this to us. Justice, she explained, is when we make peace with those who've done injustice to us."

Perched on the side of a mountain, Jesus looks over the gathering crowd and launches into a poetic assault on "the way we've always done it." The rich seem favored by God—but Jesus says the poor and desperate are the favored ones. Self-promoters seek power and wealth—but Jesus says the humble receive a priceless inheritance. The winners get to make the rules—but Jesus says the peacemakers reflect his heart. "I knew Jesus had called our family to love our enemy," says Sami. "He didn't say make peace with them; *he said love them*."

Wonder	**Jesus**	**Do**
Read straight through the Beatitudes. What do you learn about Jesus' heart?	"First say, 'May God's peace be on this house'" (Luke 10:5)	Make a "Christogram" *(above at top)*—the Greek letters ICXC, short for Jesus.

Pray: Jesus, I know peace is elusive but love is a calling.

Firing the Prison Guard

Read Matthew 18:21-35

Americans have the world's highest rate of social anxiety disorder—the "fear of negative evaluation by others." In Japanese culture, social anxiety is fueled by *hazukashii*, a revulsion for bringing shame to the family name. Likewise, the Chinese are so fixated on avoiding "negative evaluation" that they have more than 100 unique ways to describe shame.

When Jesus says "love your enemies" and "do good to those who hate you," the meaning also extends to the mirror (Luke 6:27). The voice of our "accuser" often sounds a lot like our own, because we are our own worst enemy. In response to their questions about the limits of forgiveness, Jesus obliterates his disciples' "reasonable" limits on grace by setting a new standard—*infinity*. The obvious focus of this grace is outward, toward others, but it's even harder to extend it to ourselves. He came to release prisoners from their bondage, and sometimes we are our own worst prison guard.

Like Peter at the Last Supper, we are reluctant to offer our "dirty feet" to Jesus, who is waiting with his basin and towel. But Jesus wants us to know, "Unless I wash you, you won't belong to me." It's when we, the "chief of sinners," receive his forgiveness that we cement our "belonging" relationship to Jesus. Feet cleaned by him can walk over sin and remain unstained.

Wonder	**Jesus**	**Do**
How have you been your own worst enemy at times, and why?	"No, not seven times... but seventy times seven!" (Matthew 18:22).	On a receipt, write a self-accusing word, then circle "paid" at the bottom.

Pray: Jesus, show me what "seventy times seven" means for me.

How I Treat My Friends

Read Luke 24:35-49

In the last year of her life, Teresa of Ávila and her Carmelite nun companions left their convent in Ávila to plant new outposts in Burgos and Grenada. After heavy rains the narrow hillside roads flooded, eroding the canyon edges. The travelers surveyed the situation from their carriage; they'd need to abort their journey. But Teresa cheerfully proclaimed: "As [we are] engaged in doing God's work, how could [we] die in a better cause?" And then the aged saint left the carriage and forged into the water…

The current was so strong that she lost her footing, and was on the point of being carried away when our Lord sustained her. "Oh, my Lord!" she exclaimed, with her usual loving familiarity, "when wilt Thou cease from scattering obstacles in our path?" "Do not complain, daughter," the Divine Master answered, "for it is ever thus that I treat My friends." "Ah, Lord, it is also on that account that Thou hast so few!" was her reply.

On the eve of his execution, Jesus assures his disciples: "I no longer call you slaves…Now you are my friends." Not a universally comforting thought, as it turns out. The gap between Jesus' love and his apparent indifference toward our suffering is a petri dish of doubt. But on Teresa's deathbed she prays, "O my Lord and my Spouse, the hour that I have longed for has come. It is time to meet one another."

Wonder
How has doubt been both a friend and an enemy to you?

Jesus
"Why are you frightened?…Why are your hearts filled with doubt?" (Luke 24:38).

Do
Search online for the Andy Grammer love song "Wish You Pain" and listen.

Pray: Jesus, sometimes (I have to admit) I well understand Teresa's point.

Too Much

Read Hebrews 11

When my daughter was 10, she came home from school bubbling over about her friend's upcoming trip to Hawaii. After describing the happy bullet-list of experiences her friend was about to enjoy in paradise, she asked, "When will we be going to Hawaii?" as if she was requesting a glass of water. When I responded, "That's asking for way too much," her eyes clouded over with confusion.

Children can't comprehend "too much." This is why Jesus says, "The Kingdom of God belongs to those who are like these children" (Mark 10:14). Asking for too much turns the key in the kingdom of God's lock—it's Jesus' definition of "great faith." For example…

- Matthew, a notorious sinner, asks Jesus to join him and a bunch of his sinner friends for dinner—and Jesus does (Matthew 9).

- Peter asks Jesus to make it possible for him to walk on water—and Jesus does (Matthew 14).

- A man living with the death sentence of leprosy asks Jesus to cure him—and Jesus does (Matthew 8).

- Martha asks Jesus to raise her dead brother Lazarus from the dead—and Jesus does (John 11).

My daughter asked for way too much because she believed I could deliver. She hadn't yet learned that my capabilities are tied to limited resources. But those limitations are not true of Jesus.

Wonder
Jesus encourages us to make "bigger asks" of him. What's yours?

Jesus
"Miraculous signs will accompany those who believe" (Mark 16:17).

Do
Search Google Images for your "too much" hope. Print and use it as a bookmark.

Pray: Jesus, I've been afraid to ask too much of you, but no more…

On Santa's Lap

Read 1 Corinthians 12:1-11

At a gathering of mall Santas, a roomful of bushy-faced men-in-red made a list of the weirdest things children have ever requested while sitting on their laps, including…

- a gallon jar of pickles

- a gumball machine full of avocados

- a remote-control buffalo

- plutonium

- to know how elves reproduce

- lasagna

It's the un-boundaried excess in these gift lists that delights us. But as we age into adulthood, we're infected by reasonable-ness. C.S. Lewis says, "If we consider the unblushing promises of reward and the staggering nature of the rewards promised in the Gospels, it would seem that Our Lord finds our desires, not too strong, but too weak. We are half hearted creatures, fooling about with drink and sex and ambition when infinite joy is offered us, like an ignorant child who wants to go on making mud pies in a slum because he cannot imagine what is meant by the offer of a holiday at the sea. We are far too easily pleased."

When our longings seem unreasonable or unreachable, we descend into disappointment. But it's our persistent pursuit of joy in the face of pain that is our "spiritual form of worship."

Wonder
What's the most outlandish gift you ever asked Santa for?

Jesus
"Keep on asking, and you will receive what you ask for" (Matthew 7:7).

Do
Give your mall Santa a goody bag—snacks, a drink, and a Scripture passage.

Pray: Jesus, have I "settled" for less than what you have for me?

The Spirit's To-Do List

Read John 16:5-15

What's cramming your holiday to-do list today? Whatever's on it, you're likely not the only one who's giving, um, "suggestions" for it... Our to-do's reflect our responsibilities to others. And the same is true for the Trinity's to-do list. In his last coaching session with the disciples, Jesus is preparing them to follow the inside-out guidance of his Spirit. So he ticks down the "honey-do" list he has pinned to the Spirit's refrigerator...

- *To convict us of sin and righteousness and judgment*—at the top of that list is this blunt assessment: "They do not believe in me" (John 16:8-11). When we don't live like Jesus is who he says he is, that's the root of our sin.

- *To help us "bear the truth" and "guide us into truth"*—our Spirit-dependence is the key to our lives. And so we listen, lean in, and respond to the Spirit's nudges (John 16:12-13).

- *To act as a permanent "bridge" in our relationship with God (John 16: 23-24)*—the Spirit's functional role is to be our Comforter, Counselor, Helper, Advocate, Intercessor, Strengthener, and Standby.

- *To help us understand Jesus and everything he taught*—the Spirit will "testify" and "glorify" and "speak plainly" about Jesus, disclosing everything the Father and Son are doing (John 15:26-27; 16:14-15).

Of course, there's one difference between the Spirit's to-do list and ours—on one of those, every box is checked.

Wonder	**Jesus**	**Do**
What's the most important thing on your to-do list today?	"[If I don't] go away... the Advocate won't come" (John 16:7).	Look at your to-do list. Ask the Spirit to add or subtract something.

Pray: Jesus, thank you that I'm on your to-do list.

No Fear

Real Luke 2:8-20

It's pitch-dark, and the shepherds are on high alert, studying the terrain for predators stalking their flock. Their eyes are down, not up. So the blinding arrival of an angel bathed in "the radiance of the Lord's glory" shocks and terrifies them. "But the angel reassured them. 'Don't be afraid!' he said. 'I bring you good news that will bring great joy to all people' " (Luke 2:10).

Of course, "Don't be afraid" is easy for the scary angel to say…

In the 15 seconds between the two blasts in the 2013 Boston Marathon terrorist bombings, three people suffer mortal wounds and 264 are seriously injured. The world is an eyewitness to trauma. Two days after the bombings, Jeff Greenberg, a University of Arizona psychologist, described the psychological "script" we follow when we're afraid. *First, we react in disbelief:* "I can't believe this is happening." *Then we assess our vulnerability:* "Could this terrible thing happen to me?" *Then we discount our vulnerability:* "I don't live in Boston—there are no terrorists here." *Then we manufacture solutions:* "We should pay more attention to security issues and increase our vigilance."

The eyewitness shepherds, like us, can't stop their protective impulse from kicking in when trauma descends on them. They are paralyzed until they hear the words "good news" and "great joy" and "baby wrapped in strips of cloth." Only the vulnerability of Jesus can entice us to move past our fear and into worship.

Wonder	**Jesus**	**Do**
What is paralyzing you right now?	"The blind see, the lame walk…the deaf hear, the dead are raised to life" (Matthew 11:5).	If you have a creche, position the shepherds facedown instead of standing.

Pray: Jesus, you made the paralyzed man walk—I invite the same.

The Safety Fallacy

Read Psalm 23

I'm meeting with a friend for lunch, and as we get ready to leave, our waitress stops, lowers her voice, and offers a familiar (and strangely cheery) caution: "Be safe!" As she turns away, I remark to my friend, "That's such a strange way to say goodbye!" Of course, we're hyper-vigilant about safety in our culture. "Be safe" is a universally accepted farewell. Our culture is brimming with perceived danger—though we personally experience very few of the threats that keep us awake at night. In response, we demand better security, stiffer criminal penalties, higher walls, and hyper-control over our environment.

But "Be safe!" is not a kingdom-of-God imperative. The message of the Incarnation is a prod to adventure into the darkness, not retreat from it. Jesus invites us to walk with him into the "valley of the shadow of death" because (as David reminds us) his "rod and staff" will bring comfort to us. In his hand the Good Shepherd carries two metaphoric necessities—a staff to rescue and a rod to defend. That's why his hello's and goodbye's so often convey the opposite of "Be safe!":

"Be a testimony to me" (Luke 5:14).

"Go in peace" (Luke 8:48).

"Take nothing for your journey" (Luke 9:3).

"Proclaim the kingdom of God!" (Luke 9:60).

"Be awake and alert!" (Luke 21:36).

Wonder
What are the unintended consequences of using "Be safe" for "goodbye"?

Jesus
"How can anyone enter the strong man's house...unless he first binds [him]?" (Matthew 12:29, NASB).

Do
Instead of "Be safe!" try, "Be Christ's!" or "Stay awake!" or "Live large!"

Pray: Jesus, you are my safety.

The Lonely Ornaments

Read Luke 4:31-41

On a winding road through low brush and prickly pine, with a snow-covered range of mountains before me and a frozen river snaking next to me, I see a large Christmas-tree ornament hanging from a limb that's nudging the road. And then another one, 50 feet later. And then every 50 feet for almost a mile. After the first one, I wonder about the back story—how did this lonely ornament, a piercing beauty in a dull winter landscape, find its place along this "road less traveled"? I am dragged forward by these syncopated miracles. The looming shapes crystalize, one after the other, like a string of pearls around nature's throat. Something stirs inside, an invitation into hope…

And true hope *does* feel like this—less cheery than solemn, less bombastic than quiet, less obvious than subtle. Its impact skewers us. When the prophet Isaiah describes the coming Messiah, he is also describing the ornaments by the road, strung out in the haphazard wilderness: "His name will be the hope of all the world" (Matthew 12:21).

To the man possessed by a demon, screaming at Jesus in the synagogue, hope feels like a hurricane moving out of his soul and into the void. To Simon Peter's mother-in-law, battling a high fever, hope feels like the oppressive heat of summer giving way to a crisp fall breeze. And to the villagers in Capernaum, sick with worry over their disease-ravaged family members, hope feels like a sunrise driving away a lonely, sleepless night.

Wonder	**Jesus**	**Do**
What is stirring your hope today?	"The Scripture you've just heard has been fulfilled this very day!" (Luke 4:21).	Study your reflection in an ornament. Remember he's "the hope within you."

Pray: Jesus, hope seems elusive to me, so show me its face.

The Divine Vintner

Read 2 Corinthians 4:7-10

Washington Post food columnist Ben Giliberti explains the difference between a "bulk vintage" and a superior wine: "Great wines come from low-yielding vineyards planted in marginal climates in the poorest soils. Though hard on the vines, these tough conditions are good for the wine, because vines that are stressed must work harder to produce fruit, which leads to fewer but more concentrated and flavorful grapes. By contrast, the vines used for bulk wines have it easy. [The] fertile soils in ideal climates in…such regions are great for producing tons of grapes to fill up the bulk fermentation tanks, but not at all great for producing the complex, intense flavors needed to make great wine."

The tough conditions that produce rare wine also produce martyrs and saints and "beautiful messes" like you and me. Paul tells us we are "struck down, but not destroyed… so that the life of Jesus also may be manifested in our body" (NASB). During my summer as a camp counselor for at-risk kids, I discovered one of them had stolen a butcher knife, intending to murder me in my sleep. On the day he planned to do it, I discovered the hidden knife. On my first two-day break, I drove into town and walked for hours in silence. Jesus, I knew, was forming in me a new capacity for loving others in the "marginal climate" of my soul. In my weakness, he was making me strong.

Wonder
In your life, what feels like a "marginal climate" and "poor soil"?

Jesus
"There is so much more I want to tell you, but you can't bear it now" (John 16:12).

Do
Taste-test the difference between a "bulk vintage" and "rarer" wine.

Pray: Jesus, I'm a struggling grapevine longing to be made a "rare vintage."

The Waiting Game

Read John 11:1-44

As Christmas morning draws near, time slows down. The waiting, especially if you're a child, seems torturous. There are few things we hate more than waiting, yet we do so much of it—more than 37 billion hours every year. When Timex asked people how long they'd wait in a wide variety of situations, they discovered our patience lasts…

- 13 seconds before we honk at a car in front of us that's stopped at a green light,

- 26 seconds before we shush noisy folks in a theater,

- 45 seconds before we ask someone who's talking too loud on a cellphone to "keep it down," and

- 13 minutes for a table at a restaurant.

According to MIT operations researcher Richard Larson, the world's leading expert on the science of waiting, the length of our delay matters less than *how* we bide our time. We tolerate "occupied time" (walking to the airport baggage claim) far better than "unoccupied time" (staring at the baggage carousel). So often, waiting on Jesus feels like unoccupied time. We wait, but what's really happening? Is Jesus actually doing anything?

The people of God waited for millennia on the Messiah, and it formed their hearts. John Ortberg writes, "Waiting is not just something we have to do until we get what we want. Waiting is part of the process of becoming what God wants us to be."

Wonder
What are you waiting for, and what is it producing in you?

Jesus
"Didn't I tell you that you would see God's glory if you believe?" (John 11:40).

Do
Spot someone waiting in line; ask Jesus what to pray for, then pray.

Pray: Jesus, in the unoccupied time of my life, form strength in me.

Two Temples

Read Matthew 12:1-8

N.T. Wright, the British apologist and theologian, offers an
unconventional explanation for why Jesus goes ballistic
in Jerusalem's Temple, heaving over the tables of the
moneychangers and whipping them into a panicked retreat. Yes,
he's infuriated by the shysters who've turned this place of holy
connection between God and his people into QVC. But he's also
proclaiming, says Wright, "that this town isn't big enough for two
Temples."

The Jerusalem Temple is an outpost oasis of God's presence
in the desert of humanity. But now *Jesus* is that outpost. In the
Incarnation, Jesus supplants the Temple—"I tell you, there is
one here who is even greater than the Temple!" (Matthew 12:6).
Soon the Spirit of Jesus will make his home inside the hearts of
his followers. In the words of Paul, "Do you not know that you
are a temple of God and that the Spirit of God dwells in you?"
(1 Corinthians 3:16, NASB).

We enter into the Holy of Holies when we enter into Jesus. He
in us, we in him. Openness and invitation line the path into our
embodied Temple, and our vulnerability is the only cover charge.
Jesus does not believe in velvet ropes.

Wonder	**Jesus**	**Do**
Tears are an intimate invitation to Jesus. What brings your tears, and why?	"I am able to destroy the Temple of God and rebuild it in three days" (Matthew 26:61).	With hands over your face, breathe deeply; imagine you've entered your refuge.

Pray: Jesus, thank you for making yourself at home in my mess.

The Hedgehog Concept

Read 1 John 2:26-27

In *Good to Great*, author Jim Collins studied 11 companies that beat the odds and vaulted out of longtime mediocrity into longtime excellence. One transforming catalyst, shared by all, is something Collins calls the "Hedgehog Concept." It's based on an ancient Greek parable: "The fox knows many things, but the hedgehog knows one big thing." Companies that embrace one simple purpose, then pursue it with passion, succeed. Conversely, those that skitter from one purpose to another stay mired in mediocrity.

In the church, our transformation is often framed as the result of hard work and discipline—if we follow all the Bible's "shoulds," we'll leverage the best version of ourselves. But transformation requires exposure, not industry. Jesus is like plutonium—the closer we get to him, and the longer we stay there, the more he "radiates" us. Paul says both religious and secular leaders miss that: "The rulers of this world have not understood it; if they had, they would not have crucified our glorious Lord. That is what the Scriptures mean when they say, 'No eye has seen, no ear has heard, and no mind has imagined what God has prepared for those who love him' " (2 Corinthians 2:8-9).

What is the "it" these leaders don't understand? Paul answers it in the preceding paragraph: "I decided that while I was with you I would forget everything except Jesus Christ." This is Paul's Hedgehog Concept, and today we remember it is ours as well.

Wonder
How would someone close to you define your "Hedgehog Concept"?

Jesus
"Unless a kernel of wheat is planted in the soil and dies, it remains alone" (John 12:24).

Do
Search "Zurbaran 'The Lamb of God' " online. Print it, and turn it into an ornament.

Pray: Jesus, radiate my soul as I draw near to you.

Till We Have Faces

Read Romans 3:23-28

Taped to my computer stand is a photo of me as a 3-year-old. Against a fake-nature backdrop, I'm holding a ball and managing a weak smile. My hair is curly, orange, and big. I'm ridiculously freckled. And I'm wearing a shirt-and-overall ensemble that's vaguely Scandinavian. Sometimes I stare into that little guy's eyes, looking for the "me" in there. He feels lost and alone and insignificant. And over time, that boy came to believe there was an empty void where his soul was supposed to be. He lived in fear that someone would expose this "soul leprosy" in him.

So what's a lost boy like him to do? Well, he looks for a mask to hide the face he's missing. Later I read the C.S. Lewis book *Till We Have Faces*, a retelling of an ancient Greek myth and a metaphor for maturing in Christ. I was drawn to it by the promise of the title—I wanted a real face. Meanwhile, I was determined to try harder to be better. But, like the "Rich Young Ruler" who demanded a fast-pass into eternity, I never asked myself, *Why am I trying so hard?*

My mask-wearing life was possible only as long as Jesus behaved himself. But he didn't. "The lion of the tribe of Judah" ripped off that mask, exposing my yawning emptiness. And then he filled me. And then he gave me back my face.

Wonder
Do you wear your own face or a façade most of the time?

Jesus
"You will receive power when the Holy Spirit comes upon you" (Acts 1:8).

Do
Find a photo of you as a child and stare into your eyes. What are they telling you?

Pray: Jesus, will you give me the face you already see in me?

The God of Story

Read Revelation 1:12-18

> *Twas the night before Christmas, when all through the house*
> *Not a creature was stirring, not even a mouse...*

The first words of Clement Moore's 1822 poem "A Visit from St. Nicholas" hint at the author's vibrant, playful imagination. The poem has a simple structure, with a beginning, middle, and end. The narrative suspense drives to a grateful conclusion. But would all that still be the case if, instead of Clement Moore, the poem had been written by 66 authors over 1,500 years? That is, of course, what the Bible is—66 books written in a broad range of genres: history, poetry, how-to, romance, mystery, thriller, and mysticism. It's a mind-bending collection of disparate stories that makes sense only because it has one "General Editor" tying all of it together. It's the story of God, written miraculously.

1. *The Beginning*—The establishment of mankind and of laws to guide our existence (Genesis through Job).

2. *The Middle*—Poetry, wisdom, and prophets (Psalms through Malachi).

3. *The End*—The coming of Jesus (the kingdom) and the establishment of the Church (the entire New Testament).

The Bible is ultimately an epic love story—a great hero rescuing his beloved from certain death. It is the Word on paper revealing the Word in the flesh and Spirit. Jesus is living and active, and he is editing the narrative of our lives even now.

Wonder
What do you know for sure about the Bible's General Editor?

Jesus
"I am the First and the Last. I am the living one" (Revelation 1:17-18).

Do
Read aloud "The Night Before Christmas" (find it online). What reminds you of Jesus?

Pray: Jesus, it's the night before Christmas, and all through me you're stirring.

Love Varietals

Read John 3:13-19

Today we celebrate Christmas, remembering a liberation greater than the D-Day invasion of Normandy: "For this is how God loved the world: He gave his one and only Son, so that everyone who believes in him will not perish but have eternal life." With our feet straddling two kingdoms—the kingdom of this world and the kingdom of God—we must choose between competing "love varietals" (the love of God and the love of the world). To understand the heart of Jesus, we pay attention to the contrast between the ways he loves and the norming standards of our culture's love songs...

Love, filtered through a cultural lens, means "I'm in love with your body" and "Is it too late now to say sorry, cause I'm missing more than just your body?" and "I don't know how to be there when you need me." But Jesus loves the Gentile woman who asks to eat "the crumbs off the master's table" because of her courage, and he loves the moxy of the friends who lower a paralyzed man through the roof, and he promises his anxious disciples "I will not abandon you. I will come to you." He loves...

• the disappointed and desperate.
• the mess-ups who've embarrassed themselves.
• the stressed and worried.
• the broken who are fixated on their inadequacies.

Because Jesus loves all of us as if there were only one of us, we are all (like John the apostle) "the disciple Jesus loves."

Wonder
Is it hard or easy for you to feel loved by Jesus, and why?

Jesus
"If you love me, obey my commandments" (John 14:15).

Do
Make a shiny ornament a truth-mirror. With a marker, write "Jesus loves me" on one.

Pray: Jesus, you love me, this I know...

Appalling Imperfection

Read Romans 12:6-21

Earl Palmer, retired pastor of First Presbyterian Church in Berkeley, California, once countered critics who dismiss the church for its irrelevant footprint in the culture with this metaphoric defense:

When the Milpitas High School orchestra attempts Beethoven's Ninth Symphony, the result is appalling. I wouldn't be surprised if the performance made old Ludwig roll over in his grave despite his deafness. You might ask: 'Why bother? Why inflict on those poor kids the terrible burden of trying to render what the immortal Beethoven had in mind? Not even the great Chicago Symphony Orchestra can attain that perfection.' My answer is this: The Milpitas High School orchestra will give some people in that audience their only encounter with Beethoven's great Ninth Symphony. Far from perfection, it is nevertheless the only way they will hear Beethoven's message.

The only way a thirsty, suffering world will ever hear the music of the Gospel is through the body of Christ, arguably the worst "high school orchestra" ever to disgrace a bandstand. If performance standards are really the most important measure, then the church is in trouble. But Jesus is determined to trade the perfection of his solo performance for the possibility of playing in an orchestra with us, the screechy violin players in the kingdom of God's ragtag symphony. He's looking for musicians who want to play, not critics too afraid to pick up an instrument.

Wonder	**Jesus**	**Do**
What's something you'd like to do but won't because you're "unqualified"?	"Teach these new disciples to obey all [my] commands" (Matthew 28:20).	Ask a small child to draw a picture of Jesus for you. Tape it to your refrigerator.

Pray: Jesus, I can hardly play my instrument, but I want to be in your band.

Becoming What You Love

Read 1 Corinthians 6:15-17

St. Clare of Assisi said, *"We become what we love and who we love shapes what we become. If we love things, we become a thing. If we love nothing, we become nothing. Imitation is not a literal mimicking of Christ, rather it means becoming the image of the beloved, an image disclosed through transformation."*

This is what the Apostle Paul means when he declares, "I am convinced that nothing can ever separate us from God's love. Neither death nor life, neither angels nor demons, neither our fears for today nor our worries about tomorrow—not even the powers of hell can separate us from God's love" (Romans 8:38). This notorious persecutor of the early church is describing the relational force that has reinvented his life. Knocked blind by Jesus and rescued from hatred, he's become what he loves.

In a financial services commercial for Mass Mutual, a single dad navigates his own grief while sacrificing, over and over, to be there for his two little girls. He plays dress-up, sits for tea parties, pitches softball, fills laundry baskets, and dons an apron to bake cookies with his daughters. The narrator delivers the company's tagline, an echo of St. Clare: *"Who* matters most to you says the most about you." It is *who* we love, not how we discipline ourselves, that marks our identity.

Wonder
What's something you really love? How has that shaped your personality?

Jesus
"The student who is fully trained will become like the teacher" (Luke 6:40).

Do
You are a seed Jesus is nurturing into his image. Tape a few seeds to this page.

Pray: Jesus, I'm convinced nothing can separate me from my love for you.

Outside Karma

Read 2 Timothy 1:8-10

Karma is an Eastern religious concept. It means, essentially, that we get what we deserve. It's why we tell our kids at Christmas, "If you're good, you'll get. If you're not, you won't." In an interview with journalist Michka Assayas, U2 frontman Bono describes the tension between karma and grace: "At the center of all religions is the idea of karma. You know, what you put out comes back to you: an eye for an eye, a tooth for a tooth… And yet, along comes this idea called grace to upend all that 'as you reap, so you will sow' stuff. Grace defies reason and logic. Love interrupts…the consequences of your actions."

Though grace is central to the message of Jesus, we refuse to let go of karma. A little over half of Americans believe that if people are generally good, or do enough good things for others during their lives, they'll earn a place in heaven. Many more of us who know "the right answer"—that Jesus' gift of grace is our only hope—live as if everything still depends on our own goodness. Jesus tries to surgically remove this karma-cancer: "Unless your righteousness is better than the righteousness of the teachers of religious law and the Pharisees, you will never enter the Kingdom of Heaven!" (Matthew 5:20).

Karma is a dead end; grace is our only hope.

Wonder
In what ways do you still cling to the "you get what you deserve" belief?

Jesus
"What is impossible for people is possible with God" (Luke 18:27).

Do
Money marks what we "deserve." With a $1 bill, make a paper airplane and fly it into a crowd.

Pray: Jesus, I want to live outside of karma and inside your grace.

The Why's of Love

Read Romans 4:13-25

Marketing consultant Simon Sinek, author of *Start With Why*, explains, "People don't buy *what* you do; they buy *why* you do it." Unless we discover the *why* behind a person's words and deeds, we'll never move from a benign affection to a consuming passion. Our path into intimacy with Jesus starts with a Q&A...

Q: Why does a good shepherd leave his whole flock to rescue the one sheep that has lost its way?

A: The heart of Jesus is focused on individuals, not crowds.

Q: Why does Jesus tell Peter to pay their Temple tax by extracting a coin from the mouth of a fish?

A: The heart of Jesus is playful.

Q: Why does Jesus have so little patience for religious elites?

A: The heart of Jesus longs for authenticity, not performance.

Q: Why is Jesus so willing to lose fans and followers?

A: The heart of Jesus is humble and secure.

Q: Why does Jesus delay meeting an urgent need to heal and elevate a woman locked in shame?

A: The heart of Jesus is generous to "the least of these."

Q: Why does Jesus tell the Parable of the Prodigal Son?

A: The heart of Jesus is quick to forgive/restore/celebrate.

Wonder	**Jesus**	**Do**
Why does Jesus forgive the soldiers who are executing him?	"Because [you] love me, my Father will love [you]" (John 14:21).	With a pen, dimple the word "Why?" on this page—repeatedly push the point in.

Pray: Jesus, I've discovered the *why* behind everything you say and do.

Finding Our Moral GPS

Read John 14:1-14

Jesus promises his frightened disciples that he's "going to prepare a place for you…so that you will always be with me." But Thomas is craving a GPS equivalent—he wants to know the destination and directions to the "place" Jesus is preparing for them. So Jesus tells him, *"I am your GPS."* We have to be *in him* to find the life we're meant to live.

As we stumble headlong into a new year, we're briefly open to assessing what we're doing right and what we're doing wrong. Ethicist Margaret R. McLean says we make that assessment in one of three ways: "First, there are those folks who think that the results make all the difference. Why won't you lie? It will hurt people… Second, there are those people who follow the rules. Why won't you lie? There's a rule that says to always tell the truth… And, thirdly, there are those individuals who aren't much interested in either results or rules. They are interested in the kind of person you are—a person of compassion or courage. Why won't you lie? Because I'm an honest person."

The fatal flaw in all three approaches, according to researchers at Northwestern's Kellogg School of Management: "People do not necessarily have strong, stable moral compasses." Instead of results, rules, or reputation, Jesus wants us to ingest him, the only moral GPS we can trust. When we do, we infuse right-and-wrong from its original source.

Wonder	**Jesus**	**Do**
Jesus asks, "Why can't you decide for yourselves what is right?" (Luke 12:57).	"From now on, you do know [my Father] and have seen him!" (John 14:7).	Plug Jesus' hometown ("Nazareth, Israel") into your map app; listen to the GPS instructions.

Pray: Jesus, help me live out your right-and-wrong from the inside out.

The Mouse and the Elephant

Read John 20:30-31

An end-of-year parable that first appeared in a 1936 comic strip called "Funny Fables," published in the Cleveland Plain Dealer—it's called "The Mouse and the Elephant":

One day a great-big elephant and an itsy-bitsy mouse went for a walk. They admired the flowers and birds all along the way. Soon they came to a bridge. And as they crossed the brook, the bridge trembled and shook under the weight of the elephant. "Gosh," squeaked the mouse when they were on the other side of the stream, "didn't we make that bridge shake!"

In this fable, we are the mouse and Jesus is the elephant—an important distinction as we cross the bridge into a new year full of possibility and predicament. We way overestimate our ability to "shake the bridge" and way underestimate the "weight" of Jesus.

To right-size our faith, we embrace Bernoulli's principle of physics. Here's how it works: Fill a long plastic tube with air by blowing directly into the opening, and you'll discover it takes great effort. But hold the tube 10 inches away, then sharply blow into the opening, and it fills immediately. That's because the thrust of air speeds up the molecules in the tube, lowering the pressure and sucking a huge volume of air into it. We can trust our own lung power, or we can use our tiny offering of strength to poke the elephant.

And when we trust the elephant, he will shake our bridge.

Wonder
What's something you've been unable to overcome by yourself?

Jesus
"I have given you authority over all the power of the enemy" (Luke 10:19).

Do
Practice Bernoulli's principle with a "produce bag" from your grocery store.

Pray: Jesus, shake my bridge and throw your weight around in my life.